The Politics of Food

The Politics of Food

Don Mitchell

James Lorimer & Company
Toronto 1975

ISBN 0-88862-083-7 paper
   0-88862-084-5 cloth

Cover photograph: Michael Casen Emery

Design: Lynn Campbell

James Lorimer & Company, Publishers
35 Britain Street
Toronto

Printed and bound in Canada

Canadian Shared Cataloguing in Publication Data

Mitchell, Don.
   The politics of food / Don Mitchell. --

1. Food industry and trade — Canada. 2. Food prices — Canada.
3. Farm produce — Canada — Marketing. 4. Agriculture and
state — Canada. I. Title.

HD9014.C3M58   338.1'0971
ISBN: 0-88862-084-5; 0-88862-083-7 (pbk.)

Contents

Acknowledgements

In writing this book I received help from a large number of people of whom I can list only a few. Stan Barber of the Saskatchewan Milk Control Board and Fred Longstaff of the Saskatchewan Egg Producers Marketing Board helped give me insight into those areas of public policy. The Sample Survey of the University of Regina shared their research findings on agribusiness. Roy Atkinson of the National Farmers Union offered helpful observations on the dairy issue, and Clarence Lyons provided background on the Canadian Food and Allied Workers' dispute with the three big meat packing companies. Fred Gudmunson arranged interviews with grain company and Canadian Wheat Board officials in Winnipeg.

I especially acknowledge the assistance provided by the Ontario Arts Council, and the co-operation and assistance of Jim Lorimer as publisher and adviser.

Finally I wish to thank the staff of the Moose Jaw Public Library who always go out of their way to be helpful in locating information.

To Martha
for support and understanding

I

Introduction

Throughout the period from 1972 to 1975, the issue of food occupied part of the crowded centre-stage of Canadian politics. For most observers the critical concern was inflation. For others, it was the state of underdevelopment in agriculture and the boom-and-bust cycle of farm markets and prices. Still others have regarded Canada's approach to international trade as a problem in the context of a world food distribution crisis. All of these food-related issues and others are linked through the agriculture and food 'system' and its various parts. It is the 'parts' of the system, in conflict, which determine the politics of food. The political drama of the 1970s has engaged farmers and farm workers, food industry workers, agribusiness, governments, and consumer groups in continuous tension and conflict.

Inflation and the Politics of Consumerism

For the majority of Canadians, as consumers, the main issue in the politics of food has been prices. In 1972, the federal government was boasting that the average family in Canada spent only 18 per cent of its disposable income on food items. By 1975 the average family was spending 25 per cent of its income on food, and eating less well.[1] But 'average' families are hard to come by, and in fact the worst burden is borne by the low-income segment, the 26 per cent whose income is less than $5,000 per year.[2] All the commodities regarded as essential have seen sharp increases at the retail level: bread up 37 per cent, beef up 36 per cent, eggs up 46 per cent and milk 23 per cent, all between August 1972 and August 1974.[3] And Mrs. Plumptre gave notice in late 1974 that consumers could look forward to a general across-the-board increase of another 16 per cent in food products in 1975. The fact of

---

TABLE 1

CONSUMER PRICE INDEX

	August 1972	August 1973	August 1974	% increase
Beef	161.5	204.3	220.0	36
Bread	137.9	145.1	189.4	37
Eggs	102.3	149.7	148.1	46
Milk	152.1	168.7	188.5	23

SOURCE: STATISTICS CANADA

---

general inflationary price trends is clear. What is less clear is the seriousness of the impact of higher food costs on Canadian society. The blurring occurs because the concept of every Canadian as a consumer ignores the existence of social class.

For consumers in general, there are many levels of exploitation in the modern marketplace. All consumers are encouraged by the manipulations of advertising to buy more of everything from convenience foods to diamond rings and suburban homes. But the more serious exploitation is the direct financial rip-off in which the prices of essential consumer items like food are inflated by the combined costs of advertising, deceptive packaging, luxury supermarkets and profits at every level of the production cycle. This exploitation is borne most heavily by the working class for the simple reason they spend a higher proportion of their income on food and other essentials than do consumers with management and professional-level salaries. Food company presidents, confronted by organized consumer protest over prices, have been known to say, "Of course I understand, I'm a consumer too." Corporate executives *are* consumers, but the level of consumption on a $50,000 annual salary does not lend itself to the usual frustration at the supermarket check-out counter.

Approaching the food industry as consumers, we are in the end powerless to implement the structural changes we may recognize as necessary in the food system. In certain contexts, of course, we may have the freedom to make choices about what we buy or don't buy. But in the critical areas of food, clothing, and shelter, we *must* consume and therefore have no real bargaining power. Mass consumer boycotts of particular products or companies have been tried with some limited success, but require mass organizing efforts which are impractical for most grievances. It took Caesar Chavez and his farm workers several years, through an internationally organized boycott of California farm products, to gain initial recognition of the rights of the farmworkers' union. The National Farmers Union has been promoting a consumer boycott of Kraft products since 1970 in support of demands for collective bargaining by dairy farmers. Although it has made a dent in the company's image, it has so far failed to erode its profits. Kraft, with 1974 profits of 18.3 per cent return on investment, had the highest profit ratio among all food companies in Canada.[4]

The supermarket system takes greatest advantage of those who have the least choice. For example while sirloin steak prices were increased 31 per cent from January 1972 to January 1974, hamburger (the luxury product in the shrinking protein diet of the poor) was increased by 59 per cent. Supermarkets knew sirloin steak was optional but hamburger a working-class necessity. The consumer movement drew life in Canada in the 1970s as the apparent political centre from which people could fight back against inflation, especially of food prices. Its tactics were to present briefs and statements, demand consumer representation on marketing boards and other government agencies, and advise consumers on how to eat and save. But the reality of the corporate capitalist system of production and distribution has been that we possess power in accordance with what we own in productive property or what we produce. The conflict within the system, in food production and elsewhere, is primarily *between* those who own and those who produce. As consumers we are affected by this conflict, and may indeed have some political influence on the results, but our direct economic power is limited. We become passive observers and even victims to the main struggle. Unless consumer organizations begin to mount an organized challenge to the corporate bias of state power in Canada, they will have little real impact.

Underdevelopment in Agriculture

In apparent contradiction with consumer advocates who underline as key the issue of food price inflation, there are those in Canada who argue that agriculture is underdeveloped and that it requires rapid adjustments including *higher* food prices. Where Herb Gray and Beryl Plumptre have sometimes represented the first school of thought, Eugene Whelan has stood for the second. Their continuing debate, formally staged before the Ottawa press gallery, underlines a contradiction which surfaces repeatedly in the politics of food. This contradiction is inherent in an agriculture and food system which is evidently wasteful, inefficient and expensive, but just as evidently underdeveloped and exploitative of the people and resources involved in it. The focus of discussion has been agricultural policy. The overdevelopment argument cites the pricing power of marketing agencies and over $500 million in federal subsidies as evidence of waste and overprotection.[5] By their argument, the system has encouraged inefficient farmers to stay in production and has forced processors and, ultimately, consumers to pay inflated prices for farm products. The solution, in their view, lies in withdrawal of government from agriculture and a return to pure free market competition.

In contrast, the underdevelopment arguments stress the necessity of catching up in agriculture to the standards and approaches of the rest of society. They cite low and erratic farm prices and incomes over the years, the abandonment of land by farmers, and the conversion of farmland to other uses as a reflection of underdevelopment. They too see the solution in terms of a change in government policies for agriculture, in this case toward greater intervention to assure price stability, and stable markets.

Farmers themselves are split on this debate, as are economists and politicians. Most people are probably just confused by what appears to be opposite conclusions being reached from the same total body of evidence.

In examining the politics of food, some of this confusion may be overcome. At the outset it should be clear that some of the contradiction exists because within the broad agriculture and food system there are competing and unequal sectors. Farmers, wage workers in the food industry, and agribusiness management are all engaged in pursuit of the same flow of wealth generated by the production and distribution of food products. Their relative power is examined in later chapters in the specific context of various commodities, but on the general question of underdevelopment or overdevelopment, some indicators may be useful as introduction.

Despite improved farming methods, new technology, massive and growing public subsidies, and increasing per-unit crop yields in every commodity, farms in Canada reflect a state of underdevelopment. The trends of rural depopulation, farm production declines, and generally lower standards of net-income for farmers in relation to industrial workers are evidence of a weak sector of the economy. (Farm incomes in the ten years to 1973 averaged 70 per cent of manufacturing wages.)[6] Food shortages are growing in key commodities. In milk products both Canada and the United States have fallen short of domestic consumption needs because production has declined sharply. It means little that superior feeds and animal husbandry have improved the individual milk production capacity of the Holstein cow, when 77,000 farmers gave up milking cows in

Canada from 1966 to 1971, liquidating their herds in the process.[7]

Production declines in Canada in 1974 occurred in milk products, pork and cereal grain. Canadian farmland has been converted to other uses at the rate of roughly one million acres per year from 1966 to 1974. Farmers left the land at a rate which caused a net reduction of 10,000 families per year over the same period.[8] All of this adds up to a generalized state of underdevelopment in Canadian agriculture which reduces our capacity to maintain world trade in food commodities at past levels or to feed ourselves adequately.

Production declines and production planning are a result of decisions by governments. A policy of permitting underdevelopment in North American agriculture, coupled with a higher standard of consumption, has resulted in a growing dependence on outside sources of supply. Canadian food imports from countries such as Australia, New Zealand, Brazil and South Africa are increasing while our own production declines. From these countries we import fresh, frozen and canned meat products, butter, fruit, vegetables, and sugar — almost all of which could be produced here. 1973 agricultural imports to Canada from these four countries alone totalled 365 million, up 40 per cent over 1972.[9]

The point is not that our growing pattern of food imports is a major factor in national survival in the 1970s. We are still a net-exporter of food commodities because of our large grain shipments. The point is that current trends and policies toward agriculture are rapidly downgrading the capacity to produce food in advanced capitalist countries like Canada and the United States. This causes the agribusiness suppliers of North American markets to draw on increased production from their subsidiaries in developing countries. Canada and the U.S. deny food commodities to that portion of the world facing starvation through waste and underdevelopment of North America's own agricultural resources.

This underproduction in Canadian agriculture exists despite considerable efforts by farmers to adapt to available technology. A 1969 study on Canadian agriculture productivity was done for the Economic Council of Canada by L. Auer. It showed that total production had increased 50 per cent in Canada in the 1950s and 1960s. Individual productivity among farmers increased 6 per cent per year because of larger farms, improved methods, and mechanization. But despite the adjustments, Canadian production fell increasingly farther behind the rest of the world on a per-unit basis. In wheat yields Canada ranks twenty-eighth in bushels per acre, compared to twentieth in the immediate post-war period: we produce about one-third the yield of European countries. In milk production, Canadian cows are 15 per cent below the average in the U.S. Egg production per hen is on average 20 per cent lower, and beef production showed 20 per cent lower per one hundred animals, although the two countries were almost equal in beef production during the 1940s. [10]

The effect of underdevelopment and declining production is to create shortages and an upward pressure on food prices at all levels. These higher prices to farmers for their products, although not directly proportionate to retail increases, should encourage farmers to increase their production. To some degree they do. But at the same time higher food prices in supermarkets and on international trade goods begin to outstrip the ability of lower-income consumers to pay. As a result of being bid out of the marketplace by high prices, these people contribute to a drop in per-capita consumption in key but expensive commodities such as beef, milk and sugar. All of these commodities saw a drop in consumption in Canada in 1974. Ultimately the drop in consumption leads to surpluses again in farm products. These surpluses are artificial alongside the malnutrition and starvation of millions, but their effect on the farmer is to reduce the value of his commodity and start him on another round of depression and bankruptcy.

The continuous cycle of boom and bust is of no apparent consequence to consumers since retail prices never decline to a depressed level. But for the farmer the round of shortage and surplus, high and low prices, is the treadmill of his existence and central to his politics. By 1975 the prospect of record-breaking grain crops around the world stood to deflate the buoyant price of wheat and other cereals. By doing their job too well, farmers were faced with the destruction of the relative prosperity they enjoyed in 1973 and 1974. This is just one of the contradictions of the agriculture sector in the food system which bears on the politics of farmers, examined in Chapter 2.

The evidence of underdevelopment in the agriculture and food system is not restricted to agricultural producers. It applies as well to wage workers in farm labour, also discussed in Chapter 2, and to the 200,000 workers in the food and beverage industries. The average wage for workers in food manufacturing in 1974 was $167 per week, in comparison to a general average for manufacturing employees of $184 per week.

Food manufacturing employs a high proportion of women workers. It also uses more immigrant labour and has a higher frequency of seasonal lay-offs than manufacturing generally. Food processing industries are generally more labour-intensive than other manufacturing sectors; i.e. they have a high ratio of people to machines on their assembly lines. The combination of lower than average wages, poor working conditions and labour intensity suggests that the Canadian food manufacturing industry is in some ways underdeveloped in relation to the standards of North American capitalism.[11]

But if the evidence is strong in suggesting that the agriculture and food system is relatively underdeveloped, can we then conclude that rapid increase of retail food prices between 1972 and 1975 was necessary? This was basically the position of federal agriculture minister Eugene Whelan and others in explaining and defending food price inflation. It was necessary, they say, to stimulate flagging production and improve the standards, stability, and working conditions of farmers. Whelan has implied that farmers got the benefits of inflation, a contention to be measured more concretely in the discussion of prices and incomes in various areas of commodity production.

Overdevelopment of Agribusiness

In contrast to the symptoms of stagnation and low-income for the productive workers on the farms and in the factories and stores, there is also evidence of overdevelopment in some segments of the agriculture and food system. The large-scale owners of capital who dominate food related industries have managed an impressive accumulation of capital and assets. The proliferation of factories, warehouses and shopping centres is evidence of over-capacity and inefficiency. The owners have been blessed with accelerating profits throughout the period of high inflation and they promote as part of their system the further speculative earnings of commodity and real estate trading. As a group, the capitalists engaged in the agribusiness sector in Canada are not *basically* different from the class they represent. They do have some distinctive features. They are closely knit through interlocking directorates, joint ownerships and direct subsidiaries. They have a relatively high degree of Canadian ownership. There is a close link between agribusiness holdings and the sources of finance capital, the banks and trust companies. And, finally, there is a high degree of integration of operations both vertically and horizontally as illustrated in Chapter 3.

The critical overall feature of agribusiness in Canada and elsewhere which will repeatedly be demonstrated as important is its character of oligopoly. The concept of a rival group of firms dominating a market through concentrated ownership — what economists mean by the term oligopoly — is distinct from a single firm domination or monopoly. The key difference from the point of view of price movements is that where monopoly power can be exercised to adjust prices upward or downward according to conditions of supply and demand, an oligopoly usually adjusts prices upward only. In the absence of formal understood pricing agreements among the rival firms, price cuts may symbolize competitive pricing and the beginning of a price war. This does no one any good: while it may increase the proportion of the profits pie going to the leading competitor, it reduces the overall size of the pie. Oligopolies steadfastly avoid price competition.

Politicians and Government

The issues and conflicts surrounding food are translated to the formal political stage by politicians and officials both elected and appointed. Much of the discussion, particularly in the latter half of this book, is devoted to examining the role of the state in the agriculture and food system. Some personalities such as Eugene Whelan and Beryl Plumptre stand out, by virtue of the positions they have held, as having great influence on the destiny of food prices and farmers. In reality their impact is somewhat more limited — though not unimportant. What we come to realize on closer scrutiny is that the underlying struggles in the politics of food are not fully reflected in the surface skirmishes of the Whelans and Plumptres. When it comes down to the crunch they are, in spite of their entertaining differences, on the same side of the conflict. Their direction is established by the same basic set of interests which also controls their purse-strings. As we examine the role of government in relation to agriculture, agribusiness and the international trade in food commodities, the politicians begin to appear to be pawns in the game. They are not altogether devoid of power but the ways in which they can exercise it are greatly predetermined by the faceless authority of an international system of private wealth.

Notes to Chapter 1

1. An average of 25 per cent spending on food occurred by 1975 as a result of a 50 per cent increase in food prices over three years while the overall price index was up 33 per cent.

2. Based on 1973 Taxation Statistics, Department of National Revenue.

3. These figures on per cent increases in food commodities are based only on the Consumer Price Index and do not include the federal and provincial subsidies applied in this period to domestic bread wheat, cattle and milk.

4. *Financial Post*, survey of 100 largest companies, 1974.

5. $500 million was the figure attributed by economist J.D. Forbes in his 1974 report on marketing policies done for the Consumer Council of Canada. Dairy subsidies alone were $250 million by 1974.

6. Based on Statistics Canada comparisons of average manufacturing wages and net farm income earnings from 1963-1972.

7. The 1971 Census of Agriculture in Canada shows a net reduction of 77,000 in the number of farmers milking cows in Canada as compared to 1966.

8. Figures on land conversion and depopulation are averaged for the period 1966-71 and then projected as an estimate for the period to 1974.

9. Trade figures are taken from the 1972-73 Department of Agriculture Report on *Trade in Agricultural Commodities*. The expanded trade with non-European overseas countries is significant but, as indicated in Chapter 9, our biggest supplier and market remains the United States.

10. The study by L. Auer, *Productivity in Canadian Agriculture*, 1971, was commissioned by and for the Economic Council of Canada. Mr. Auer was on staff with the ECC.

11. Statistics and conclusions on the state of employment in food manufacturing are derived from Statistics Canada bulletins on Employment, Earnings and Hours, Nos. 72-002. Women made up 29 per cent of all workers in food manufacturing in 1974 compared to 23 per cent in all manufacturing.

II

Farmers: A Class Divided

The basic role of the farmer is well understood. He produces raw foodstuffs which the rest of the society can process and consume, or in the case of Canada use as an export staple in exchange for manufactured goods. Farmers collectively, although they now represent less than seven per cent of the population, remain a key sector of the Canadian economy. Because of the richness of agricultural resources we are roughly self-sufficient in essential commodities like cereals, meats and dairy products.

The traditional farmer operates as an independent capitalist-producer, usually owning his own land and equipment and providing most of the labour himself. The trend away from independent units to corporate farms which hire wage-labour, though significant, is still small as a proportion of total Canadian agriculture.

Although basic food production is still characterized by the independent producer, there has been something of a revolution in rural Canada over the past twenty to thirty years as the full force of industrial technology has been made to apply. Post-war trends, externally imposed on the farming community and aided to some extent by the politics and ideology of farmers themselves, have gradually but drastically restructured agriculture. Whether farmers are regarded as the helpless and powerless victims or as willing participants, the changes created have been profound. If logically extended to the future they could eliminate the working farmer and develop a system of corporate-owned agriculture, accompanied by 'managers' and industrial farm wage workers.

Prior to the post-war trends of mechanization and specialization which brought agriculture to its current state, a strikingly different farming community existed, particularly in western Canada. Its life-style and politics reflected an earlier stage of industrial technology, more limited capital resources, and a less complex relationship between farmers and the national economy. Farmers and their communities were more united in their problems and their politics.

This period began about the turn of the century with the settlement of western Canada and the introduction of mechanized horse-drawn machinery. It ended with the more general use of tractor power in the late 1940s and 1950s and the race to enlarge farm production units through land expansion, ever-larger equipment, and the wide use of fertilizers and pesticides.

This earlier period of agriculture was in sharp contrast to the post-1950s era both in terms of the production unit itself (i.e. the circumstances of the farmer and his family) *and* in terms of the broader economic forces and the political response of farmers and their organizations to them.

The life-style and politics of the rural communities in the first half of the century was shaped by the farming operation. In western Canada, homestead policies under the Dominion Land Act coupled with the location of grain shipping points every eight to ten miles on railway branch lines meant that farms and communities were close together. The small towns which served as commercial trading centres also became social, political and religious centres as did the even more concentrated local school districts.

The farming operation was labour-intensive, involving both family labour and hired wage labour during the growing and harvest seasons. Each farm was largely self-sufficient in food commodities in co-operation with neighbouring farms. (Beef rings, for example, were established in which each family in a certain area would take turn slaughtering a steer and distributing the meat in equal portions to the neighbours. This provided everyone with fresh beef every two or three weeks despite the absence of refrigeration.) Farms were diversified in their operations, including field crops, livestock, poultry, and milk cows, so that each family member had specific chores to carry out. The use of horses for field work required extra labour, but also had the effect of regulating the family work-day since the horses needed periodic feed and rest and couldn't be worked after dark.

Family involvement in farm labour and regulation of the work-day had an effect on the farming community and its activities. Sports days, community suppers, political meetings and religious gatherings were planned around the work day and the growing season and involved entire families. There was an egalitarian aspect to social activity and politics based on common problems, common work demands and the necessity for co-operation at a community level during peak labour demands in the farming operation. Harvest bees, building bees, and the collective handling of livestock were commonplace examples of necessary co-operation.

It is important not to romanticize this period in agricultural history, although many would argue that despite the physical hardships it had some qualitative advantages over the present. It was also physically exploitative at times to the point of real suffering. The point is to recognize that the nature of the farmers' involvement in production and the social network of their community gave rise to a much different political self-conception as they assessed their relationship to the rest of the society. Different, that is, from the state of farmer politics in the 1970s.

The common problems faced by farmers in the west went far beyond the grief of struggle with wind, hail, frost, insects, crop diseases, weeds, and prolonged drought. They came up against the combined power of the railways and the grain trade which moved the prairie crops from local delivery points to flour mills and export terminals. Between 1901 and 1950, western farmers organized a series of powerful producer organizations around the primary issue of marketing. From the Territorial Grain Growers to the United Farmers and Farmers Union movements and the partisan politics of the Progressive party and Co-operative Commonwealth Federation, prairie farmers, sometimes joined by colleagues in other regions, fought against monopoly power over agriculture prices and marketing conditions. Their demands ranged from state regulation of handling and grading procedures to nationalization of the entire elevator and railway system and a public marketing board for grain. The common thread of the farm movement and the individual consciousness of farmers was a strong anti-monopoly bias. Their solutions ranged from self-help co-operatives to massive state intervention, but they managed to unite in a succession of political formations because they shared common assumptions and problems in their own community. For example, the Progressive Party, which first ran nationally in 1921 on a 'Farmers' Platform,' took shape in less than a year but managed to sweep every rural seat in Saskatchewan with 62.6 per cent of the vote, and elected 65 members federally. United Farmer parties were elected to government provincially in Alberta and Manitoba in the 1920s, and the CCF carried 55 per cent of the vote in rural Saskatchewan to take power in 1944. The common ideology of each of these farm-based movements was an attack on the monopoly power of banks, railways, and large manufacturers. Over a period of time the movement was successful in building protective agencies of limited power. Institutions such as the wheat pools and farm product marketing boards were allowed to co-exist with private capitalist enterprise, and provide limited stability and protection for farmers in the economy.

Farmers in the first half of the century geared their political demands to the marketing side of agriculture rather than the 'cost of production' side. In part this was because the agencies affecting price and market conditions were more apparently exploitive in their dealings with farmers. Daily price changes and conflicts over grading, weights, and dockage confronted the producer every time he delivered products to the market. But there is a more basic reason why 'cost of production' was less of an issue than marketing. It was much less of a problem. The major factors forcing up costs of production in all commodities after 1950 were the capital costs of land and machinery. But in the first half of the century the production unit was more stable and less expansionary. Each farmer had as much land as he and his family could physically handle with the use of horse-drawn equipment. It made no sense to compete to buy land which would require more horses, more labour than the family could provide, and more equipment and buildings. The price of machinery was gradually inflationary but purchases were restricted to replacement of essential implements. This meant the farmer could depreciate his costs over several years knowing he would be buying a binder or cultivator of similar size and cost. It was only after the demise of horse-power and the lifting of physical limitations on how much a man could farm that costs of land, machinery, and other farm production costs began to increase uncontrollably and became a major problem.

To summarize, until the end of the Second World War farmers were able to identify certain common enemies and their concern centred primarily around issues of marketing their products. They had solid social communities from which to organize and they shaped strong and united farm organizations and political groups which won important concessions over the years. After 1950 all of that changed. The agricultural community was torn economically and politically by post-war trends, and there has been a growing disparity between large and small production units. Two major and conflicting tendencies emerged in the farming community, so that by the 1960s there was no longer a single political position which could be said to characterize the 'farmer view'. The ideological and class differences were so wide that even broad farmer populists like Alvin Hamilton and Eugene Whelan could not successfully bridge the gap.

A number of critical trends combined to change the political face of agriculture after 1950. They generally related to the phenomenon of the cost-price squeeze. Some of these trends greatly influenced the upward push on food costs but their greatest impact was on the social and political base of the farm community itself. By the 1970s, farmers could no longer be fairly characterized as a single group with a single identifiable set of problems. The tremendous disparity in income and living standards between the owners of large-scale production units and traditional small farm enterprise is greater than for any other occupational group. In rough terms the largest five per cent of farm units in Canada in 1974 produced 20 per cent of farm products and had net earnings which would average $20,000 to $25,000. (This was high by working-class standards but low in relationship to capital invested. Their farms would be valued at over $150,000.) In contrast, over 60 per cent of all farms in 1971 had gross earnings of under $10,000, which represented less than $5,000 in net income.[1] The economic disparities to some extent overlapped with the political divisions in rural Canada. It was clearly the large-scale production units which were emerging as a new political force on the Right in contradiction to traditional farm organizations. The character of the new politics bred by the changes of the past twenty years carried with it some dangers for the future. Grain farming by the 1970s was essentially a one-man operation using large capital equipment. Family labour was not involved except during peak periods of activity such as harvest. Younger family members were leaving agriculture and the rural communities at an earlier age, after completing basic education. The farm operator worked longer hours during the growing season and often lived off the farm in larger centres in the off-season. As a result he was less involved in community activities and there were fewer activities to be involved in.

The communities themselves had physically disappeared at the level of hamlet and village. Services were systematically withdrawn to larger centres as schools, hospitals, post offices, retail services, and finally marketing facilities like grain elevators and railway branchlines were closed and removed. It is true that communities are defined by the interaction of people and not by buildings. The communities were still there as part of a larger population unit, but the basis of human interaction had radically altered. There was no social purpose to an agricultural community per se when the economic services, recreation facilities and social institutions had been centralized to an urban environment. Farmers became an extension of an already defined urban community with its own power structure, social network, and political tradition.

The conditions of capital-intensive agriculture for the large farmer add to his isolation and independence from other farmers. His self-conception of farmer-businessman operating in 'the grains industry' or 'the cattle industry' for a profit moves him to identify more closely with the non-farm components of his commodity area. He becomes a partner of the agribusiness sector of the food industry.

The change in farmers' political attitudes came gradually, but systematically. It was most notable in the prairie wheat-producing region which once fostered the radical wing of the national farm movement. But it was an inevitable trend within all regions and commodities as farms became larger, more capital-intensive and more integrated with the interests of corporate agribusiness. Farmers were split between the traditional anti-monopoly populism which the agrarian movement had always emphasized, and a new farmer-businessman consciousness which allowed for a closer integration between farm production and other agricultural interests. In the prairie wheatland the former tendency was reflected in the NDP's rural support base and the National Farmers Union, while the latter was reflected in the Palliser Wheat Growers and support for the Liberal Party.

Through the 1960s the shift in the political base among farmers was readily apparent. The National Farmers Union, which merged existing provincial farmers unions into a national structure in 1969, maintained the fight for expanded state intervention, marketing boards, price stabilization, and collective bargaining rights for farmers. Representing about 10 per cent of all farmers in direct membership, the NFU was strongest in southwestern Ontario, central Saskatchewan, and pockets of northern Alberta including the Peace River region which spills into B.C. NFU members tended to be middle-size farmers plus a few larger producers with a tradition of radical politics. Their tactics consisted of both formal polite representations to the federal government, and massive rallies and tractor demonstrations. They represent nominally all commodities in all regions, but their main punch has been in grain policy in challenge to Otto Lang, Wheat Board Minister. By 1973 tensions reached the point where Lang would no longer speak to NFU gatherings to which he had been invited.

The NFU relied heavily on the traditions and loyalties of the hard-core activists of the farm movement to sustain itself. Its farmer members, like their more conservative rivals in the various commodity groups, lived and worked in communities which had been diffused and isolated. Sustained involvement and organizational focus became difficult at the local level and leadership was very much centralized into national and regional offices.

The hope for the NFU, so far as the non-farm work force in Canada was concerned, lay with its continued opposition to the commercial monopolies of agribusiness. Resistance by NFU men and women to the inevitable encroachment of agribusiness directly into agriculture could increasingly take collectivist forms in self-defence. Individual farmers couldn't compete dollar for dollar with the agencies of multi-national corporations engaged in land purchase. Farmers either had to demand and fight for state intervention to regulate the land resource and ultimately, perhaps, establish co-operative farms, or they might lose control of production to larger units of private capital.

At its 1974 convention, the NFU established a land policy which called on governments to consider maximum limits on farm size and systems of land tenure which gave consideration to public ownership. This policy, which led at least one Ontario delegate to resign in protest, was not a hard-line declaration. But it did extend the discussion of land beyond the narrow confines of private ownership. The NFU's own commitment to "preserving the family farm" forced it toward a position of land control policies.

In contrast to the NFU, the commodity groups which speak for the larger producers have no romantic illusions about "the family farm." These groups, such as the Canadian Cattlemen's Association and the Palliser Wheat Growers Association, have a strong ideological commitment to the unrestricted ownership of private farmland.

The Palliser Wheat Growers formed in 1969 in opposition to the NFU. Largely based in Saskatchewan, its 1974 membership was less than five per cent of all grain permit holders or about one-third the membership strength of the NFU's Saskatchewan section. But despite a limited membership it quickly gained influence with Ottawa far beyond its numbers because it reinforced federal policy objectives.

The membership strongholds for Palliser include the large wheat farm districts of the Regina plains. This area of south-central Saskatchewan had been sliding politically to the Right since the provincial election sweep of the CCF to government in 1944. In 1944, seventeen of the eighteen provincial constituencies in this area voted in CCF members. In 1960, thirteen of the seats were still CCF but in the 1964 and 1967 elections they went overwhelmingly Liberal and were the main factor in turning the CCF government out of office after twenty years of uninterrupted power. Despite re-election of an NDP government in 1971, many of these areas such as Lumsden, Milestone and Rosetown remained Liberal Party strongholds. In the federal election of 1974 the Assiniboia constituency in the same area elected Otto Lang's executive assistant, largely on the strength of votes from large wheat producers.

The areas of large grain farms also had the greatest population shift, a six per cent decline from 1961-66 compared to one-and-a-half per cent in the province's rural districts overall. This population outmigration had been a contributing factor to the political shift since it was the middle and smaller farmers who were retiring. They would have been part of the pre-1950 political experience and more inclined to the anti-monopoly populism of the CCF and NFU. The younger, larger operators are more consistently conservative and attracted to the Palliser organization and its thinking.[2]

Palliser members adopted the farmer-businessman perspective in their policies and programs. Their president from 1970-74 was a farm-machinery dealer and a governor of the Winnipeg Commodity Exchange as well as a farm owner. They became engaged in a close informal working relationship with the CPR, Commercial Grain Companies, and the federal government departments of Transportation and Agriculture. In their support of reorganizing grain handling and transportation they provided a political base for the Lang strategy, discussed here in Chapter 4. Palliser members channeled investment capital off the farm into corporation shares, and companies reciprocated by taking out Associate memberships. The Associate status of $300 per member was made available to any non-farm corporation and was well received by the summer of 1974 when Palliser was clearly on record as favouring an integration with agribusiness. Palliser supported "open marketing" of feed grain in opposition to the Canadian Wheat Board in 1974, and they led the demand for removal of the long-standing Crow's Nest freight rates on grain. They worked closely with Otto Lang to design and try to execute a plan to replace the 3,000 or so country elevators on the prairies with a system of large inland terminals, forcing a fifty-mile truck haul for farmers. (See chapter 4.)

In general both Palliser and its counterpart the Canadian Cattlemen's Association contradicted the traditional populism of western Canadian farmers which resisted the power of monopolies over farm prices and marketing conditions. The Cattlemen's Association continued to preach free market theory despite the crisis of the international beef industry in 1973 and 1974 and Palliser appeared to want the same conditions in the grains industry.

Cost-Price Squeeze

The economic force which reshaped both the political attitudes and class position of the farming community was the post-1945 cost-price squeeze. The cost-price squeeze was a process in which the rate of increase in the combined costs of producing a commodity were rising faster than the gross return received by the farmer for the commodity when he sold it. This cut into the margin of net-income between sale price and costs of production which the farmer and his family had left with which to survive. The late 1940s was not the first period in agricultural history when the cost-price squeeze on farm income was a problem. The phenomenon was as old as industrial agriculture. But for the first time after 1945 there seemed to be a solution other than a simple increase in the market price of farm commodities. (Increases in farm product prices were never attained to the satisfaction of farmers *before* 1945, but they had perceived this as the primary solution to their problems.) In the post-war era the new technology offered new solutions to declining net income. With larger machinery, fertilizers, chemical sprays, and the physical capacity to farm more land, farmers could expand their *volume* of production to increase revenues. By increasing their per-acre yield with new farming methods and by doubling the average size of farms, farmers increased their productivity an average of six per cent per year between 1945 and 1970. In the early stages this "improved efficiency" as a response to the cost-price squeeze appeared to be a solution. For a short time it was.

Not every farmer responded in the same way to the pressures of the post-war cost-price squeeze. The critical and dominant response was to increase volume of output in whatever commodity he was engaged in. This in turn meant seeking more land. One 1971 survey of farmers in a Saskatchewan municipality indicated that 85 per cent of the farm operators had expanded their farms since they began farming and 60 per cent had more than doubled their holdings.[3] (The largest part of the increase in the capitalization of farms was due to land investments, a problem elaborated later in the chapter.) The farmers who expanded their operations were in the majority. They became the 'high risk' entrepreneurs who would exchange debts for capital equipment and land on the gamble that the productivity advantages would pay dividends. Politically these farmers were the activists in both the traditional anti-monopoly organizations like the NFU *and* the more conservative farmer-businessman commodity groups.

Other farmers responded to the pressure of rising costs by maintaining a small land base. They scrupulously avoided cost outlays for land, buildings and machinery. They tried to offset declining net-income by making their farms more labour-intensive and self-sufficient by keeping a small number of pigs, milk cows, chickens and, when possible, engaging in off-farm work. These farmers were among the 150,000 in Canada who by 1971 still had gross income from cash receipts of less than $5,000 and net earnings estimated at under $3,000.[4] Although poor in cash income and living standards, these farmers remained relatively debt-free in comparison to those who bought land and expanded.

Small farmers view the land base in their small holdings as the security for retirement. They are on average older than larger farmers, less inclined to take risk. Socially and politically these farmers are isolated and independent. They are more tied to the farm by work demands and have less money for social and recreational events or to support farm and political organizations. With self-sufficient operations, low volume of market sales each year, and avoidance of debts, these small farmers have less to be interested in in the capitalist market-place.

Then there are those who responded to the cost-price pressure by migrating out of the farm community, selling their land to expanding units. Many of these farmers were at or beyond retirement age, and others left to search for jobs in an urban setting because their farms were not large enough to prosper. From 1966 to 1971 alone there was a net decline of 500,000 people from farms in Canada, a reduction of 24 per cent. Not all the land left behind was integrated with existing units. In some cases farm families left because land was bought for urban expansion, recreation or other development. Of the 4 million acres converted out of farming in Ontario and Quebec from 1966 to 1971, *2.4 million* was prime cultivated land.[5] What happened to those who left farming for economic reasons before retirement age is largely a matter of speculation. In general they faced a hostile and unknown culture and at middle-age were forced to compete on the labour market with no formally recognized skills and little education. Canadian cities have an abundance of ex-farmers whose material circumstances actually declined when they left farming although the move was motivated by a desire to improve their family income. In the twenty years from 1941 to 1961 Saskatchewan, the province with the largest proportion of farmers, had a total outmigration of 350,000 people, more than all other provinces combined.[6]

Regardless of their particular response, Canadian families who lived and worked on farms in the period from 1945 on underwent a difficult period of adjustment. The impact was felt beyond the farm community and ultimately affected the consumer cost of food, first positively and then negatively.

It is clear in retrospect that the conditions surrounding the cost-price squeeze were controlled and directed in a way by which farmers ultimately could only be the losers. The primary external influence was the federal government. In the war and immediate post-war period the federal government was interested in boosting productivity and trade in agricultural products both to satisfy and profit from the food needs of war-torn western Europe. There was also concern about post-war domestic inflation in food products. These two objectives, increased productivity and stable prices, led to a range of policy initiatives. On the one hand there were measures to assist capital expansion in agriculture through farm loans, particularly to veterans, and industry was encouraged to develop and promote new technology. On the other hand, measures such as the continuation of the Canadian Wheat Board and the Price Stabilization Act in 1944 were aimed at keeping prices down for farm commodities. In general, the combination of controlled farm market prices and rising produc- tions costs forced farmers to accept a massive capitalization of agricultural production in the post-war period.

The farm price of commodities advanced only 17 per cent from 1949 to 1970, with the price of wheat virtually frozen from 1945 to 1972. Farm income gains *had* to come from increased volume if they came at all. But they didn't come substantially because gains in efficiency by way of improved productivity were lost to the continuous pressure of farm input prices and the crushing burden of debt.

The facts are that during this period the efficiency and productivity gains were not transferred to farmers. Farmers managed to increase their average per-capita output by six-fold between 1951 and 1966 and they increased the total volume of Canadian agricultural production by 40 per cent. But net farm income remained below the average for manufacturing wages in Canada. And during this period there was a 50 per cent decline in the number of farms from 733,000 in 1941 to 366,000 in 1971. In other words half the previous number of farmers produced 140 per cent of the volume of food but their relative standard of income improved only marginally.

If farmers failed to benefit dramatically from a more highly industrialized system of agriculture, it still seems probable that the consumers of Canada and the world gained advantage in the form of cheaper food products. For a time this was true. By supporting half the farm population at the same standard, on average, as 1950 (some better, some worse), we were able in 1970 to spend less of our earnings on food that we had in 1950 and before. This was true in spite of the accumulated earnings of non-farm agribusiness which profited immensely from the process of industrialization. But the era of 'cheap food' encouraged by government policy and made possible by productivity gains of farmers was in contradiction to uncontrolled inflation in the price of farmland, the biggest single factor in the cost of food production. The 15 per cent rate of inflation in food commodities beginning in 1973 has only served to further exaggerate land values and add to the inflationary pressures.

Land: The Problem at Its Source

The greatest single drain on capital during the period of industrialization of agriculture was not machinery but land. The land question was central to the cost-price squeeze and the land tenure system reinforced the economic divisions and cutthroat competition which increasingly characterized the farm community after 1945.

The original policies governing land tenure, framed in the Dominion Lands Act of 1870, were aimed at rapid disbursement of large areas of undeveloped farmland to immigrant settlers. They served the purpose well, attracting over a million-and-a-half claimants to unsettled parts of the country in less than two decades, 1900 to 1920. The overseas claims of Dominion Government advertising were of course exaggerated but the basic promise of free land was kept. Each settler gained title to 160 acres of "homestead" provided he established residency on the land over three years after filing an original claim. He could then purchase the adjoining 160 acres of land for three dollars per acre. This policy was aimed at maximizing the population in agricultural regions and providing security of tenure. It was based on the American system which aimed at maximum utilization of the land resource. Other, less measurable benefits have also been cited:

> They felt also that farm-owning operatorship would give the greatest measure of security to the cultivator and would provide the most effective organization of rural life. Quite as important they felt that farm-home ownership would furnish the type of political environment and the degree of political stability necessary for a strong democracy.[7]

The homestead policy obviously worked for the purposes of the Canadian Government in the period from 1870 to 1930 when land settlement was fairly much completed. It was also generally satisfactory to immigrants, particularly those from Europe for whom land ownership was extremely important. But with the advent of more mechanized, capital-intensive agriculture and with competition for a scarce land resource the old system of land tenure became a disaster. In the years from 1945 to 1974, land values went up from approximately $25 per acre to $100 as a provincial average in Saskatchewan. In Ontario, farmland was selling by 1974 for $500 per acre and more in areas close to urban centres.[8] These costs paid out over time add sharply to overall costs of production. But surprisingly land policies are the least considered aspect of agriculture by governments, consumer groups and farmers themselves.[9]

Land represents 60 per cent of the total capital investment in farms as of 1971. It was the largest contributing factor to the increase in accumulated debt for individual farms in Canada, which rose from $3,168 in 1960 to $12,875 in 1971. It also contributed much of the $5 billion collective debt of Canadian farmers accumulated by 1972. Annual interest payments alone have risen from $250 per farm in 1961 to $1400 in 1973.[10]

It would be impossible to calculate the sums which have gone into the payment to Canadian lending agencies for debts related to land purchases over the thirty years after 1945. What is clear is that the market value of farm land continued to rise uncontrolled in response to competitive bidding for its use not just by farmers but by land and development companies, 'hobby' farmers from the city, and petty land speculators. Land speculation will continue to be a major source of inflation in the cost of food production until a new system of land tenure is devised.

To some degree, changes in land tenure are being forced by the prohibitive costs of land ownership and by the desire of non-farmer owners of farmland to generate revenue by renting it to farmers. A modern version of 'share-cropping,' in which a farmer farms land in exchange for a share of the crop produced, is becoming more commonplace. This system, although cheaper for farmers, is also inefficient in that it must provide landlords with an income which is not based on any productive contribution beyond the holding of a land title.

A 1971 study of land tenure in Saskatchewan provided some rather startling data on the question of land tenure.[11] In direct comparisons on the cost of land ownership versus rental among grain farmers in 1969, rental arrangements were found to be cheaper per acre than land ownership by 25-30 per cent. The usual rental agreement assumes that a one-third share of the value of production goes as rent to the owner of the land, who pays the taxes. In the Brown-Bens study of a Saskatoon area, the absentee landlords were made up of widows (22 per cent), retired farmers (21 per cent), businessmen or professionals (21 per cent), active farmers (13 per cent), miscellaneous, including corporations, real estate firms and the Saskatchewan Government (23 per cent).

Rental became more common over the years as absentee land ownership has increased. Only 56 per cent of the farmers in Saskatchewan in 1971 had title to all the land they farmed and 73 per cent of the farmers in Canada had complete title. The fact has been that rental or ownership makes little difference to most farmers in terms of security of tenure. An estimated two-thirds of all farmland is under mortgage to one or other of the major lending agencies, primarily the federal Farm Credit Corporation. The land under mortgage can be repossessed if conditions prevent farmers from keeping up payments to their mortgage holder.

Brown and Bens found that the rental option was pursued most by already large farms. It was not generally available to smaller farmers who were unable to invest in larger equipment on the basis of a short-term lease. Most of the farmers renting land were prepared to buy it as soon as it became available. Brown and Bens sum up their findings this way:

Individual operators often maintain their independent status at the expense of opportunities for greater efficiency and net-income. Farm operators appear to prefer obligations to lenders over obligations to landlords. This is so even though rental may be a less burdensome way to acquire the services of farmland.

Despite the extra cost, farmers prefer to own their land for ideological reasons and as a security for retirement in the absence of effective pensions. There is a general confidence based on the evidence of the past thirty years that speculation will inflate land values continuously and provide a 'capital-gain' for the retiring farmer on his original investment. But the capital-gain aspect of land turnover is what attracts the large and small-time speculators as well.

The relationship of land policy to the cost-price squeeze and to food price inflation has been ignored by government and farm organizations because of the very basic commitment to private ownership of land. The right to own, buy, and sell land on an unrestricted open market is sacred to the notion of 'free enterprise.' Such a system applied to farmland requires refinancing of agricultural resources every generation with the brunt of costs borne initially by the farmer, and ultimately in the form of higher food costs. The speculative value attached to the land resource as it becomes more scarce is automatically included in the cost of food. And the original selling price of land is tripled by the cost of mortgaging over twenty-five years at rates of interest in the range of ten per cent. Nevertheless, despite the crippling burden of the present system, no new system of land tenure has been conceived since 1870.

Saskatchewan Land Bank

The nearest example to a new system of land-tenure began in 1972 in Saskatchewan. The Saskatchewan Government Land Bank program, modelled largely on the proposals of the Brown-Bens study of land tenure, purchases land as it becomes available on the market. It leases the land out again to existing farmers wishing to expand their operations or to new farmers. There are restrictions on eligibility for Land Bank leases, with farmers having assets beyond a certain level ($60,000 in 1973) ineligible to apply. In the first two years of the plan's existence roughly 1,000 Land Bank purchases of land were made and leased out. Roughly 20 per cent of these leases went to new farmers, and the remainder to expanding operations.[12]

The Land Bank program can solve the problem of an immediate major capital outlay on land for a limited number of farmers wishing to expand holdings or start into farming. It particularly can solve a dilemma in father-to-son land transfers. Retiring farmers can get a cash settlement from the Land Bank, which they need for retirement security, and their immediate family will get preferential consideration if they apply for the land for lease.

The Land Bank fails as a solution to the private ownership of land, however, because it makes allowance for the lessee to *purchase* the land as an option after five years of leasing from the government. This means the land may revert to the private market if the farmer holding a lease feels speculation on land is a profitable investment. If sufficient capital gains can be extracted through speculation on land the higher costs of ownership over rental to produce the same value of products is of no concern to the farmer. This cost difference should be a concern to consumers, however, because it ultimately shows up in higher food prices.

A second general problem with the Land Bank program has been that the Saskatchewan Government itself *borrows* the money to purchase land. The government must itself pay interest costs to lending agencies which it then includes in the assessment of rent to farmers. This means that the high cost of mortgage and interest payments is still borne within the costs of production in farming, indirectly through an annual lease fee. The solution would be for land purchases to be viewed as reclamation of a public resource to be financed directly from government tax revenues. The land resource could then be left permanently in the hands of the crown in terms of ownership, with tenure established for farmers through lifetime leases with no option to purchase. Lease fees would reflect only the cost of servicing the land, in lieu of taxes. Then the burden of refinancing the same vital resource each generation could be avoided and the flow of surplus to banks and mortgage companies ended. If even the annual interest payments on farm debts for land purchases were suddenly abolished, per capita farm net income could rise 20 per cent across Canada, or alternately food prices could be reduced by five to ten per cent.

If the Land Bank falls short as an alternative it is nonetheless a useful reform at the provincial level, one which could well be duplicated in other provinces. Along with measures to restrict foreign and absentee ownership of farmland and the setting of maximum limits on farm size, crown land assembly or 'land banks' could sharply reduce the inflationary spiral on agricultural land.

Realignment of 'Class' Among Farmers

The trends in land ownership in the period from 1945 to 1975 not only exaggerated disparities in wealth and farm size between large and small farmers; they also altered the farmers' relationship to wage-labour. The concentration of land and capital by larger producers was a general trend among all commodities. In most commodities other than grain this also meant an increase in hired wage-labour. Large farmers not only had larger capital investments by the 1970s, they also had more seasonal and full-time farm workers in their operations. They became bosses over wage-labour in addition to or instead of their traditional role as independent producers. This newly emerging status affected their political and ideological conceptions of the rest of society and brought them closer to non-farm capitalists in their attitudes and biases.

In contrast, the smaller farmers were becoming more directly linked with the general industrial work force. Their independence as farmers was eroded directly by such things as contract-farming and share-cropping for absentee landlords. At the same time they showed an increasing tendency to engage in off-farm labour to supplement inadequate farm income. Among farms with annual cash receipts under $2,500 in 1971, 45 per cent reported off-farm earnings. Average days of off-farm work among those reporting was 120 days, or almost half the total work-year.[13]

The polarization along class lines as well as the political polarization discussed earlier brings the social structure of rural Canada more closely in line with the rest of the society. We now have a situation where smaller farmers increasingly have more in common with non-farm industrial workers than with their large farm neighbours. They also have more in common with the growing number of skilled farm workers who are working for wages for larger farmers or farm corporations.

The current data on concentration of land ownership and the growth of an industrial labour force on larger farms may suggest a pattern of the future. While the vast majority of farms are individually owned and operated, the disproportionate growth of corporate farms with wage workers is unmistakeable. The overall capital and labour flow goes something like this: smaller farmers are increasing their income through labour earnings in more intensive and diversified farming operations and through off-farm employment; middle farmers are expanding income through greater use of technology and land and generally work independently without hired farm-labour and without themselves engaging in off-farm work; the larger individual and corporate farms are expanding employment of both technology and labour and control an increasing proportion of overall resources.

One fact reflecting the trends is that the ratio of farmers to farm workers is declining as large production units consolidate land, capital and labour into farm factories. As concentration displaces farmers who operated independently, the enlarged units hire skilled farm workers. The result is that the number of farm wage-workers is overtaking the number of farmers.

TABLE 2

FARMS WITH GROSS RECEIPTS OVER $10,000

Commodity	% of total number of farms	% of total production from farms
Grain	35%	60%
Chickens and eggs	38%	95%
Cattle	35%	85%
Dairy	40%	78%

SOURCE: STATISTICS CANADA 1971 CENSUS

By 1971, concentration of farm produced wealth was evident in general, but varied greatly among commodities. In each area, the farms with their total value of production over $10,000 represented 40 per cent or less of the number of farms producing that commodity but produced a majority of overall production. Chicken and egg production, which is the most concentrated, also has a higher degree of corporate ownership of production than the other commodity areas. In addition to concentration of productive capacity in the form of land and capital equipment among the larger farms, there was also a trend toward concentration of farm labour in larger farms. While farm labour generally was being displaced by mechanized agriculture between 1950 and 1971, it was being retained and expanded in the larger units. For example although the number of full-time workers dropped by nearly 20 per cent from 1961 to 1971, the number of farms employing two or more workers *increased* by 45 per cent (from 3900 to 5700) and the number of farms hiring five or more workers increased by 30 per cent (from 762 to 1,049). As a result of this trend, the overall decline in farm workers was less between 1961 and 1971 than the decline of farm operators.

In the 1961 and 1966 census years, Statistics Canada included a category of farms under *Tenure of Operator* which was called 'managers.' These were farms in which the owner was absent from the production unit, and was either a corporation or an individual entrepreneur with other interests. This category was eliminated in the 1971 census report for reasons best known to Statistics Canada, and integrated with the Tenure categories of Owner, Part-Owner, and Renter. This category change removed evidence of the trend to corporate farms which was clear between 1961 and 1966. For example while the total number of farms decreased by 15 per cent from 1961 to 1966 the number of farms operated by farm managers *increased* by three per cent. Furthermore these farms had a rapid build-up of wage labour. Although they totalled only 2,472, less than one per cent of all farms, these 'managed' farms employed 15 per cent of all full-time farm workers in 1961 and 20 per cent by 1966. They were the major contributing factor to the increase in the number of farms with two or more workers. Since their disappearance as a separate statistical category after 1966, the trend toward factory-farming is more difficult to assess accurately.

What is clear is that farming is big business for some. Large units, if not owned by agribusiness outright, have come to share its problems and assumptions in relation to the industrial workforce.

Farm Workers

In 1971 there were 127,000 farm workers in Canada, 38,600 full-time. With the growth of large production units the character of hired farm-labour has changed somewhat. Farm workers must be more skilled at handling new technology and are increasingly placed in a collective work situation with other workers. The traditional 'hired man' working for the independent farmer and becoming part of the family operation is rapidly disappearing. The old-style hired man would room and board with the farm family as part of his pay and often give a lifetime of loyal service under low pay but cheerful working conditions. The modern farm worker is more mobile and independent, often living with his own family in independent quarters on or off the farm. Wage-labour is more restricted to larger farms.

What hasn't changed is the scale of exploitation of farm workers relative to the rest of the Canadian labour force. A farm worker is underpaid, unprotected by labour laws, and subject to some of the most extreme working conditions imaginable, particularly if he is a seasonal or migrant farm worker engaged in harvest operations.

Full-time average earnings for farm labourers in 1973 were $3,620 plus board and $4,325 in 1974. These rates work out to an average of less than the minimum wage in some provinces. But since farm workers are exempt from all labour standards in every province except Newfoundland, the denial of minimum wages is neither illegal or unusual.

Labour standards include minimum wage, hours of work provisions, child labour laws, and accident and sickness coverage, all of which are violated in the case of Canada's farm workers. They have also been excluded from Unemployment Insurance and Canada Pension Plan benefits except through special voluntary arrangements.

And finally, farm workers are prevented from forming unions in most provinces, including Ontario which has the highest concentration of full-time and migrant farm workers, an estimated 60,000.

It is only in recent years that there has been any degree of concern or awareness about the conditions of farm workers. Conditions which are generally bad are magnified ten-fold for the migrant workers on the tobacco and tomato farms, the orchards, and the sugar beet farms in southern Alberta. With publicity surrounding the plight of the California grape and lettuce farm workers, some protest began to surface around conditions in Canada by the early 1970s. As well, it was becoming increasingly difficult for farms to get labour under the wages and conditions available. Farmers and growers themselves began to make some adjustment and improvements.[14]

A federal government report on migrant farm labour in 1973 fully acknowledged the severity of working conditions for migrant farm workers. But the only changes enforced in the following year were those governing imported workers brought in under federal work visas from Mexico, the Caribbean, and Europe. Canadian migrant workers, or immigrants brought in privately, (and usually illegally) had no protection or standards. Angry spokesmen for the Migrant Farm Workers Association complained in fall 1974 about the lack of government response to appalling conditions a year after they were recognized and described in a federal manpower report. The MFWA also chided organized labour and church groups which were supporting the cause of California farm workers while ignoring the plight of French-Canadian migrants in southwestern Ontario. A main focus of criticism by migrant workers was housing conditions:

> On one farm, four men and two women live in a shack 20 feet by 25 feet with no washing facilities, tattered mattresses on the floor and a fly-infested outhouse nearby.[15]

Farm workers also have a stake in agricultural policy. As conditions are stabilized and improved for landowners, standards may improve for farm labour as well. This will happen through the combined organizing efforts of farm workers themselves, by enforcement of federal and provincial labour standards and by the need for farmers and agribusiness to compete for wage-labour with the non-farm industrial sector. As the proportion of farm workers to farm owners increases and farms continue to get bigger the class relationship of capital to labour will follow the pattern of other industries.

Independent farmers who fit the mould of neither capitalist nor worker are and will remain politically unpredictable. They will be in general an influence toward change on both the Left and the Right. Individually, depending on their material circumstances, their organizational ties, and their political experience, they will tend to share working-class objectives or those of the oligopolies. They will either be supportive of state intervention in marketing, pricing and the ownership of agricultural resources including land, or else fiercely supportive of 'free market' non-intervention by the state and a closer integration with the private oligopolies which represent agribusiness. Observers outside the farming community need to be aware that the differences of class and politics among farmers are as deep as they are. It is no longer possible to make a generalized analysis about the politics of farmers as a single force.

Notes to Chapter 2

1. All figures are drawn from 1971 Census data on Agriculture in Canada.

2. These observations are based on empirical data gathered through extensive interview questionnaires with farmers in South Central Saskatchewan as part of an M.A. thesis project. The interviews were combined with an analysis of population and voting trends and a breakdown of the membership base of major farmer-organizations. Related references include: Sanford Silverstein, "Occupational Class and Voting Behaviour: Electoral Support of a Left-Wing Protest Movement in a Period of Prosperity" in Seymour Lipset, *Agrarian Socialism: The Co-operative Commonwealth Federation in Saskatchewan*, 2nd edition, revised (Toronto, Doubleday, 1968); James McCrorie, *In Union Is Strength: A History of the Saskatchewan Farmers Union* (Saskatoon, Modern Press, 1965); Don Mitchell, "Oligopoly and the Cost-Price Squeeze: Assessing the Causes of Rural Decline" (unpublished M.A. thesis, University of Regina); and James McCrorie, "Change and Paradox in Agrarian Social Movements: The Case of Saskatchewan" in Richard Ossenburg (ed.), *Canadian Society: Pluralism, Change and Conflict* (Toronto, Prentice-Hall, 1971).

3. From a survey of Lake Johnston Municipality No. 102 for M.A. thesis research in 1971.

4. Statistics Canada, 1971 Census data.

5. Ibid.

6. Migration data within Canada is provided in John Porter's *Statistical Profile*. Porter also describes and documents the condition of rural-to-urban migrants in *The Vertical Mosaic*. A more specific reference to declining income and social status of ex-farm-operators is provided by the Centre for Community Studies, University of

Saskatchewan. This study examines the impact of out-migration by small farmers in Northern Saskatchewan as a result of the organization of community pastures by the federal government in the early 1960s.

7. Hadley Van Vliet, "Land Tenure Problems," *Scientific Agriculture* 7 (March 1941).

8. Land value figures are based on annual reports of the Saskatchewan Department of Agriculture and a 1974 *Financial Post* article on the problem of escalating land values in southern Ontario.

9. Mrs. Plumptre and the Prices Review Board, after three years of quarterly and special reports analyzing food costs, had yet, by mid-1975, to deal with the critical question of land tenure and inflated land values as they affected food prices.

10. Articles by R.S. Rust in the federal Department of Agriculture's periodical *Canadian Farm Economics* give detailed statistics on capital values, debt, and interest costs for Canadian farmers.

11. Jacob Brown and Robert Benz, *Land Tenure is Saskatchewan* (Regina, Queen's Printer, 1971).

12. Information on Land Bank transactions is based on the 1974 annual Report of the Saskatchewan Land Bank plus a CBC radio interview with Land Bank officials in November 1974.

13. Statistics Canada, 1971 Census data.

14. The Canadian Federation of Agriculture at its 1975 convention called for a labour standards code for farm workers. Their concerns were based less on humanitarian inspiration than on the necessity of self-interest. Farm workers are increasingly less willing to accept existing conditions. The CFA proposal called for a maximum work year of 2,800 hours, or 54 hours a week. They also suggested workers have minimum wage benefits and some form of workmen's compensation. But the fact they were unprepared to propose farm workers be included under existing provincial labour standards as they apply to urban workers suggests a continuing second-class role.

15. Canadian Press story, September 18, 1974, quoted by Mike Lemire of the Migrant Farm Workers Association.

III

Agribusiness

Agribusiness is the term often used by farmers in Canada to describe all industries and agencies which own, manage, or profit from activities directly related to agriculture. By that broad definition agribusiness encompasses a large proportion of the Canadian economy and exercises an equally strong political influence with the Canadian state.

The two broadest categories within agribusiness are the farm supply sector — those industries which manufacture and distribute all the goods and services necessary to complete basic food production — and the food and beverage industry — those industries which buy raw materials from farmers and process, package, and distribute them. The farm supply interests deal with farmers as a consumer market. Farmers have annual expenditures of roughly $500 million in connection with their farming operations and are major consumers of energy, manufactured goods, transportation services, credit, and specialty items like fertilizers and chemical sprays for field crops. The expenses paid out by farmers are a central source of profit to agribusiness suppliers who make up a vast network of farm machinery manufacturers, banks, feed-mills, oil companies, fertilizer companies, and so on.

Food and beverage industries combined represent the largest source of manufacturing employment in Canada, with over 200,000 workers. Among the hundred largest companies in the area of manufacturing, utilities, and resource firms in 1974, sixteen were food and beverage manufacturers. In retail merchandising, the largest three corporations as measured by reported sales in 1974 were supermarket food chains.[1] In addition to the 'pure' agribusiness corporations in the farm supply and food and beverage industries, there are many companies in

Canada which earn a portion of their overall profits from involvement in some aspect of the food cycle. Through their subsidiaries or departments, fully half of the hundred largest resource, manufacturing or utilities corporations are major agribusiness participants. For example Ford Motors, largest manufacturer in Canada, has a farm machinery division which ranks fourth largest in the world. Ford also specializes in the marketing of farm trucks. Imperial Oil, the largest resource industry, not only produces petroleum products for the farm market with fuels, oils, and greases, but also owns a subsidiary which manufactures and sells fertilizer across Canada. Canadian Pacific is a direct beneficiary of grain marketing activity through its railway holdings, but it also owns a large fertilizer plant through its subsidiary Cominco, speculates on farmland through Marathon Realty, and profits on farm fuel sales as a major shareholder of Husky Oil.

Obviously the scope of agribusiness is massive and includes not only the various levels of productive activity which go to make up final food products, but a good deal of essentially non-productive activity as well. The extensions of corporate interests in the form of land and commodity speculation, the science of air-filled packages and food advertising, and the over-capacity of factories and stores are features of agribusiness which are non-productive and inflationary.

The corporations engaged in food-related activities share the dominant characteristics of North American enterprise. They have concentrated markets among few sellers, and the waste and inefficiencies of a marketing structure which on the whole is neither competitive nor rational. The fact of oligopoly in agribusiness is undeniable, even by liberal economists. The evidence of the application of the collective power of corporate rivals in their shared markets is considerable, even relying only on the results of government inquiries. Oligopolies in agribusiness have used their power advantage to create the main conditions of the cost-price squeeze on farmers. They have also, through administered prices, exploited the general condition of inflation in the early to mid-1970s. And they have added unnecessarily to the cost of food products by such specific practices as double-ticketing of in-store merchandise and by a general avoidance of price competition. Despite all the pressures of rising costs and falling consumer demand in the period from 1973 to 1975, the food industry consistently added to its profit margins and maintained the luxury of massive advertising, promotions, and new openings of stores and plant facilities. Only when a full-scale recession hit parts of the country in 1975 did the accelerating profits and waste of the food empires level off.

Historical Background

Agribusiness has deep roots in Canadian economic history which parallel the development of an agricultural economy. Industrial agriculture was developed in the period from 1870 to 1930 primarily to develop grain as an export staple. Grain was shipped in raw unprocessed form then as now. But there was also a high degree of self-sufficiency in Canada in processed agricultural products to serve the limited domestic market. In other words, although the development of agriculture was aimed at supplying a trading commodity, its existence in the colony encouraged a measure of self-reliance uncharacteristic of the overall Canadian economy. Food surpluses in agricultural regions encouraged small indigenous food processing plants to establish themselves to serve local markets. European immigrants applied their traditional skills and limited capital to set up abattoirs, grist mills, cheese factories, and small creameries in any community with a thousand or so residents.

This pattern of hundreds of small food processing plants across the country, and larger plants in sizable urban centres, was well established by the 1920s and existed in sharp contrast to the near absence of other forms of manufacturing, particularly in the west. The reasons for this self-sufficiency trend in contrast to general dependency were obvious. Food was a perishable commodity and couldn't be supplied by imports even from other regions. Because the market was guaranteed locally and the technology relatively simple, local entrepreneurs were prepared to take risks they could not take in the manufacture of hard consumer goods, or of farm implements which were being manufactured in Britain and central Canada.

The significance of a highly decentralized food and manufacturing sector in which local market areas were self-sufficient became apparent during the period of capital consolidation in Canada after World War I. At that time Canadian finance capital poured into take-overs and centralization of food manufacturing industries in a way which was uncharacteristic of manufacturing investments generally.[2] From the early part of the century to the present, the dominant source of capital investment for agribusiness in Canada has been Canadian banks, investment corporations, and the network of Canadian capitalists centred in Toronto's Bay street. The proportion of U.S. and other foreign capital is growing today in food industries, as elsewhere. But in contrast to the general levels of foreign ownership found in manufacturing and resource industries, the proportion of U.S. ownership of the food and beverage and farm supply sectors is small. This distinct feature of Canadian agribusiness probably developed because of the existence in the early 1900s of already established local industries and markets, which could simply have their ownership transferred through purchase.[3] In other areas of manufacturing and resource development, Canadian capitalists were faced with *initiating* activity through investment, assuming a greater risk. This they were prepared to leave to U.S. multinationals, through the creation of a branch-plant system of ownership. The fact of higher proportions of Canadian ownership has no immediate relevance to consumer or Canadian workers. Canadian-based food corporations are no more responsive or accountable to the needs of Canadian people than the branch-plant expressions of American capitalism. No one is really aware in a day-to-day sense that Swift Canadian, Canada Safeway, or Kraft Foods are U.S. subsidiaries; while Loblaws, Dominion Stores, Canada Packers, Burns Foods, and Massey-Ferguson have their financial bases and head offices in Canada.

But the factor of substantial Canadian ownership may have relevance as a distinguishing characteristic of agribusiness relative to other sectors in terms ot the type and extent of integration within the industry. The tightly-integrated food empire in Canada, knit through interlocking directorships, subsidiary holdings, and protected and guaranteed markets and supplies, is facilitated by the cosiness of Bay Street capitalists. Financial institutions, primarily Canadian banks, are intimately connected to every level of agribusiness activity from farm supply industries to supermarkets to a degree not found in many other industries.

Concentration and Integration

Two measurements of oligopoly power which are pronounced in agribusiness are the degree of market concentration among the major rival firms and the total integration of markets and ownership through all levels of the industry. Concentration measures the absence of competition and the ease with which the dominant firms can administer prices and mutually participate in exploitive market practices without fear of challenge. Integration measures the absence of competition as well, and illustrates the power of a closed system of gauranteed markets and guaranteed supplies. Potential efficiencies of centralized market power are turned to profit advantage for the integrated conglomerates over their weaker independent rivals.

In measuring the extent of concentration of market control a relevant factor is the scope of the market involved. In some goods and services there is a national market, such as with automobiles, farm machinery, or petroleum distribution. There may be some regional variations in the pattern of market concentration but generally these are nationally defined markets. With other markets such as grocery retailing, or fertilizer suppliers and feed mills, the market is more regionally defined. In these cases either the nation has been divided through an informal understanding by the major rivals, or else the market conditions are sufficiently distinct in each region that they have attracted regionally specialized companies rather than nationally uniform ones. In either case the relevant measure of concentration must be adjusted to the size of market to which the major rivals are committed whether that be national, regional or even metropolitan.

With the above qualification it is safe to say that virtually all aspects of agribusiness are controlled by oligopolies. In the farm supply sector, 67 per cent of the tractor and combine market is supplied by the four major manufacturers. Fertilizers in western Canada are supplied by only six manufacturers, and two of those (Imperial Oil and Cominco) have 55 per cent of the market. Fuel supplies emanate from the U.S. multinational oil companies, with the exception of Co-operative Refinery Products in Regina, which supplies less than five per cent of farm fuels, oil and grease to the national market. Feed-mills are concentrated among the major grain companies, plus the meat packers such as Burns and Canada Packers. Canada Packers has 26 feed mills across Canada, while Burns is concentrated in the west. While there are some 800 feed mills in Canada, the four largest have 30 per cent of the market.

In the food processing sector, the three major meat packers have 55 per cent of the national market, seven companies account for 85 per cent of all fruit and vegetable processing, four companies have 77 per cent of the flour milling capacity and four companies have 96 per cent of all breakfast cereal manufacturing.[4]

In 1968 the federal Department of Corporate and Consumer Affairs undertook a survey on concentration in manufacturing industries. They discovered that food and beverage industries were among the most concentrated. Ranking among the top 50 industries of 154 surveyed in levels of concentration were breakfast cereal manufacturers, breweries, tobacco products manufacturers, macaroni manufacturers, vegetable oil mills, distilleries, sugar refineries, flour mills, wineries, biscuit manufacturers, and agricultural implement dealers. All of these had better than 60 per cent of the markets under three or four large firms.

Finally at the level of retail distribution, in terms of regional concentration, the major supermarket chains have anywhere from 50-80 per cent of the market to divide between them. In Alberta, Safeway stores have moved from an oligopoly position to a near monopoly in Edmonton and Calgary with 75 per cent of the market and local retail co-operatives as the only significant alternative. Safeway dominates the west generally, with the combined Weston chain (Loblaws, O.K. Economy, Shop-Easy) running a distant second. In Ontario, Dominion Stores are the leading chain, with Loblaws, Steinberg's, and A and P trailing. In Metropolitan Montreal, Dominion Stores and Steinberg's have 56 per cent of the market between them. These two chains also dominate the Quebec market as a whole but with less concentration.

A 1968 Royal Commission on consumer problems and inflation in the prairie provinces pointed an accusing finger at the concentration of the retail grocery trade as a source of industry failings:

> Grocery retailing today is seriously deficient on at least four counts: profits are excessive; excess capacity has added to costs; advertising has favored a concentrated structure, created monopoly power and increased costs; and the promotion of the luxury store has inflated gross margins.

The "Batten Commission," as this report became known after its chairman Judge Mary Batten, is one of numerous government studies intended to rediscover oligopoly in the food industry in this century, but from the consumer point of view it is probably the most instructive.

The concentration of markets is the most visible aspect of agribusiness power and the best understood. Less known is the power attained through vertical integration in which companies at various levels of activity are owned or controlled by a single financial empire. This factor of vertical control combines numerous market concentrations into a multi-tiered system of corporate power. Agribusiness, with half a million employees, can be boiled down to a few closely linked 'groupings' of financial and industrial interests.

Two outstanding Canadian examples illustrate the character of agribusiness in terms of integration, the Bank-of-Commerce-Argus-Canada-Packers network, and the Weston family empire. Between the two of them they own or control an estimated $5 billion in assets and as much as $15 billion in sales annually. Based on per capita income figures in 1973, the combined earning power of all Canadian men, women and children was roughly $60 billion annually. So these two giants generate fully one-quarter of that total in sales.[5]

Argus and Friends

The largest and most complete industrial grouping in Canada is the network involving the Canadian Imperial Bank of Commerce, Argus Corporation (with its numerous holdings including Massey-Ferguson, and Dominion Stores), and Canada Packers plus all of its subsidiaries. Each of these incorporated entities is massive in itself. The Bank of Commerce is the second-largest national bank with assets totalling $16

billion. Dominion Stores is the largest supermarket grocery chain in
Canada with 400 outlets and sales of $1.3 billion annually. Massey-
Ferguson is the largest Canadian-owned manufacturing firm with sales
of $1.5 billion in 1974 and Canada Packers is the largest food
manufacturer with 1974 sales also at $1.5 billion. The massive
combined market power of all of these firms in a working relationship
is a staggering prospect.

The strategy of the Argus Corporation, which is a holding
company bringing together some of the leading lights of Bay Street
capitalism, has been to direct and control their investments through
selective ownership of blocks of shares in numerous large corporations. Argus itself is owned by a number of investment firms which
are in essence 'front groups' for the ranking capitalists. Back in 1960
the late Wallace McCutcheon admitted that 30 per cent of the Argus
shares, the controlling block, were held by just four men — E.P.
Taylor, John McDougald, W.C. Philips, and Wallace McCutcheon. Of
these, McDougald remains the central figure and master strategist.
Under McDougald, the Argus Corporation reaches out in several
directions, owning sometimes as little as 10 per cent and up to 48 per
cent of shares in the firms they control. By block voting at
shareholders' meetings, Argus has no difficulty electing its core elite
to company boards of directors, thereby controlling the finances and
policies of the firms.[6] *Financial Post* data on investments by Argus
compared to the pattern of interlocking directorships of the thirteen
Argus board members readily confirms that Argus controls what it
invests in. Some of the major companies in which Argus holds
substantial shares include Dominion Stores, Domtar, Massey-Ferguson, Hollinger Mines, B.C. Forest Products and Standard Broadcast
Ltd. Each of these companies in turn has major subsidiaries. Argus
dominates these companies through its directorship block.

The pivot of power begins with McDougald. In addition to being
the chairman and president of Argus, he holds thirty-four other
directorships including chairman of the executive committee in each
of Dominion Stores, Massey-Ferguson, Hollinger Mines, Standard
Broadcast, and General Bakeries (a company in which Dominion
Stores has 60 per cent shares and McDougald personally has another
11 per cent). At the same time the presidents and managing directors
of these companies, the central leadership in their operations, are all
Argus board members as well. For example Al Thornbrough, president
of Massey-Ferguson, W.C. Thornton Cran of Standard Broadcasting,
Albert Fairley of Hollinger Explorations, and Tom McCormick of
Dominion Stores were all on the Argus board of directors in the early
1970s.[7]

In total the Argus Corporation is able to control a group of

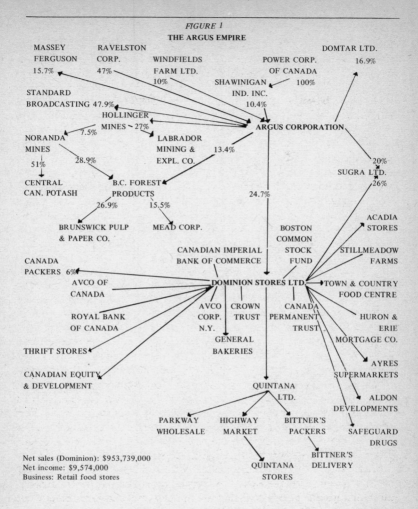

FIGURE 1

THE ARGUS EMPIRE

Net sales (Dominion): $953,739,000
Net income: $9,574,000
Business: Retail food stores

FIGURE 2
CANADA PACKERS

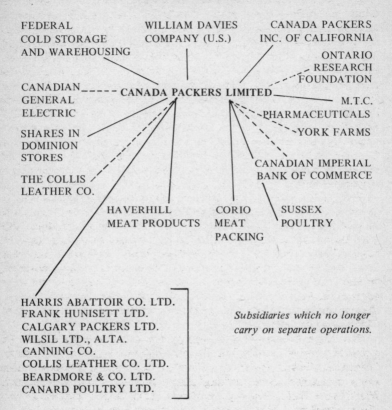

FEDERAL COLD STORAGE AND WAREHOUSING

WILLIAM DAVIES COMPANY (U.S.)

CANADA PACKERS INC. OF CALIFORNIA

ONTARIO RESEARCH FOUNDATION

CANADIAN GENERAL ELECTRIC

CANADA PACKERS LIMITED

M.T.C. PHARMACEUTICALS

YORK FARMS

SHARES IN DOMINION STORES

THE COLLIS LEATHER CO.

CANADIAN IMPERIAL BANK OF COMMERCE

HAVERHILL MEAT PRODUCTS

CORIO MEAT PACKING

SUSSEX POULTRY

HARRIS ABATTOIR CO. LTD.
FRANK HUNISETT LTD.
CALGARY PACKERS LTD.
WILSIL LTD., ALTA.
CANNING CO.
COLLIS LEATHER CO. LTD.
BEARDMORE & CO. LTD.
CANARD POULTRY LTD.

Subsidiaries which no longer carry on separate operations.

Net sales (1971): $919,178,000
Net income: $9,589,000
Major products: Packing house products and by-products, canned foods, farm products.

corporations with assets in the range of $2.5 billion, although its own assets amount to 'only' $100 million.

Part of the key to the Argus success and influence, beyond the direct investments of its central shareholders, is its ability to generate finance capital. The small Argus board of directors has representatives on four national banks; one each on the Royal, Bank of Montreal, and Bank of Nova Scotia, and six on the Canadian Imperial Bank of Commerce. The six Argus directors on the Bank of Commerce, which include McDougald, Thornborough, Fairley and Thornton Cran, are joined by seven other directors from Argus-controlled companies. Together they provide the core of leadership on an overall board of fifty bank directors, many of whom are token regional representatives. By its influence within the Canadian Imperial Bank of Commerce, Argus is assured of substantial backing on capital expansion plans by its major corporations, while the bank secures a market for industrial loans.

The social elite of the Toronto Club, of which McDougald is president, may be part of a shrinking capitalist class in Canada but they remain powerful in the sectors in which they are involved. The Bay Street Tories like E.P. Taylor and Maxwell Meighen (son of former Tory Prime Minister Arthur Meighen), along with the other few dozen of the old-guard finance and investment tycoons, continue to wield an impressive degree of power through banking and trust companies, key areas of manufacturing, and merchandising. Argus, through its vertical links and interlocks, typifies the hard crusty core of Canadian capitalism.

The Argus-Dominion Store complex is partly integrated with its suppliers through ownership. General Bakeries supplies the bulk of Dominion's bakery products in Quebec and Ontario. Dominion also owns a smaller meat packing plant (Bittner's), and a wholesale distribution firm, Parkway Wholesale. Like Argus, Dominion has direct interlocks with financial institutions with board members as directors of the Royal Bank, Crown Trust, Canada Permanent Trust, and the Canadian Imperial Bank of Commerce. But the major practical integration, from the perspective of controlling and guaranteeing supplies, comes through Dominion's relationship with Canada Packers.

Canada Packers is the second major shareholder of Dominion Stores with 500,000 shares, 6 per cent of the total and the only other block share owner besides Argus. Canada Packers is independent from Argus in terms of ownership and control. What exists is a working alliance through joint ownership in Dominion Stores and a mutual tie-in to the Canadian Imperial Bank of Commerce. In its own right Canada Packers is the largest food manufacturer in the country. It is fully integrated from farm production to wholesale. Its president, W.F. McClean, is also a vice-president of the Canadian Imperial Bank of Commerce, the Argus anchor bank.

Canada Packers food processing plants include red meat and poultry production, dairy products, vegetable oils and margarines. Through its subsidiary York Farms Limited, CP produces a full range of fruit and vegetable products both canned and frozen. Its access to Dominion Stores completes the perfect circle.

The marriage of convenience between the nation's largest processor and largest retailer is not simply an informal relationship involving preferential treatment of one by the other. Canada Packers and York Farms have formal contractual obligations through which, for example, York Farms supplies all the "Dominion" store brand frozen fruits and vegetables as well as selling under the York label (at a higher price). Canada Packers is the primary supplier for Dominion Stores meat counters, a commodity which Dominion focussed on in its promotions, "Mainly because of the Meat." Canada Packers' assured retail markets provide it with an advantage over its national rivals Burns and Swift, and render the selling prospects of smaller abattoirs through supermarkets unlikely at best.

Canada Packers' market power extends back toward production on the farms as well, an aspect of agribusiness to be considered in the context of farmer-agribusiness conflict later. CP's feed mills chain and livestock and poultry operations are as much a part of the corporate maze as the interconnections on Bay Street.

The Weston Family Empire

George Weston Limited and Loblaw Companies Limited, the main holding companies for the Weston family empire, represent assets between them of $1.2 billion and 1974 sales of $3.8 billion. The difference between Weston's operations and those of Argus-Dominion-Store-Canada-Packers alliance is that Weston is bound together through a pyramid of wholly-owned subsidiaries, internal directorship links, and finance capital generated largely from within the organization. The Argus group, in contrast, is held together through strategic blocks of minority shares, interlocking directorships, and bank finance capital. Another distinction between Weston holdings and Argus is that Weston is more fully tied to food industry pursuits. It too has major non-food subsidiaries, however, such as pulp and paper manufacturer E.B. Eddy Limited.

The similarity of Weston to Argus is its use of directorship links as a means of ensuring solidarity in the 'family.' The board of directors of George Weston Limited fan out and hold director and executive

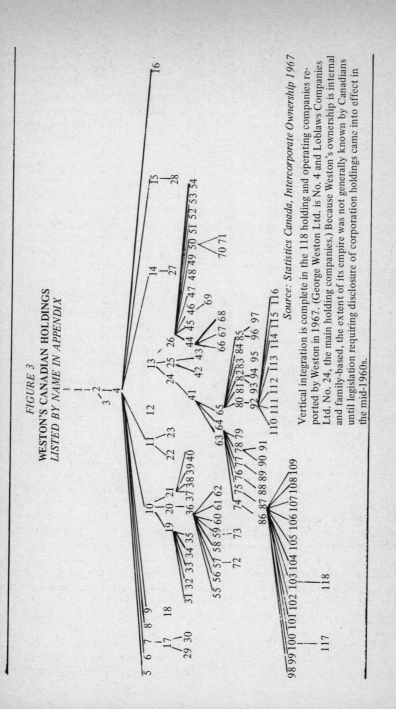

FIGURE 3
WESTON'S CANADIAN HOLDINGS
LISTED BY NAME IN APPENDIX

Source: Statistics Canada, Intercorporate Ownership 1967

Vertical integration is complete in the 118 holding and operating companies reported by Weston in 1967. (George Weston Ltd. is No. 4 and Loblaws Companies Ltd. No. 24, the main holding companies.) Because Weston's ownership is internal and family-based, the extent of its empire was not generally known by Canadians until legislation requiring disclosure of corporation holdings came into effect in the mid-1960s.

FIGURE 4

VERTICAL INTEGRATION: THE CASE OF WESTON		AVERAGE PROFIT LEVELS 1962-1966
RETAIL FOOD OUTLETS	LOBLAWS GROCETERIA O.K. ECONOMY STORES SHOP-EASY STORES HIGH-LOW FOODS ECONOMART	RETAIL OUTLETS AVERAGE PROFITS 15.9%
WHOLESALE DISTRIBUTION	KELLY-DOUGLAS ATLANTIC WHOLESALES B.C. PACKERS WESTFAIR FOODS	WHOLESALE DISTRIBUTION AVERAGE PROFITS 13.2%

FOOD PROCESSING	McCORMICK BISCUITS—
	  WESTON BAKERIES
	EPLETT DAIRIES
	NABOB FOODS
	WILLARDS
	  CHOCOLATE CO.
	NELPACK FISHERIES
	SEAL COVE CANNING
		BAKERY PRODUCTS
		MANUFACTURING
		AVERAGE PROFITS
		11.3%
		DAIRY PRODUCTS
		MANUFACTURING
		AVERAGE PROFITS
		15.2%
		CONFECTIONERY
		MANUFACTURING
		AVERAGE PROFITS
		13%

SUPPLIES AND SERVICES	SNO-BOY COOLERS
	UNIVERSAL
	  REFRIGERATION
	CANADIAN
	  FOLDING CARTON
	DISPLAY FIXTURES LTD.
	CLOVERDALE PAINT
	  AND CHEMICALS
	WITTINGDON REALTY
	  AND CONSTRUCTION	

positions in Weston Bakeries, William Neilson Ltd., Loblaws, Tamblyn Drugs, Kelly-Douglas, B.C. Packers, and McCormicks Limited, all of which are Weston subsidiaries. Collectively the 10 George Weston Limited board members held 63 directorships in 1974, all but two of which were with subsidiaries or affiliates of Westons. Three of the central board members are Westons; Garfield, Galen and Gary, father and sons.

Unlike Argus, there are no directorships held in banks by the Weston men and only one with a trust company. As with Argus, the controlling elite of the Weston companies are based in Toronto, which headquarters most of the companies.

The Cost-Price Squeeze

The power of agribusiness, as exemplified by Argus and Weston, is exercised in at least three areas of importance to ordinary consumers. One is the economic pressure placed on farmers in the farm supply and food processing sectors. Second is the political influence exercised on government and state agencies, third is the direct inflationary influence the exercise of oligopoly power has on consumer prices between farm gate and supermarket.

As described in Chapter 2, farmers are in the middle of industrial agriculture. They are caught defenceless between the farm supply sector, which influences costs of production in agriculture, and the corporate food industry, which determines farm product prices. Both of these sectors of agribusiness are oligopolies and each exploits the weakness of farmers by using its market and pricing powers. In the farm supply sector or 'cost' industries, the farmer is a captive consumer for the farm machinery firms, feed mills, and fertilizer companies. Their proven ability to administer prices has been outlined in a number of studies, most notably the Royal Commission on Farm Machinery Prices which reported in 1969. (Some of the Commission's findings are described in Chapter 4 as they affected cost-price pressures in the wheat economy.)

In general the attitude of farm suppliers appears to be one of responding to what the market will bear. Fertilizer and machinery prices parallelled the increased in gross farm incomes in 1973 and 1974. By advancing prices against farmers the 'cost' industries provide an upward pressure on food prices both directly, by increasing the farmer's cost of basic supplies, and indirectly, by forcing farmers to try to get bigger. When farmers try to enlarge their operations the effect, as described in Chapter 2, is to increase the capital cost of land by forcing competitive bidding over a scarce land resource.

By virtue of their individual status as consumers of manufactured goods, farmers have no choice but to pay the established price of farm supply oligopolies. This price goes up rapidly when times in agriculture are good (i.e. farm product prices are up), and it goes up less rapidly when farm incomes are depressed. But the cost of farm supplies never goes down. Under these circumstances periods of short-term boom for the farmer, as in the two years from 1973 to 1975 for grain farmers, may be bad news for consumers because they are times when the 'cost' industries take advantage of farmer wealth and accelerate their farm-supply prices.

But if the weakness of individually competing farmers in the marketplace leads to an upward pressure on costs of production, it is equally true that the industries on the other side, the food manufacturing sector, take advantage of farmers by a downward pressure on farm commodity prices. Low farm product prices mean a saving in the cost of raw material for the dairy, meat-packing, canning, and frozen foods industries, and so on. These 'price' industries, by maintaining a downward influence on farm prices, have over the years managed to increase the non-farm margin of mark-up on food products from 40¢ of the retail food dollar in 1951 to 65¢ in 1971. This was accomplished without greatly disturbing the general levels of retail food prices at least until 1972. Unfortunately any consumer savings this exercise of oligopoly power by food processing firms represented were at the expense of farmers and their communities.

The period of 1956 to 1971 will go down as the era of the 'cheap food' policy. It was a period when the open-market system worked hardest against farmers through the combined market powers of 'cost' industries and 'price' industries and the resulting 'cost-price squeeze' on farm income. But the advantages of the improved-volume and low-priced system of agriculture did not go to consumers. Food prices increased 36 per cent from 1956 to 1968, generally in line with the overall rate of inflation. Where the advantage of low-priced agriculture did go was toward an expansion in food processing and merchandising. The boom period for supermarket construction, development of convenience foods, and expansion of existing processing facilities went on with abandon in this period, gradually eating up a larger share of the consumer food dollar and contributing to over-capacity. The build-up of an elaborate and inefficient food marketing system was costing consumers throughout the 1960s, but it didn't show up as a problem until farm product prices were forced upwards in 1973. Then there was a 37 per cent increase over two years in the retail price of food.

For the first time since 1945, 1973 increases in farm prices outstripped the increase in farm costs of production. But this change did not affect the ability of the food processing sector to sustain and actually expand its margin of mark-up. Canada Packers managed to increase 1973 profits 36 per cent above 1972 despite sharp increases in the price of cattle. What higher farm prices *have* meant is that the farm *supply* sector is now rapidly expanding. Pursuing a market that can't last, Massey-Ferguson announced a $60 million expansion plan in 1974 and all farm machinery firms were increasing factory production in anticipation of sales increases from 10-50 per cent. The short-term build-up in the farm supply sector could lead only to further over-capacity of factory facilities, but with administered pricing these extra costs could be passed on to farmers.

The squeeze that 'cost' industries and 'price' industries place on farmers is more obvious and dramatic when both are part of the same vertically integrated conglomerate. Canada Packers is a good example, selling to farmers through feed mills and buying back their cattle or hogs for slaughter at the packing plant. Canada Packers goes the further step of competing directly with the producer through custom feed-lots and poultry farms. In essence CP operates their own production units or factory farms on a contract basis without having to invest directly in agricultural land. Farmers or farm corporations handle large numbers of Canada Packers animals for a management fee. An example is Alberta-based Parkland Beef, which operates a string of feed-lots, with $1 million sales in that province in 1973. Parkland custom-feeds cattle on contract for Swift, Canada Packers, and other commercial entities. Only a small proportion of the packing plants' total supplies come through their own custom feeding arrangements. But the significance of the arrangement is the flexibility it gives CP and the other packers in their price offerings to farmers for supplies bought at company buying stations or public stockyards. Knowing they have a certain volume of guaranteed deliveries from custom feed-lots, the packers have increased flexibility in their handling of price offerings in the overall market.

In an open market situation, as exists for cattle, the combined influence of the national company buyers largely determines the day-to-day level of prices. They make the majority of purchases on the public stock-yards and increasingly through direct producer deliveries to company plants. Buyers for these companies are instructed by their regional head offices on bidding limits.

Where producer marketing boards have been established, as with poultry and with hogs in several provinces in 1973, the direct control by the national packing plants over day-to-day prices for products is reduced but not eliminated. The major buyers still can influence the market price downward by refusing to accept delivery above certain price limits. This forces the public marketing boards and commissions to yield. But the extreme market manipulations and the rapid

up-and-down price levels are reduced, along with the windfall profits
the companies have gained from market instability over the years.
Under these circumstances the processing companies are inclined to
expand directly into production, as they have in turkey and eggs.
Direct farm production by agribusiness under marketing boards not
only guarantees a supply to company processing plants, it also allows
for another level of profits because stable and controlled market
prices make basic production more profitable for all operators.

Two areas of integration for Canada Packers not yet considered are
commercial feed mills and overseas packing plants. The twenty-six
commercial feed mills owned by Canada Packers sell feed to a range of
farmers, but primarily to cattlemen. Cattle operators in turn sell
much of their livestock to Canada Packers. The potential result is that
if a market shortage developed for cattle, with the packing plants
having to pay an abnormally high price to farmers, Canada Packers
could recover its advantage by increasing the price of feed back to the
same operators. In the reverse situation, however, where external
factors such as higher world grain prices forced an abnormal increase
in the price of commercial feeds, there is nothing to ensure that cattle
price offerings by the packing plants would be adjusted to compen-
sate. In short, in areas where Canada Packers or other national
companies function as both a major buyer of livestock or poultry and
a major seller of feed, they have all the advantages. A manipulated
squeeze on producers is not only possible but probable. In Newfoundland in November 1974, a group of producers and an area Member of
Parliament called for an inquiry into what they alleged to be
price-fixing among Canada Packers and three other feed-mills after a
series of identical and simultaneous price increases.

The international holdings of Canada Packers represent 20 per cent
of their total sales, and consist of slaughtering and processing plants
for meat in Australia, Mexico, and West Germany as well as trading
companies in the U.S., England, and West Germany. These operations
involve sales in the countries in which they are located as well as
exports to North America. The importation of these overseas meat
products has a downward influence on North American cattle prices,
based on the experience of 1974. Therefore if Canada Packers, as an
example, were to market low-grade ground beef into Canada from
Australian subsidiaries at a time when cow-beef was already in
domestic surplus, they would have the effect of further depressing
cattle prices for Canadian producers. This would be to the tremendous
advantage of their Canadian plant operations. In October and
November 1974, Australian frozen beef generally was having a
depressing impact on the Canadian market. What is unclear is what
proportion, if any, of this overseas product came from the subsidiary

holdings of CP. This was not one of the questions investigated by either Beryl Plumptre or the special Beef Commission which was appointed by Parliament in 1975.

The Political Pay-off

The politics of agribusiness through traditional lobbying tactics has been self-rewarding. With agribusiness representatives in both major parties, (like the late Tory Senator Wallace MacCutcheon, formerly in the Diefenbaker cabinet, and James Richardson in the Trudeau cabinet) the pipeline of influence has been fairly direct. In addition to involvement in the Canadian Manufacturers Association, food industries have their own lobbies such as the Grocery Products Manufacturers Association, the Meat Packers Council, the National Dairy Council, the Bakery Products Council, and the Retail Grocers Association. There are also lobbies for industries which service the food industry such as the Packaging Association of Canada and the Canadian Association of Advertisers.

In the continuing charade of parliamentary inquiries and Royal Commissions, the food industry lobby is kept busy presenting its case to government agencies and committees. Two-thirds of the briefs to the 1973 Committee on Trends in Food Prices came from the industry lobbies and from representatives of individual food companies. The remaining third of the briefs covered government agencies, farm organizations, and labour and consumer groups. (Incredibly enough, there were no briefs presented by food industry workers like the Canadian Food and Allied Workers Union, the United Fishermen, or Retail Wholesale and Department Store Union. Briefs were scheduled primarily by invitation.)

Aside from defending its case against the accusations of inflation, the food industry lobby has concerned itself with ripping off the Canadian tax system. Tax concessions to manufacturing industries announced in John Turner's 1972 budget cost the Canadian Government an estimated $900 million in lost revenue. A large proportion of that cost goes to domestic and foreign-owned food processing and farm supply manufacturing firms, perhaps as much as $200-300 million. Turner's argument for the tax break was that it would encourage expansion (something the food industry already had too much of), and would create jobs. What it did instead was increase the profit earnings of manufacturing companies by 35 per cent in 1973 over 1972.[8]

The other area in which the food industry has cashed in disproportionately is federal incentive grants under DREE and other programs. Agribusiness is still relatively more decentralized than other

TABLE 3

LETHBRIDGE AGRI-BUSINESS EXPANSION FUND 1969–1973

COMPANY	FEDERAL GRANT	ANNUAL PROFITS (1973)
1) Swift Canadian	$4,000,000	$9,600,000
2) Western Canadian Seed Processers (Subsidiary of Burns)	$82,500	$5,000,000 (Burns)
3) Vauxhall Foods	$1,800,000	————(unknown)
4) Canada Packers	$506,000	$19,100,000
5) Canadian Dressed Meats (Subsidiary of Burns)	$550,350	$5,000,000
6) Karnair Industries	$1,334,880	———

SOURCE: FINANCIAL POST

industries and can often locate its operations, or parts of them, in precisely those areas which the federal government has designated for assistance. Allocation of DREE grants bears no relationship to the size of the company applying or its profit and loss statements. So we find that the major beneficiaries of corporate welfare are the giants of agribusiness. An example of the extent of handouts is provided by the city of Lethbridge in southern Alberta. Lethbridge was named as a "designated area" in 1969. Already an industrial centre for food-related industries, it saw existing companies, and some new plants, bite into the federal government for over $10 million in less than four years, plus an additional $8.4 million in low-interest provincial government loans. Seventeen companies took advantage of these programs. Lethbridge may be an exaggerated example, but it is not an isolated one. Centres throughout the prairies, Quebec, the maritimes and parts of Ontario are havens for corporate welfare.

The economic and political power of agribusiness is obviously not a special or isolated phenomenon. Nor are the tactics of doing business for profit illegal or morally reprehensible if we accept the standards and values of the system of which agribusiness is a part. By accepted business standards, food industry profits are reasonable and price leadership or co-operation among rivals is normal and legal unless done openly and formally. And the tricks and manipulations of the retail trade are acceptable mass-merchandising practices used in any industry. In short, business is business as usual in agribusiness circles and perhaps no one should complain.

But people do complain, both those who do not question the basic rationality of capitalist enterprise and those who do. The reason they complain, and provide a political climate of opposition and challenge to the food industry, is because they have documented grievances of normal business practice which hurt people. They are exploited as producers of food, as food industry workers and as ultimate consumers of food products. The nature and extent of grievance is perhaps best illustrated by an examination of some key commodity areas. In the following three chapters on bread, beef, and the dairy industry, we see how the generalized power of agribusiness is brought directly and impressively to bear, and exactly who suffers in the process.

Notes to Chapter 3

1. All references here to the 100 largest companies are based on the *Financial Post's* 1974 survey of the largest utility, resource, and manufacturing firms plus a separate survey in the same issue on retail distributors. Ownership links are established through the Statistics Canada summary on *Intercorporate Ownership*, 1969.

2. The trend of capital consolidation can be followed in the history of any of the large Canadian food manufacturers as provided by *Financial Post* corporation card index. An example of the beginning and end of a cycle is Burns Food's meat-packing operations in Saskatchewan. In 1918 and 1919, Burns bought existing plants in Regina and Prince Albert. In February 1974 they closed their Regina plant and laid off 230 workers. In March 1975 Burns closed its processing plant in Prince Albert, leaving only a hog-killing plant and laying off 300 of 350 workers.

3. This same pattern of consolidating Canadian capital is much less true of the centralization which occurred in some food manufacturing, notably dairy processing, in the 1960s and 1970s. The primary source of investment and expansion in dairy has been through U.S. branch-plant take-overs. The two most aggressive rivals in the dairy industry are U.S.-based Kraft Foods (and subsidiary Dominion

Dairies) and Beatrice Foods, as elaborated in Chapter 6.

4. Concentration figures are derived here from a number of sources including the 1968 Consumer and Corporate Affairs study on Concentration in Manufacturing Industries, the Barber Commission on Farm Machinery Prices, the Manitoba Department of Agriculture Study into the Fertilizer Industry, and figures cited by Henry Aubin, writing in the *Montreal Gazette* in September 1974 about food manufacturing and retail distribution.

5. The figures on gross assets and sales are estimates based on *Financial Post*'s Corporation Index for 1974. In terms of sales the total volume involves all sales of each of the major subsidiaries. This means that in some cases the total sales value involves double counting of the same commodity as it goes through two or more stages of production and distribution. For example, Weston Bakeries sales are in large proportion ot Loblaws Groceterias who resell the products.

The more relevant measurement is not sales but profits. These are more difficult to estimate because of the relationship between 'holding' and 'operating' companies within a single financial network. In the case of Weston many of the operating subsidiaries show low profits, but George Weston Ltd., the holding company, shows a consistently strong profit position.

6. Control tactics of the Argus men are described in Porter's *Vertical Mosaic* as part of his analysis of Canada's economic and social elite.

7. *Financial Post*, Directory of Directors, 1971.

8. *Financial Post*, September 8, 1973.

IV

Our Daily Bread

The built-in class bias of bread, in terms of its use by low-income families as a basic food staple, has made it a high priority issue within the politics of food at the federal level. When the Canadian Bakery Council projected in August 1973 that bread prices would rise 15 per cent in September and another 20 per cent in October in response to world grain prices, the Trudeau cabinet was relatively quick to respond. They responded by subsidizing the price of bread wheat to the milling-baking industry. The skirmishes between federal agencies and the baking industry over policies and price movements continued through 1974, with the basic result that the price impact was partially blunted and absorbed by the public treasury.

Retail bread prices increased 37 per cent in Canada between August 1972 and August 1974. This increase was separate and above the cost of a subsidy estimated at $160 million per year for bread wheat starting in 1973. Bread prices are deceptive because the cost of subsidies to the milling industry, borne by the federal government and wheat producers, must be added into any true calculation. At 6-8¢ per loaf, as estimated by the Prices Review Board, the additional cost of the bread subsidy makes bread among the most inflated of all commodities, with an increase of about 60 per cent over two years.

The analysis of price movements in the wheat-bread economy is just one focus for discussing an industry which encompasses roughly half the nation's agricultural producers, a major sector of agribusiness processing and farm-supply, and has in wheat the largest agricultural export commodity accounting for almost 50 per cent of total farm products exported. In general the direction of the wheat-bread industry is influenced externally by the world wheat economy and internally by public policy and the power of various levels of the industry to exercise influence on government. Wheat producers, farm input manufacturers, grain marketing and handling agencies, flour mills, commercial bakeries and the national railways all play a critical role in the direction of the industry and its price and profit levels.

The period from 1972 to 1975 saw some spectacular upheavals in the grains economy in the wake of high international prices and world food shortages. The international aspects of the issue are critically linked to national markets and prices for wheat and bread. They are discussed briefly here, and are elaborated in the discussion of Canada's role in the world food crisis in Chapter 9.

World market and price are critical because of the high proportion of Canadian production of wheat which is tied to an export market. Our fading reputation as the 'bread basket of the world' stemmed originally from our role as supplier to Britain and Western Europe in the first half of the century, particularly during the two world wars. And although we now produce less than 5 per cent of the world wheat crop, we still export 80 per cent of what we produce. All of which means that the roughly 10 per cent (60 million bushels) of Canadian wheat which is used domestically for bread flour and other cereal products is subservient to the marketing policies established for the export trade, and to the international price of wheat. This price for the Canadian industry is officially set by the Canadian Wheat Board, but it is unofficially determined by the open market price of U.S. wheat.

The long-standing 'single price system' for wheat, in which domestic market prices were tied directly to the competitive export market price, has meant bargain prices for industrial consumers of wheat in Canada. Flour mills, breakfast cereal manufacturers, feed mills and pasta manufacturers have all benefited substantially from the generally depressed world wheat price of less than $2.00 per bushel from 1945 to 1972. As well as the advantage of low price they were spared the costs of overseas transportation borne by their European counterparts.

For wheat producers and their organizations, however, this pricing system was long a sore point. They understood and lived with the price set by the Canadian Wheat Board (CWB) for export grain, knowing that it had to reflect world market conditions if the Board was to ensure overseas sales. But they couldn't see why Canadian flour mills should get the advantage of these depressed prices when the price level bore no fair relationship to the farmers' cost of production. Farmers saw bread and flour prices constantly rising with no increased return to themselves. What they argued for was a 'two-price system' in which all domestically consumed wheat would reflect a cost of production increase to farmers. A domestic price of at least $1.00 per

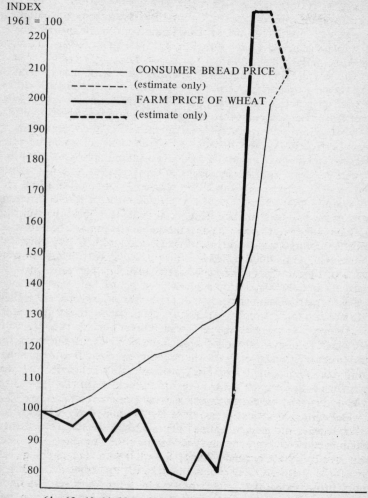

FIGURE 5

WHEAT AND RETAIL BREAD PRICE TRENDS

INDEX
1961 = 100

CONSUMER BREAD PRICE
------------- (estimate only)
FARM PRICE OF WHEAT
━ ━ ━ ━ (estimate only)

61 62 63 64 65 66 67 68 69 70 71 72 73 74 75

*1973-74 price increase for bread occurred *despite* freeze on price of wheat at $3.25 per bushel in Sept. 1973 for domestic market.

SOURCES: STATISTICS CANADA, SASK. DEPT OF AGRICULTURE

bushel over the export price was viewed as a minimum demand. This would better enable farmers to bear the brunt of depressed prices and unstable sales on the international market. The demand for a two-price system was consistently ignored by federal politicians, notwithstanding repeated election promises by western candidates for all parties, until 1970. Success of a limited and qualified nature was ultimately achieved under Otto Lang whose role in this matter is discussed in detail below.

The existence of a depressed price on grain should have been of great benefit to Canadian consumers of retail cereal commodities but, as farmers pointed out, bread, flour, breakfast cereals, and macaroni were all subject to the normal pattern of inflation from 1945 to 1972.

When international factors encouraged the price of wheat to advance from $1.55 in 1971 to $5.60 in 1973, all domestic price trends in cereals, and in animal products from milk to beef-steak, were thrown into chaos. The main cause of this international price change was the condition of rapidly increasing world production and consumption of grain, which left world export stocks as a shrinking proportion of overall needs. The public policies of both Canada and the United States (the major grain exporting countries) further reduced grain stocks. In this unstable situation, the Soviet Union fell short of its needs due to a crop failure in 1972. World supplies were bid up in price. This led to increases in animal feed prices as well, since there was competition directly over cereal supplies for human versus animal consumption and indirectly over land use for either. The inflationary spiral which overtook all food commodities after 1972 was based, as we will see in greater detail in Chapter 9, on a combination of real factors of supply and demand and the exaggerated impact of speculation on the commodity markets. But the problem from the point of view of both producers and consumers was the permanent dislocation caused by *the combination of free market commodity pricing and administered pricing of processed foods.*

The pattern of wheat prices since the Second World War has been at odds with the general pattern of inflation in North America over the same period. Only agricultural resources and products, like land, wheat and livestock, have their price fate determined so completely by shifts in supply and demand and by the speculative activity of grain brokers and petty investors. Other goods and services under capitalist production and markets are priced by the companies involved, primarily according to costs of production and profit objectives.

Supply-and-demand pricing for wheat has been chaotic in two directions. When the market reflects complacency in the face of surplus stocks of wheat, the resulting depressed prices ($1.50 per

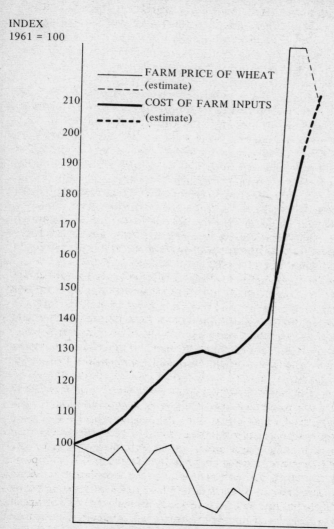

FIGURE 6
COMPARISON OF WHEAT AND COST OF FARM INPUTS

INDEX
1961 = 100

——————— FARM PRICE OF WHEAT
– – – – – (estimate)
━━━━━ COST OF FARM INPUTS
▬ ▬ ▬ ▬ (estimate)

210

200

190

180

170

160

150

140

130

120

110

100

1961 62 63 64 65 66 67 68 69 70 71 72 73 74 75

SOURCE: STATISTICS CANADA, SASK. DEPT. OF AGRICULTURE

bushel) create the conditions of rural poverty, depopulation of agricultural regions, and a national 'cheap food' policy at the expense of wheat producers. On the other hand, when the market reflects shortages and speculative bidding for available supplies, the resulting inflated prices ($5.00 per bushel) create the conditions of rising cost of production in land and farm supplies, consumer price inflation in food commodities, growing incidence of malnutrition among low-income people, and a cost-price squeeze in grain-feeding industries such as dairy, poultry and beef operations.

The near tripling of the farm price of wheat from 1971 to 1975 *did* make rich men out of some large grain producers. (At the same time, grain prices had the reverse impact on cattle, hog, poultry and dairy producers who as grain buyers faced major cost increases not generally covered by the price adjustments in milk, beef and pork, poultry, and eggs.) At the same time the impact of rising costs of production has increased the price of growing a bushel of wheat for the market from an estimated $1.60 in 1972 to an estimated $3.00 in 1975. The result is that a price of $3.50 per bushel becomes the short-term minimum (as of 1975) with an index tied to cost of production increases each year. Maintaining the 1975 rate of rising farm production costs of 15 per cent per year, the 1975 world price of $5.00 per bushel would become a *minimum* price by 1978.

The cost of farm inputs has followed a pattern entirely separate from the selling price of wheat. By 1969, when the price of wheat was $1.29 per bushel, a drop of 27 per cent from 1961, costs of farm inputs had risen by 30 per cent over 1961. Farm net-incomes in 1969 were at their lowest point for grain producers in twenty-five years. From this low the 'boom' of 1973 and 1974 was all the more dramatic as wheat prices actually temporarily outstripped the rising costs of farm inputs.

Over the longer term a comparison of wheat prices to rising farm-input costs illustrates that in the post war period farmers were not taking as much revenue in on a per-bushel basis as they were paying out to suppliers. But, as set out in Chapter 2, they compensated for low prices by improvements in productivity and enlargement of farms. This led in turn to still higher costs.

The factors which pushed up costs of production for wheat at an accelerated rate after 1972 were farm machinery, land, fuel, fertilizer and debt costs (related primarily to land and machinery). The graph below shows the general rate of inflation of these items from 1961 to 1975. Passenger cars are illustrated in contrast to trucks and farm machinery which involve comparative labour and raw material costs but which have a much higher rate of inflation.

The point is illustrated by a summary of farm gross receipts,

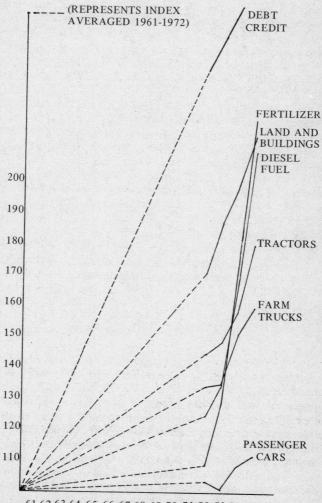

FIGURE 7
COMPARISON OF FARM INPUT COSTS

INDEX
1961 = 100

- - - - (REPRESENTS INDEX
AVERAGED 1961-1972)

DEBT
CREDIT

FERTILIZER
LAND AND
BUILDINGS
DIESEL
FUEL

TRACTORS

FARM
TRUCKS

PASSENGER
CARS

200
190
180
170
160
150
140
130
120
110

61 62 63 64 65 66 67 68 69 70 71 72 73 74 75

SOURCE: STATISTICS CANADA, CONSUMER PRICE INDEX

TABLE 4

**FARM COSTS, CASH RECEIPTS, AND NET INCOME
IN SASKATCHEWAN, 1956–1972**

Year	Total # of farms	Farm Operating costs	Total Farm Cash Receipts	Net Income
*1956	103,391	$ 3,100	$ 5,000	$ 2,500
1957	102,000	3,100	5,200	2,100
1958	100,000	3,300	6,000	2,700
1959	98,000	3,500	5,800	2,300
1960	96,000	3,900	6,000	2,100
*1961	93,924	3,700	6,500	2,800
1962	92,000	4,200	7,700	3,500
1963	90,500	4,800	7,700	2,900
1964	89,000	5,000	9,200	4,200
1965	87,500	5,700	10,200	4,500
*1966	85,686	6,500	11,100	4,600
1967	84,000	6,800	11,500	4,700
1968	82,000	7,400	10,900	3,500
1969	80,000	4,800	9,000	1,200
1970	78,000	7,700	9,300	1,600
*1971	75,970	8,000	11,900	3,900
1972	76,000	8,400	15,800	7,400

*Precise number of farms is known for census years only.
Totals for other years are estimates based on the trend.

SOURCE: SASKATCHEWAN ECONOMIC REVIEW, 1972.

operating costs, and net-income in the 'wheat' province of Saskatchewan. What the accompanying table indicates is that despite tripling of
farm cash receipts on Saskatchewan farms between 1956 and 1972,
most of the advantage has gone out in increased operating costs. These
include costs of land and buildings, equipment purchase and repair,
taxes and rent, fuel, fertilizer, and chemicals. Net-income was erratic
and averaged only $3,850 per farm in the fifteen years up to 1971.
Over the same period the number of farms declined by almost 30,000.
    Each of the major cost items, with the exception of land,
underlines the power and advantage of industrial oligopolies in their
relationship to private producers.

Farm machinery. The farm machinery market is dominated by four firms: John Deere, Massey-Ferguson, International Harvester, and Ford. These firms between them shared 67 per cent of the North American market for tractors and combines, the major cost items in grain farming. The Barber Report on farm machinery reported that tractor and combines prices were up 36 per cent in the seven-year period studied, compared to 10 per cent for autos. The Report also demonstrated an absence of price competition among any of the eleven North American manufacturers in operation in the 1960s. Through a practice of 'price leadership' led by John Deere, all companies had near-identical prices for tractors in each horsepower range. This was despite the companies' widely varying per-unit costs of production for tractors. Individual tractor costs varied according to total production runs. The range of production runs for tractors was from 7,000 units per year to 153,000, yet the prices established by the oligopoly covered the costs of the smallest and most costly plants. The larger plants were placed in a superior profit position, and farmers paid an unnecessarily high retail price.[1]

Investment per farm in farm machinery on grain farms reached an average of $20,000 by 1975. Canadian manufacturers were advancing prices of all implements by 10 per cent per year and of combines by 17 per cent in 1973. Clearly farm machinery costs were a leading edge for rising production costs taking advantage of a buoyant grain economy and the short-term prosperity of farmers to extract improved earnings. These earnings reflect both higher sales volume and higher prices. Massey-Ferguson, largest Canadian-based manufacturer of farm machinery, had 1973 profit increases of 80 per cent over 1972. The link between farm income and implement sales and profits is illustrated in the five-year table below.

Fertilizer. Fertilizer is a chemically based soil additive prepared in order to meet the specific needs of varying types of soil and designed to increase yields. With higher prices for grain there is a much heavier demand for fertilizers. Farmers tend to have the cash to pay even though the companies exaggerate prices in response to demand. A *Financial Post* article in March 1973 captured the essence of the industry's attitude. Headlined *Agribusiness a 'hot crop' prospect*, the article outlined the potential gains for investors in agribusiness as farmers scrambled to increase their production.

> . . . Moreover they have the money to do so. These bright new prospects down on the farm are already being reflected in higher fertilizer prices.

The fertilizer price increases of 100 per cent from 1971 to 1975 reflect both genuine cost increases to the industry and a good deal of

TABLE 5

FARM INCOME AND IMPLEMENT SALES

YEAR	FARM INCOME		IMPLEMENT SALES	
	Total ($ billion)	% change from previous year	Total ($ million)	% change from previous year
1973	3.3	+80	656	+29
1972	1.9	+11	508	+26
1971	1.7	+18	403	+17
1970	1.4	+9	344	−16
1969	1.6	−9	410	−7

SOURCE: STATISTICS CANADA

price manipulation, according to a study by the Manitoba Government which reported in March 1974. There are six companies engaged in fertilizer manufacturing in the wheat-producing region of Western Canada. Two of these, Cominco (CPR) and Imperial Oil, have 55 per cent of total capacity. This high degree of concentration enables pricing ". . . characterized by non-competitive techniques initiated by the recognized price leaders."[2] Specifically, the report details the practice of all companies in pricing their prairie market on a standard assumption of maximum freight rate costs for delivery. They then exchange orders with plants close to the customer. For example, the Simplots plant in Brandon, Manitoba, might exchange orders for southern Alberta or southwest Saskatchewan with Western Co-op Fertilizers in Calgary. The effect of this practice of dividing the market geographically while charging prairie-wide freight costs is a windfall for the fertilizer oligopoly. However, it created a price differential of 15-20 per cent between Manitoba farmers and neighbouring North Dakota farmers for identical products. The resulting farmer protest helped spark the Manitoba inquiry as well as a federal investigation by the Restrictive Trade Practices Commission under the Anti-Combines Act.

Energy. The rise in the world price of fossil fuels in 1973-74 hit the prairie wheat farmer at two levels. Firstly, the direct costs of gasoline and fuel oil represent 13 per cent of the farmers' total production costs. Secondly, the rise in overall energy costs helped to inflate the manufacturing costs of other farm inputs such as fertilizer, which requires a large volume of natural gas in processing. The federal Agricultural Economics Research Council predicted in 1974 that overall farm cost increases of 25-50 per cent would result from a doubling of the price of domestic crude oil in Canada. Although the doubling of crude oil prices was staged out by agreements between the oil producing provinces and Ottawa over the two years 1974-76, the increase was being used as an explanation by agribusiness manufacturers for price increases in early 1974. This was especially true of the fertilizer industry which uses both fossil fuels and natural gas.

The cost problem in energy is complicated by the serious question of supply. At rates of production and export recorded in the early 1970s Canada's conventional supply of crude oil was projected to be exhausted by 1985. With federal policies announced in December 1974 that exports in oil would be curtailed by 1982, the deadline for exhaustion of conventional supply may be extended but the basic problem remains. Wheat production is a heavy consumer of fossil fuels. (In Saskatchewan more than 40 per cent of total fuel consumption is by farmers.) Field work with heavy machinery is not easily convertible to other forms of energy. This means that higher costs of fossil fuels from tar sands development or offshore oil or imported oil will be borne disproportionately by the agricultural sector.

In terms of price, the index of diesel fuel costs from 1971 to 1975 showed a rise of more than 60 per cent. This increase was double the rise of the previous ten years but was minimal in relation to future trends based on the announced pricing policies of both levels of government and the oil cartel.

Land and debt costs. Land costs have already been discussed as a critical factor in the general cost-price squeeze on farmers. In terms of the wheat economy specifically, the impact has been staggering both over the long term since 1945 and in the recent short term since 1972. Land prices in the prime wheatland of the Regina Plains reached up to $300 per acre in 1974 and the provincial average for land prices in Saskatchewan rose to $100 per acre from $32 in 1956. At these prices, land alone if bought and financed over a thirty-year period represents up to $1.50 per bushel in the cost of wheat produced. The main beneficiaries from land transfers are real estate brokers who on arranging sale of a two-section farm on the Regina Plains could net $19,200 with a 5 per cent commission. This cost must ultimately be added to the cost of food along with the payments of interest that follow the transaction.

The cost of mortgage credit is the most inflationary of all farm service costs. Based on index 100 in 1961, mortgage money was at 300 by 1975. The average per farm debt payment was up 400 per cent in 1973 over 1961. These debt totals, reflecting the capital burden of land, machinery, and operating costs, represent a second level of production costs. Ironically, but not surprisingly, the level of debt burden is not reduced but *increased* during times of improved gross earnings. Farmers take on new commitments to expand at higher land prices and higher interest rates. Borrowing by farmers from the federally funded Farm Credit Corporation increased by two-thirds in 1973 to a yearly total of $300 million, and short term bank loans to farmers increased 21 per cent in the first half of 1973 over 1972. This was during a year when gross farm income was up by 80 per cent over the previous year!

In summary, these production cost increases add up to the necessity of *permanently* higher prices for wheat and all related commodities. But it should be clear that, above and beyond farm net-income, the higher wheat price carries the extra profit and inefficiencies of the farm machinery, fertilizer and oil cartel. It carries the weight of parasitic real estate brokers, land speculators, and mortgage companies. And it carries the weight of an irrational system of private land ownership in which productive agricultural land must be refinanced every generation at increasingly higher costs.

All of these costs enter into the consumer price of cereal products before wheat has even left the farmer's yard and begun to work through the wheat-bread cycle. Yet none of them have been effectively challenged by government, by consumer groups, or by farmers themselves. Farmers, powerless to resist higher costs set by outside agencies, have opted instead to fight for their own price gains in the marketplace. But contrary to some current interpretation about the role of marketing boards, the experience of producer-influence in marketing of wheat has not meant artificially high product prices.

The History and Politics of Grain Marketing, Handling and Transportation

The grain marketing system has been a source of political conflict historically between prairie producers and federal government policies. Far from being settled, the conflict has taken on new dimensions in the mid-1970s as federal initiatives aim at reorganizing the elevator and transportation systems for grain in ways which favour the interests of railways and the private grain trade but represent higher costs to the producer. Before examining the struggle over this matter its historic context needs elaboration.

As long as the western wheat economy has existed, farmers have sought income protection and guarantees through marketing reforms. Since before 1900, the recurring focus of farmer protest and farm organisations has been on demands for public regulation, control, or ownership of the grain handling system. This has resulted in a considerable degree of public influence in wheat marketing and prices and the development of farmer-owned co-operatives to handle wheat in competition with the international private grain trade.

The history of the marketing issue is best documented by Vernon Fowke in *The National Policy and the Wheat Economy*. He illustrates the painful path of progress over the years by which farmers extracted concessions from reluctant governments. The Winnipeg Grain and Produce Exchange (1887), the Canadian Pacific Railway and the private elevator companies had a free rein in the determination of prices, freight-rates, grade and weight standards at local elevators prior to 1910. The farmer was confronted with a local monopoly at every shipping point. The CPR guaranteed the monopoly position of elevator companies by refusing to allow farmers to load their own wheat at loading platforms. Forced to use the elevator, the farmer was also forced to accept the weight, grade and dockage of the elevator agent. It was not uncommon for farmers to haul wheat thirty or forty miles with horses to discover the elevator price-offerings had dropped below the cost of production. He could then sell at a loss or return home with the load, hoping for a better price another day. No matter what he decided, he lost money. The organized protest of the Manitoba and Northwest Farmers Union (1880s), the Territorial Grain Growers Association (1901-1905), and the Grain Growers Associations of each of the three prairie provinces (1905-1920s) led to a series of government regulations in grain trade and transportation. The response of the Ottawa government always began with an inquiry or commission into farmer grievances and ended with compromise solutions. In 1900 and 1912 the Manitoba and Canadian Grain Acts established a Board of Grain Commissioners which set standards for grading and supervised box car distribution and generally served as a supervising and appeal agency over the grain marketing system. Farmers had demanded nationalization.

Crow Rates. In 1897 the government entered into an agreement with the Canadian Pacific Railway. The CPR was proposing a railway from Lethbridge to Nelson, B.C., through the Crow's Nest Pass. The line provided mutual advantage in that the CPR would have access to the rich mining investments in the Kootenays while the federal government avoided the risk of further U.S. penetration. In the Crow Rates agreement, the federal government subsidized the railway $11,000 per mile to a total of $3.4 million while the company agreed to certain maximum rates on grain to the Lakehead and farm machinery to western Canada. In addition to the federal subsidy, the railway obtained a land subsidy from the government of British Columbia.[3]

The rates agreed to by the federal government were generous at the time and showed no apparent favour to farmers. The CPR actually reduced their rates 10 per cent below the Crow Rate in 1903 and maintained them there until 1918. Then, under pressure from the railways, the government suspended the Crow's Nest provisions and authorized rate increases which brought rates 25 per cent above the 1897 statute. Finally, in 1925, the government amended the original Act to limit the fixed rates to grain (freeing the rates on farm machinery), but enforced them on all export routes and included the CNR. Thus the west coast ports and the port of Churchill were included on the routes and the statutory rate was left in the hands of Parliament and fixed from 1925 on at the original 1897 rate. Since then the railways have consistently worked to undermine the Crow Rate agreement, and the issue is still current in the 1970s, along with that of the reorganization of grain marketing.

Wheat Board. Throughout the early period after 1900, the grain marketing and selling function was left entirely in private hands. Grain dealers operated through the trading facility of the Winnipeg Grain Exchange and adjusted prices daily. Demands by the grain growers' movement for nationalization of the commercial elevator system were avoided by government, but a number of partial reforms emerged, largely at the hands of the farmers themselves.

The Grain Growers Grain Company was established as a farmers co-operative initially in Saskatchewan in 1906 and later in Manitoba and Alberta. This was followed by the Manitoba Government Elevator Company (1910), the Saskatchewan Co-op Elevator Company (1911) and the Alberta Farmers Co-op Elevator Company (1913). The voluntary co-operatives in competition with the private grain trade fell far short of public ownership, but they did provide a more direct and honest basis for dealing.

A further advance in public marketing came during World War I when the Board of Grain Commissioners was authorized to sell wheat at fixed prices in government-to-government contracts with the allied powers. The Winnipeg Grain Exchange was closed for two years and under pressure of wartime demand, prices were maintained at a level 70¢ higher than the average Exchange price in 1916. In the post-war period of 1919, because of rising prices and uncertain markets, the government intervened again, this time through a separate Canadian Wheat Board. This was farmers' first experience with public marketing and, not surprisingly, they liked it. The Wheat Board paid farmers an initial price on delivery of the wheat of $2.15 per bushel. They then pooled the returns from the sale of the grain to exporters (which averaged $2.63 per bushel) and distributed the additional 48¢ to farmers at the end of the crop year.

Ironically, given its acclaim by producers, the Wheat Board had been set up for its one-year duration in order to keep prices from escalating. But its important feature, for which farmers were to fight for twenty-four years to re-establish, was the compulsory pooling of all sales of wheat with the returns distributed equally to the producer. This was in contrast to the grain-exchange system of pricing in which the price was free to float on a day-to-day basis. The fluctuations in price were caused by the buying and selling of 'futures contracts.' The farmer received whatever price was quoted in Winnipeg on the day of his elevator delivery, less freight, handling charges and dockage. The price was generally if not always low in the fall, rising as the crop-year advanced. (The crop-year runs from August 1 to July 31.) This pricing cycle meant farmers had to either sell at lower prices in the fall, thus avoiding storage costs, or hold their grain, absorbing the costs and possible damage in storage, in hopes the price would rise. But since each individual farmer was faced with the same dilemma the net result was that when the price *did* rise in the Winnipeg Exchange everyone would attempt to deliver to their local elevator at once. The elevator system would become plugged with wheat and the price would once again decline. The net effect of the system was that most farmers sold their crops at well below the average export price.

The combination of the good experience with the 1919 Wheat Board and the marketing disasters of the early 1920s (when wheat averaged less than $1.00 per bushel) united prairie wheat producers in opposition to the Grain Exchange system and the old-line parties which supported it. In the federal election of 1921 it was the marketing issue which swept the Progressives to Parliament with thirty-nine seats in the prairies.

The unity demonstrated politically was applied organizationally through the Farmers Union of Canada (1921) and the older Grain Growers movements to establish their own compulsory pooling agency through pledges from farmers. The three prairie wheat pools organized in 1924-26 became the base of the drive for the Canadian Wheat Board and had majority support among farmers.

Through a central selling agency, the pools began to threaten the private members of the grain trade by selling directly to overseas customers, instead of through the Winnipeg Grain Exchange. This central agency, however, faced financial collapse in the height of the depression, as it attempted to absorb for a time the falling prices and collapse of markets which characterized 1930-31. In two years the combined wheat pools lost $25 million because of overpayments to farmers in relation to the world price.

The near-collapse of the pools led to renewed and more vigorous demands for a compulsory pool to replace the voluntary co-ops. In 1930, 48,000 Saskatchewan Wheat Pool members voted 71.3 per cent in favour of a compulsory pool. After 1,500 of them stormed the Legislature, the provincial government, followed by those of Alberta and Manitoba, voted enabling legislation for public marketing. But the measure was quashed in the courts as ultra vires with federal jurisdiction over inter-provincial trade.

Following the pressure from farmers, the Canadian Wheat Board was finally re-established by the federal government, first as a temporary and voluntary pooling agency in 1935 to assist the prairie pools beyond their depression debts, then as a compulsory wartime measure to keep wheat prices from escalating in the face of strong world demand.[4] Despite the role of the Board in keeping prices below temporary peaks, farmers have over the years been resolute in their support.

Two features of the Wheat Board system of marketing appealed to farmers in contrast to their experience on the open market. One was the creation of a compulsory pool of all wheat marketed, and the averaging of price. All producers received the same final price, based on the average per-bushel price of domestic and export wheat over the entire year rather than the price on the world market on the particular day they delivered their grain. The elevator companies no longer determined the price. They became buying agents for the Wheat Board, which was the exclusive selling agency. Elevator handling charges were fixed and negotiated year by year, so that windfall profits or extra charges were reduced. The farmers got whatever the world price was on average for the year, less handling charges and freight rates, which were controlled. The gamble was removed.

The second feature which made the Wheat Board system popular was the enforcement of the 'quota system' of delivery. This system enabled the Wheat Board to provide equal access to delivery for all producers. Permit books were issued through the elevator system for each farmer so that his deliveries could be recorded systematically. With each new crop year a delivery quota would be maintained on all crops based on the cultivated acreage of each farm. For example, a 'one bushel quota' would enable all farmers to deliver one bushel of wheat for each acre they had sown. As more space became available in the elevator system through the movement of wheat to export terminals the quota allocations would increase. This control over delivery meant that whatever sales were negotiated by the Canadian

Wheat Board were shared equally by producers. If export sales were poor, farmers would share the burden of carrying over farm-stored grain to the next crop year. This system contrasted sharply with the days of open market deliveries which operated on a first-come first-serve basis.[5]

But the issue of marketing was not abandoned by the private grain trade after 1943. It first tried to persuade farmers that the Canadian Wheat Board was a socialist plot imposing compulsory prices and regulations on farmers and grain companies alike, thereby destroying initiative and the free enterprise system. Speakers from the Grain Exchange criss-crossed the prairies in the late 1940s and early 1950s speaking to local Chambers of Commerce and any farmers they could interest. They used the media extensively, both radio and newspapers, to promote the 'Red Scare' in a climate which was generally ripe for such promotion. But farmers couldn't be persuaded and the government held firm. An effort to have the legislation creating the Wheat Board ruled unconstitutional failed in the courts.

Feed Grains Issue and Inland Terminals

The most recent strategy offensive against the Wheat Board system of marketing combines the federal government with the two national railways, the American-based international grain trade and the local base of free enterprise found in Chambers of Commerce and the Palliser Wheat Growers.

In rapid succession beginning in mid-1973, a number of related developments occurred under the orchestration of Wheat Board Minister Otto Lang. Marketing of feed grain opened up when Lang announced that Wheat Board control over interprovincial trade would be substantially reduced. An 'off-board' selling mechanism was created to make room for feed grain handling by Carghills and Continental Grain along with the other private grain companies.[6] At the same time, on the advice of civil servant grains policy advisors known as the 'Grains Group,' Lang began to promote and support new proposals for grain handling and transportation. Critical among these was a proposal for a string of high capacity inland terminals with long-haul private trucking. These terminals would replace the existing country elevators and the branch-line system of railways would be abandoned.

Lang pushed through his Feed Grains Policy in 1973 and 1974 over the vocal opposition of the three prairie governments, the Wheat Pools, the National Farmers Union and candidates for the federal NDP in the 1974 election. He emerged with increased political power and set out the means to expand his base of influence and complete the implementation of a "balanced, freedom of choice" approach to marketing.

The Inland Terminal concept was the vehicle Lang needed to impose policy changes which he personally favoured following his rise to cabinet in 1968 and which the railways and grain companies had been demanding for twenty years. In a matter of a few short years, it might be possible to undo both the Canadian Wheat Board *and* the Crow's Nest Freight Rates which had taken farmers a lifetime of political struggle to establish and maintain.

The political scenario around the Terminals went as follows. First, farmers were courted to support the Terminal idea as more efficient because it would facilitate both cleaning and grading grain on the prairies instead of at the port terminals, as well as loading and marshalling of railway cars through the use of so-called 'unit trains.'[7] Once farmers became interested in the idea, promoted both through the Palliser Wheat Growers and local Chambers of Commerce, pro-Terminal groups were formed. The first of these was at Weyburn, Saskatchewan, in 1973. It was followed by pro-Terminal committees in several other prairie towns and cities.

The Weyburn group formed a company which applied for and received $35,000 from the federal government to conduct a feasibility study. The results of this study were never made public and were inaccessible to anyone but shareholders in the company.

Other pro-Terminal committees applied for federal funds at the suggestion of Lang.[8] In each area they began to solicit potential members and investors among the larger farmers of the district. Lang was creating a support base of at least 200-300 farmers in each area who would become members and ultimately shareholders in Inland Terminal Associations. This provided a political network of farmers who would then have a stake in some drastic changes in transportation, marketing policies and freight rates in order for their terminal to succeed.

In the Weyburn example, the Terminal would require half the total volume of grain produced within a 50-mile radius of the city to meet its proposed annual handling capacity of 20 million bushels. In order to force farmers to haul that far, it would be necessary to close down at least half of the 93 community shipping points in the area. But this could be accomplished through rail-line abandonment.

It just happened that on January 1, 1975, 6,808 miles of prairie branch lines were unfrozen for possible abandonment.[9] 525 were immediately abandoned and 6,283 were subject to abandonment beginning in 1976, pending public hearings. Within the Weyburn Terminal radius, some 300 miles of branch lines were left 'unprotected.' These contained more than half the local shipping points.

But there were still a couple of snags in the Lang scenario. One was the fact that truck hauling had been shown to be three-and-a-half times more costly than rail line hauling in terms of energy used per ton/mile. It would cost a farmer at least 10¢ per bushel for a 50-mile haul when he could haul to his local elevator for 5¢. Also, truck hauling meant expensive road upgrading normally paid by local and municipal governments. The second problem was that most prairie residents were prepared to fight to keep their railway service which they regarded as essential to maintain many of the smaller towns.

The federal government could eliminate these objections through the lifting of the Crow's Nest Rates on railway grain hauling. This would allow the railways to overcharge for their branch-line routes, making them uneconomical in relation to trucking and providing further argument for abandonment. On the positive side, the federal government would have a large sum of money available, estimated as high as $300 million, hitherto paid out to the railways in subsidies for uneconomical branch lines. They would use this money to sweeten the pot for both local municipalities, provincial governments on the prairies and farmers themselves.

When he first proposed abandoning the Crow Rates (in Edmonton in November 1974), Lang suggested that this money could pay for highway and road subsidies and private trucking subsidies to farmers who hauled their own grain. This would undermine some of the local resistance to centralized hauling.

The big push for grain handling and transportation changes (resisted by the same coalition that lost the fight on feed grains) must still come from the pro-Terminal forces themselves. These include not just farmers and local businessmen, but the American grain companies and of course the railways. A spokesman for Carghill Grain told a group of farmers at one terminal-organizing meeting in Melfort, Saskatchewan, that if the farmers didn't build a terminal they (Carghill) would.

The issue, of course, is not between one system of grain handling versus another, or one approach to transportation versus another — although both of these questions warrant debate and raise doubts about the Terminal proposal. What is really at stake is control over the grain resource in the forseeable future. Under the Canadian Wheat Board grain had become a publicly regulated commodity with limited profit potential for either the railways or private grain trade. But with a return to the flexibility of the open market, the possibility of unloading a greater burden of the costs onto farmers and the lifting of the long-standing Crow Rates, the profit future is golden for agri-business. Production and markets can shift freely to the luxury oilseed commodities, and feed grains for livestock in Canada, both of which are already outside the Wheat Board, thanks in no small measure to the efforts of Otto Lang.

The Agribusiness Component: Elevators, Millers and Bakers

Winnipeg is Canada's grain-trade capital, and although the domestic consumption of wheat is a minor aspect of the trade in terms of volume, it is extremely lucrative. The grain-milling and commerical bakery industry is a tightly woven network within the shadow of the larger export grain trade and integral to it. The size and wealth of the grain trade bureaucracy in downtown Winnipeg is impressive. The concrete and glass of the Richardson Tower and the more modest Grain Exchange Building and Wheat Board offices house the elevator companies, flour and feed-mills, exporters and shippers, and the brokerage firms who inhabit the Commodity Exchange. Winnipeg is the nerve centre from which the national wheat economy takes its cues.

The elevator handling system itself, since the advent of the Canadian Wheat Board, has lost much of its profit potential. The major companies involved are not suffering (the Saskatchewan Wheat Pool declared a $32 million profit in 1974) but the Wheat Board control on wheat prices and fixed elevator handling charges reduced the potential of windfall gains. Most of the private national and international companies abandoned elevator handling of wheat to the large farmer-owned co-operatives.

By 1973 the three prairie Wheat Pools and the United Grain Growers owned about 79 per cent of elevator storage capacity in 4,000 local elevators. The only remaining private companies of consequence were Pioneer Grain (owned by the Richardson family) and Carghill Grain (subsidiary of U.S. Carghill, the world's largest grain trading company). Carghill only recently entered the elevator business in a major way in Canada, buying out National Grain Company in 1974. But both Pioneer and Carghill are concentrating their energy and investments in specialty crops whose markets and prices are not controlled by the wheat board. They are also part of a scheme to enlarge the marketing of feed-grains in Canada.

The domestic milling industry is fully integrated from country elevators to commercial bakeries. Along with the large international grain traders, the domestic cereal processors have de-emphasized their elevator holdings because wheat prices are set by the Wheat Board and all purchasers have equal access to stored wheat reserves. Ogilvie Flour and Maple Leaf Mills still maintain a string of elevators but primarily for the purchase of oats and corn for processing.

There are flour mills that own bakeries, bakeries which own flour mills and retail grocery chains which own both. In general, of all

domestic grain interests, flour mills and breakfast cereal manufacturers are the most centralized and concentrated in their ownership. Commercial bakeries are somewhat more diversified in size and
scale of operation. There were 35 flour mills in Canada in 1971, down
from 54 in 1961 with the number of employees reduced from 2,665
to 2,121. With fewer workers, labour costs declined as a per cent of
total operating costs in the grain milling industry over the same
period.

The four largest flour mills handle 77 per cent of the value of all
shipments in Canada. The major companies, Ogilvie, Robin Hood
Multifoods, Maple Leaf Mills and Quaker, are also heavily integrated
into other levels of the food industry. Ogilvie Flour Mills is owned by
International Utilities Overseas Investment Corporation along with
Labatt Breweries and Brascan Limited. It has a network of holdings
from grain elevators and flour mills to poultry and dairy processing
plants and part ownership in McGavin-Toastmaster Bakeries, Seagram
Distillers and the Mercantile Bank of Canada. Ogilvie's $2.8 million
in profit earnings in 1973 were an increase of 40 per cent over 1972
and attest to the advantages of vertical integration.

Robin Hood Multifoods, subsidiary of U.S. International Multifoods Corporation, is equally diverse in its Canadian interests. With
1971 sales of $433.5 million and profits of $7.4 million, Robin Hood
pursued activity in milling, feed mills, meat processing (50 per cent
share in Lakeside Packing) and pickles (as owners of Bick's of
Canada).

Quaker Oats, subsidiary of U.S. Quaker Oats, has concentrated its
Canadian operations in milling, breakfast cereal manufacturing and
the manufacture of pet foods. The parent company is involved in a
number of other separate Canadian holdings such as Alsask Processors
Limited, and has shares in banking, retail trade, airlines, and Singer
sewing machines. Quaker sales of $679 million netted 1971 profits of
$24.2 million.

Maple Leaf Mills has shared interests with both Quaker and Ogilvie,
two of its major competitors. With Ogilvie it shares ownership of
McGavin Toastmaster Bakeries and it owns the Agricultural Products
Division of Quaker Oats of Canada. But Maple Leaf Mills in its own
right is the owner of Canadian Bakeries, Eastern Bakeries, Corporate
Foods Limited, and has investments in trust and mortgage companies,
Eagle Star Insurance, Dominion Foundries and numerous feed mills
and seed companies. Maple Leaf had 1973 profits of $7.8 million, an
incredible increase of 286 per cent over 1972.

The commercial baking industry is a mixture of large and small
enterprise. There were 2,135 bakeries in Canada in 1972 but the four

largest handled 30.7 per cent of all shipments. The mortality rate among the small and medium-sized bakeries is high. The larger bakeries are directly integrated either with processors, retailers or both. For example Weston Bakeries, owned by George Weston Limited, supplies Loblaw Groceterias, O.K. Economy Stores, and Shop-Easy — all owned by George Weston Limited. Dominion Stores owns General Bakeries, its major supplier. Maple Leaf Mills owns Canadian Bakeries and is a major shareholder in Eastern Bakeries, McGavin-Toastmaster and Berwick Bakeries.

The problem for medium and small bakeries is not simply one of competing, although that may be difficult without the advantage of an integrated supplier. It is primarily a problem of gaining access to supermarket shelf space. This problem is mentioned in the Prices Review Board *Report on Bread Prices*. Unfortunately the Board does not draw any obvious conclusions about the degree of monopoly in the food industry. It merely suggests the problems of smaller bakeries should be "given serious consideration" by government "in light of their policies to develop and support regional industry and enterprise."

An indication that some competition exists in the bakery industry despite the power of larger integrated firms may be that biscuit manufacturers and bakeries pay among the lowest wages of all manufacturing industries. Compared to an average manufacturing wage of $161 per week in 1972, biscuit workers and bakery workers were earning $120 and $130 per week respectively. Both industries, not coincidentally, have a high percentage of female workers.

The Price of Bread

After considering some characteristics of the mill-baking industry which better clarify its power in relation to producers and consumers, the diagram below makes clear how a 36¢ loaf of bread slices down between production, processing, and profits and distribution which account for almost half a loaf. In line with earlier discussion on farm costs of production, the farmer's net income in 1974 amounted to 1.2¢ on a 36¢ loaf. Although not shown separately, the direct labour costs of workers in the milling industry are approximately 1¢ per loaf, as were those of the baking industry workers.

Despite the fact wheat is produced here, its price and marketing is publicly controlled from the elevator to the bakery, and despite a $160 million subsidy to the industry the state is still unwilling to control the final price of bread. This was clearly illustrated by the events of 1972-74 as they unfolded before a weary consuming public.

Bread prices, although out of line with the price of wheat, had

FIGURE 8

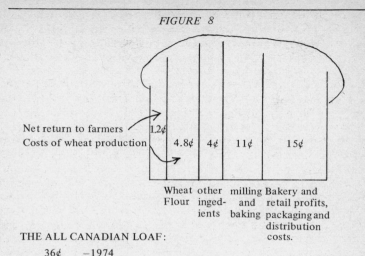

Net return to farmers ↗ 1.2¢

Costs of wheat production | 4.8¢ | 4¢ | 11¢ | 15¢ |

Wheat Flour   other ingedients   milling and baking   Bakery and retail profits, packaging and distribution costs.

THE ALL CANADIAN LOAF:

36¢   —1974

SOURCE: STATISTICS CANADA ON FARM PRODUCTION COSTS AND PRICES REVIEW BOARD ON INDUSTRY COST BREAKDOWN.

maintained an average rate of inflation since 1961, about three per cent per year. This was closely in line with flour, the main cost ingredient. Then in November 1972 there was a general increase in bread prices of eight per cent. This was followed in September 1973 by further increases of 20-25 per cent. Both the Canadian Bakery Council and the Food Prices Review Board had predicted the September increase and were anticipating a further 20 per cent increase in October unless government action was forthcoming. It was at this juncture that the federal cabinet and the bakery industry made a deal.

Wheat prices for flour have, as already mentioned, been based in the long term on the price of export wheat. This was a grievance of farmers until the system was changed in 1970. But it meant that the wheat price to flour mills remained stable until 1973. Despite the stability of a depressed world price for wheat the industry managed to inflate flour prices by 40 per cent from 1961 to 1973, and by 90 per cent from 1961 to 1975. With flour went the price of bread.

The initial 'two-price system' for domestically-consumed wheat

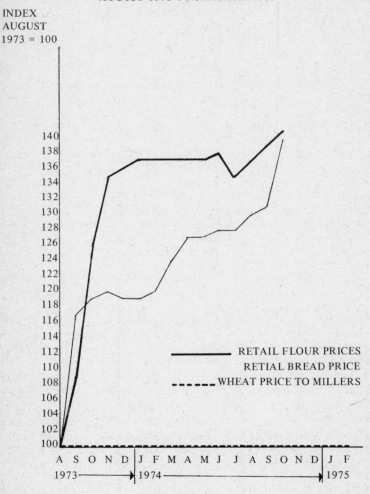

FIGURE 9

**COMPARISON OF WHEAT PRICE TO FLOUR-MILLS
WITH RETAIL FLOUR AND BREAD PRICES,
AUGUST 1973 TO JANUARY 1975**

INDEX
AUGUST
1973 = 100

140
138
136
134
132
130
128
126
124
122
120
118
116
114
112 ———— RETAIL FLOUR PRICES
110   RETIAL BREAD PRICE
108 ------ WHEAT PRICE TO MILLERS
106
104
102
100

A S O N D J F M A M J J A S O N D J F
1973 ——▶ 1974 ———————— ▶ 1975

SOURCE: STATISTICS CANADA CONSUMER PRICE INDEX

was announced by Otto Lang, Minister in charge of the Wheat Board, in 1970. The Lang policy involved a 'two-price' system in which the higher price to farmers for wheat used for domestic human consumption was paid not by millers and bakers but rather by the public treasury. The price paid to farmers for domestic wheat, ten per cent of total production, was raised to $3.00 per bushel. This was in line with farmer demands and well above the export price of $1.65. But instead of the Wheat Board charging this $3.00 price to the flour mills, cereal manufacturers and commercial bakeries, their price stayed at $1.95, the longstanding export price of the mid-1960s. The federal government paid the difference, and in the process shielded the grain milling industry to the tune of $60 million per year after 1970. So the price of wheat for flour was frozen at $1.95, ostensibly for the benefit of consumers.

In July 1973, when the world wheat price surpassed $4.00 per bushel, the federal government adjusted their policy. They released the domestic price from $1.95 so that it could float with the world price, but the federal treasury continued to pay $1.00 per bushel subsidy. In other words whatever the export price, the purchase price to Canadian millers would be $1.00 less and the public subsidy would remain at a constant $60 million per year (based on the normal 60 million bushels of domestic wheat consumption). The logic of the federal treasury in introducing this change was clear enough. As long as the price had remained fixed to the millers at $1.95, and wheat export prices continued to rise without sign of levelling off, the government stood to pay out double or triple the $60 million subsidy they had adjusted to from 1970 to 1973. Lang's 1970 policy had been to maintain a price to farmers for domestically consumed wheat of either $3.00 or the equivalent of the export price, whichever was higher. By July 19, 1973, when he changed his policy, the export price was around $4.10.

The impact on the milling and baking industry of a floating subsidy instead of a fixed, depressed price was severe. The price of wheat to millers by August 1 was $3.18. They wasted no time in passing the increase on to the commercial bakeries in the August deliveries of flour despite the fact that their wheat had been purchased well in advance of the crop year-end of July 30. (It was the millers' version of supermarket double-ticketing.) The bakeries in turn announced in August that bread prices would be hiked 6-7¢ per loaf effective September 1973, due to the higher price of flour. (Since so many of the flour mills are subsidiaries of the commercial bakeries and vice versa, the possibilities for short-term co-operative price arrangements in this situation were endless.)

It was only six weeks later, on September 4, 1973, that the federal government, pressed by the alarm calls of Beryl Plumptre's Prices

Review Board and the heat of August inflation, reversed its policy of a floating wheat-flour price. But they were too late for anything more than a compromise. The food industry had managed a 25 per cent increase in the price of bread in the eight months from January to August 1973, and they weren't about to retreat.

The deal, announced by the Cabinet on September 4, was that the price of wheat for domestic human consumption would be fixed at $3.25 for a seven-year period. The federal government would pay a subsidy above this price up to $5.00 per bushel. Farmers would be asked to absorb any difference between the $5.00 subsidized price and the current export price. As the price remained above $5.00 from September 1973 to May 1974, producers absorbed losses of up to 85¢ per bushel and the federal government paid $1.75 per bushel. Annually this amounted to $105 million from government, assuming an export price of $5.00 or better and another $50-60 million from producers. The government estimated that bread prices could have risen another 6-8¢ per loaf if the full export price were allowed to apply to flour.

Peter Wygant, Executive Vice-President for General Bakeries and spokesman for the Bakery Council (which represents 409 of 1,824 Canadian bakeries) committed the industry not to raise prices for twelve months "unless extraordinary and unforeseen cost increases occur." Otto Lang while boasting the agreement the following day in Parliament conceded under questioning that he had "no iron-clad agreement" from the bakeries.

The significance of this deal between the cabinet and the baking industry is interesting to contemplate. The federal cabinet had changed its policy on domestic wheat so as to effectively reduce the per-bushel price to millers and bakers from a September price of $4.65 (based on the export price of $5.65 less $1.00 subsidy) to the actual September price of $3.25 under the new policy effective until 1980. In other words the industry was given a windfall saving of roughly $80 million by this policy on top of the $60 million cushion they already enjoyed. In addition the government had a commitment to maintain this subsidized price of flour for seven years. In exchange for all of this, the government got an informal commitment that at least the 409 bakeries represented by the Bakery Council would try not to raise their prices any more for at least six months "unless . . . unforeseen cost increases occur."

Should the consumer who was spared the threatened further hike in bread prices have rejoiced about this arrangement? Not if he began to calculate who really paid the $100-$150 million subsidy to protect the millers from world wheat prices. The cereal manufacturing and commercial bread industry is among the most tightly integrated and controlled industries in Canada, and among the most profitable. And yet after years of living on the advantage of wheat produced by prairie farmers at depressed prices, they suddenly found their profits being sweetened by the protection of the public treasury from the perils of the world market.

It was only five months later that the Canadian Bakery Council was in the news again, this time announcing a 4¢ per loaf increase in the price of bread. The February 15, 1974, announcement claimed wages and ingredients other than flour were making a substantial increase necessary. "And," they added defensively, "Canadian bread prices will still be amongst the lowest in the world." (This calculation obviously didn't include the cost to the consumer of government and producer subsidies estimated at 8¢ per loaf.) The Prices Review Board and Consumer Affairs Minister Herb Gray attempted to prevent the increase. The Review Board produced a report on bread prices which suggested that cost increases could justify no more than a 2¢ increase in price. This report, released at the end of February, documented both direct cost factors, which amounted to 1.75¢, and a number of waste costs which amounted to uncalculated excess and inefficiency in the industry.

Whatever the merits of the Review Board Report, the Board itself was powerless to act. The best they could do was convene a meeting for March 20 with Bakery Council officials to ask them to justify the increase in public. The Council agreed, but in the meantime their members and other bakeries began to advance prices. Ironically among the first to announce an increase was Dominion Stores, whose spokesman said the 3¢ increase effective March 11 was because General Bakeries, their major supplier (and a 100 per cent subsidiary of Dominion), was increasing its wholesale price 8-10 per cent. The irony is that it was Peter Wygant, Executive Vice-President of General Bakeries, who originally stated in September on behalf of the Bakery Council that there would be no price increase for a year.

The federal cabinet was obviously embarrassed and upset by the failure of the bakers to live up to their 'agreement.' Herb Gray, with egg on his face, tried to buy time. He first tried to pass the issue to the Prices Review Board saying on March 5 "the cabinet wouldn't make any decision on whether to control prices until the bakeries and prices board had a chance to meet to discuss their differences." But later, when it was clear that the bakeries were going to push ahead regardless, Gray got on the phone and worked compromises with some of the big 'name' companies. On March 8 he was able to announce to the press that Weston Bakeries, Steinberg's, A and P, Corporate Foods and Safeway had agreed to limit their increases to 2¢ until after the March 20 meeting with Beryl Plumptre.

The March 20 meeting date was set up, like a showdown at the O.K. corral. And Beryl Plumptre stuck to her guns about the correctness of the Review Board's figures on costs to the industry. The bakeries disagreed, presenting their own estimates and arguing that a 4¢ increase was minimal to their very survival. It was a great public display. But neither the Prices Review Board nor the Bakery Council had the power either to advance or to hold back prices. Clearly there was some compromise and the exercise of forcing public discussion was not entirely useless. But the fact is the industry had and still has the unchallenged power to proceed with whatever price levels their profit position suggests. Between March and December 1974, prices were adjusted upward regularly without serious further objections from Mrs. Plumptre. There was a 7 per cent increase in March-April and another 10 per cent increase in September-October 1974. The baking industry was able to point to the rising price of refined sugar as a cause for price increases even though the original cost of sugar was less than 2¢ per loaf which, even tripled, did not account for the increases of more than 10¢ per loaf experienced between July 1973 and December 1974. Furthermore, when sugar prices declined at the end of 1974, there was no retreat on bread prices. General Bakeries weighed in with a 200 per cent profit increase over 1973.[10]

Future bread prices are uncertain because of the federal commitment to maintain the domestic price of wheat to millers at $2.5 per bushel until 1980. Presumably price increases will reflect other lesser raw material costs, labour costs and the continuing thirst for profit and expansion in the milling-baking industry. But there is also the uncertainty of how changes in grain handling and transportation will affect consumers. Clearly the proposed lifting of the Crow Rate agreement on freight rates for grain moved to the lakehead and west coast ports has implications for the domestic milling industry, as well as for cereal manufacturing firms in central Canada. Will the federal treasury bear the cost of freight rate adjustments to grain products, thereby enlarging its handsome subsidy to the industry? Or will these costs be 'absorbed' by the industry and passed on in higher retail prices? In some ways it matters not at all; it all comes back to 'consumers.' But bread is an essential low-income staple, and if public subsidies to private industry are to be applied, they apply more logically to a commodity like bread than, for example, red meats. Yet such subsidies are a cushion of extra profit to the private food industry, a problem which can only be ultimately faced through public takeover.

Notes to Chapter 4

1. Royal Commission on Farm Machinery Prices.

2. Weiss study on the fertilizer industry in Western Canada, for Manitoba Department of Agriculture, 1973-4.

3. Robert Chodos, *The CPR: A Century of Corporate Welfare* (Toronto, James, Lewis and Samuel, 1974).

4. In retrospect it may seem unusual and counterproductive to the economy for the Canadian Government to have moved to discourage the price of a major export commodity like wheat. In similar world market circumstances in 1973 the government made no effort to dampen Wheat Board price increases in response to world conditions. The difference is that in 1943 both domestic and export customers were being subsidized from the federal treasury. Domestic bread prices were frozen and millers were being subsidized for their losses by the federal treasury. Export grain to Europe was being financed under Canadian Mutual Aid. A higher price for farmers would have been justified given the difficult recovery from the depression. 1943 prices had only recovered to $1.14 from the previous five-year average of 60¢.) But unlike today when higher farm prices can be passed on to domestic and overseas consumers, in 1943 they would have been a drain on the federal budget.

5. There are numerous references on the marketing and handling of grain in western Canada. These include Vernon Fowkes, *National Policy and the Wheat Economy*, and S.W. Yates, *History of the Saskatchewan Wheat Pool*, which covers in detail the period from World War I to the early 1940s.

6. These two major companies only established a base on the prairies in the 1973-74 crop year. Carghill gained its foothold by purchasing National Grain Company, while Continental began by leasing space from federal government terminals in Saskatchewan. Both companies concentrated on getting contracts with farmers for delivery of rape-seed, flax and the other commodities not marketed through the Canadian Wheat Board.

7. "Unit Trains" are a proposal to load up to 100 cars with cleaned and graded grain on the prairies for direct loading onto ships at the ports. Its supporters claim these trains can be unloaded without the time and expense of unloading and cleaning at port terminals. Unit trains would be made practical, they suggest, by the establishment of inland terminals for cleaning and grading.

Critics argue the bottleneck in transportation is not at the port facilities but on the railway lines themselves, which are inefficient and unwilling to give priority to grain commodities under existing freight rates. While not opposed to the unit train concept, they argue that its features could be incorporated into the existing railway system without the necessity of the large inland terminals.

8. A spokesman for the Melville pro-Terminal committee was quoted in the Regina *Leader-Post* as saying "Otto" had told him to apply for the $35,000 feasibility study. The man later turned out to be finance chairman for the local Liberal Association.

9. The two national railways have been applying for abandonment of branch line service over a period of years. Since 1961 the lines were protected against abandonment and the federal government granted subsidies to cover the railways claims for losses. In 1967 the federal government announced that the freeze would be lifted January 1, 1975. When that date arrived, three categories were established for the more than 6,000 miles of prairie branch lines. 525 miles were abandoned outright. 12,413 miles were protected until the year 2000, and 6,283 miles were protected until 1976 subject to hearings.

10. *Financial Post*'s Corporation Index showed General Bakeries with a two-fold increase in net earnings for 1974 over 1973.

V

The 'Crisis' of the Livestock-Beef Industry

Nowhere, perhaps, are the contradictions of the food system exemplified more dramatically than in the livestock-beef industry. In the short period from mid-1973 to early 1975, the 'crises' in the industry included apparent shortages, apparent surpluses, high beef prices, depressed cattle prices, high cattle feed prices, an international trade war, consumer protest over the use of hormone additives, the discovery of poisonous bacteria in supermarket ground beef, and double-ticketing of in-store merchandise. Beef was the most highly politicized and controversial commodity, and the most investigated. It was the subject of seven special reports by the Food Prices Review Board, an emergency parliamentary debate, and a special Commons inquiry. It divided the producers, with the National Farmers Union and the Canadian Cattlemen's Association demanding precisely opposite solutions. In general, beef was the most erratic commodity in terms of price movements, reflecting both the hazards of the 'free market' and the distortions caused by inconsistent public policies.

Beef consumption symbolizes the good life in North America and increasingly throughout the world. It has become a measurement of living standards used by both economists and ordinary people. Annual per-capita consumption of beef has peaked in the United States at 116 pounds, and at 92.5 pounds in Canada in 1972, reflecting the world's richest average life-style. But the average has been poorly distributed, and just when many Canadians were beginning to savour some sense of prosperity, the beef market left them behind again.

It is not surprising that rising beef prices provoked consumer protest. Retail beef prices jumped an incredible 32 per cent in the nine months from December 1972 to September 1973. This equalled the cumulative price rise of the previous six years. Beef prices then levelled off slightly in the early fall of 1973 before increasing sharply again in November, December and January. A collapse in cattle prices in March and April 1974 gave some relief on retail prices, but a second high peak was reached in August 1974 and prices continued high until February 1975. At that time the market price for cattle collapsed completely and consumer beef prices returned to a two-year low.

Open consumer protest was less apparent in Canada than in the United States, but both countries experienced consumer reaction in the form of falling per-capita consumption during the period of exaggerated beef prices.[1] The rise in consumption which began after World War II was reversed, and Canadians and Americans shifted marginally to poultry, cheese and other proteins. A pattern of increasing cattle production since 1969 was in sharp contradiction to the drop-off in consumption. The fear of beef shortages which existed in 1973 was suddenly transformed into a market glut in the industrial countries around the world. Beef-exporting countries began dumping their surpluses, disrupting the domestic prices of cattle in the importing countries. Cattlemen in North America and elsewhere faced bankruptcy during 1974 and 1975, because even though beef retail prices were still 30 to 40 per cent above the level of 1972, their cattle prices had returned to 1972 levels. And, most critically, the price they paid for commercial feed was up over 100 per cent from 1972. (Feed costs represent 50 per cent of the total cost of production for beef.)

As with inflation generally, the beef price spiral was hardest on the working-class and low-income consumer. Pensioners and large families were singled out as the front line victims. It was the 'cheaper' cuts, like hamburger and stewing beef, which appeared to get selective attention for price hikes. The drop in overall consumption can be attributed primarily to low-income consumers who shifted to more purely starch diets, contributing to the growing incidence of malnutrition.

The mystery of the livestock-beef business from 1973 through 1975 lay not so much in high beef prices as in the tendency toward a growing spread during the same period between the selling price of cattle, the wholesale carcass price for beef, and the consumer price of beef cuts. By February 1975, cattle prices averaged 3.9 per cent above those of June 1973, but retail beef prices had risen an average of 9.3 per cent in the same interval. The price spread is more dramatic over the longer term: where beef prices in February 1975 were up as much as 40 per cent over the 1972 prices on some cuts, cattle prices were up only 10 per cent.

The price spread from producers to consumers was expanding throughout this period, despite federal government policies ostensibly aimed at stabilizing conditions in the industry. The confusion

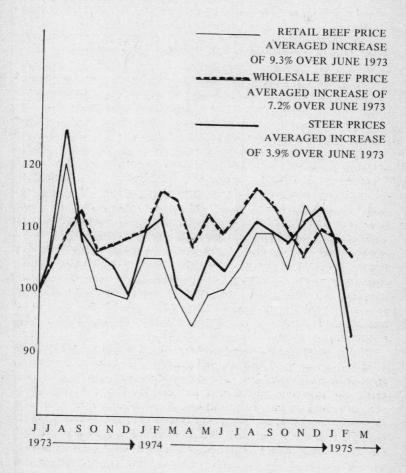

FIGURE 10
BEEF PRICE TRENDS, JUNE 1973 TO MARCH 1975

INDEX:
JUNE 1973 = 100

RETAIL BEEF PRICE
AVERAGED INCREASE
OF 9.3% OVER JUNE 1973

WHOLESALE BEEF PRICE
AVERAGED INCREASE OF
7.2% OVER JUNE 1973

STEER PRICES
AVERAGED INCREASE
OF 3.9% OVER JUNE 1973

J J A S O N D J F M A M J J A S O N D J F M
1973 ⟶ 1974 ⟶ 1975 ⟶

SOURCES: 1. CANADA AGRICULTURE, LIVESTOCK AND MEAT
                 TRADE REPORT (WEEKLY)
             2. STATISTICS CANADA, CONSUMER PRICE INDEX.

surrounding the beef crisis made little obvious sense to most observers, but in time two points emerged with some clarity. One was that the oligopolies in both the processing and retail-sales sectors were capable of protecting themselves from erratic price movements and even gaining some advantage relative to producers. This accounts for the price spread. Secondly, it was apparent by early 1974 that the crisis was as much a crisis for producers facing a cost-price squeeze as it was a crisis for consumers facing a problem of uncontrolled inflation.

How the Livestock Beef Industry Works

The cycle of production and distribution of livestock and beef products includes three general levels: livestock production, meat slaughtering and processing, and distribution. The basic production of cattle is divided into two stages and is mainly in the hands of private producers. Both processing and distribution industries are dominated by a few major firms with national markets and reflect all of the general characteristics of oligopoly.

The full cycle of livestock production involves two stages which may be carried out within a single diversified enterprise but are usually undertaken by separate specialized enterprises. These are *cow-calf* operations or 'ranching' and *feed-lot* operations. Cow-calf operations maintain a herd of breeding stock on open range land or pasture. They produce a crop of calves each year which are marketed either as veal to packing plants or as feeder-stock to feed-lots. Calves, born in the spring, are marketed either in the fall of their first year or wintered over for sale in the second summer or fall. Some cow-calf operators maintain a feed-lot as well, in which case they keep their steer calves over a second winter, grain-feeding them until they reach market weight of 1,100 to 1,200 pounds.

In a straight cow-calf operation the land base requirements are extensive, about ten acres per head, with an average of about a hundred head of cows and one or two bulls. Because feed requirements for winter feeding consist primarily of hay for cows, most cow-calf operations are fully self-sufficient, producing all feed requirements on the farm. This reduces the dependence of cow-calf operations on the fluctuations and generally inflationary pattern of commercial feed grains. The major costs of production affecting cow-calf operators are the general costs of machinery, repairs, and farm fuels, plus the cost of twine for baling hay and the cost of buildings and shelters for animals and feed. Revenues come primarily from the annual sale of calves and older cows which are 'culled' from the herd along with heifers which failed to calve or had difficulty calving. These 'culls' are replaced by a hold-back of some of the heifer calves to sustain or increase the size of the herd.

Labour demands in cow-calf operations are intensive but seasonal rather than year-round. Calving in the spring, annual fence repairs, haying in June and July, branding, dehorning and castrating in late summer, all can be integrated with field work in a 'mixed farming' operation. The vast majority of cow-calf operations in both eastern and western Canada are of this sort. These operations, usually with a hundred or so head and less, are in contrast to the large ranches spotted through southwestern Saskatchewan, Alberta, and the interior of British Columbia. The ranchers with up to 10,000 head represent the aristocracy of cattle producers in both wealth and politics, and they tend to dominate organizations such as the Canadian Cattlemen's Association. Smaller cow-calf operators are as likely to identify with the issues surrounding their grain commodities as they are with cattle, and are more inclined to support general farm organizations such as the National Farmers Union.

Feed-lots are both capital and labour-intensive. They buy calves and cattle ranging in age and weight from seven months and 400 pounds to eighteen months and 1,000 pounds. They feed animals on grain rations in enclosed areas to fatten them as quickly as possible for market at about 1,150 pounds. The scale of operation may be large or small, from five or six acres to a hundred or so acres of shelter fencing, feed bunkers, water troughs, and granaries, with the cattle themselves numbering from 200 or so to three or four thousand. Feed-lots are generally close to urban markets where they deliver regularly to buying stations of the major packing plants or to public and private stockyards where cattle are auctioned off to buyers from the packing houses.

The high capital cost of both cattle and feed and the rapid turnover of stock make feed-lot operations extremely vulnerable. Changes in the price of any or all of feed grains, feeder replacement stock or the market price for finished cattle can have disastrous consequences for feed-lot operations in a matter of days. All of these price factors are subject to the fluctuations of 'open market' supply and demand. Feed-lots are also vulnerable to disease problems and animal losses, because the animals are confined to wet and crowded conditions and there is a constant turnover of stock with each new animal a potential disease-carrier.

The high risks in feed-lot operations were accompanied by high profits throughout the 1960s and early 1970s, as general grain surpluses in Canada depressed the price of feed grain for cattle, particularly in the prairie provinces. This profit potential attracted custom feeding by agribusiness firms like Canada Packers, Swift, and

National Grain Company as well as encouraging smaller scale entrepreneurs to pool resources to set up feed-lots. Hundreds of feed-lots began operation in the late 1960s on the strength of cheap surplus grain. It was these new capital ventures which were first faced with bankruptcy and closures when grain prices began to rise sharply on the world markets in 1973.

The interests of feed-lot operators and cow-calf operators are often at variance on matters of policy. Despite this conflict they belong to the same producer organizations. Some of the contradictory positions which show up within such organizations as the Canadian Cattlemen's Association and the provincial stockgrowers' groups reflect the dichotomy of feed-lot operators and cow-calf men on marketing, trade, and price issues.

The Packers: Slaughtering and processing operations have usually been integrated within a single establishment. Larger firms, however, are tending toward a centralization policy whereby they operate bulk killing plants separately from their processing operations. The killing plants are maintained in livestock-producing regions, like Saskatchewan, while processing, canning and sausage-making are centralized to urban market centres such as Vancouver, Edmonton, Winnipeg, Toronto, and Montreal.

The largest five companies, Canada Packers, Swift, Burns, Schneider's, and Intercontinental Packers, share 60 per cent of the overall market. Although there are still 432 slaughtering and meat-packing establishments, these five — led by the three national companies, Burns, Swift, and Canada Packers — effectively determine price and market conditions.

The packing houses buy their cattle directly from independent producers or commercial feed-lots which deliver to company buying stations, or they bid for cattle at public auctions. In either case the major buyers effectively set the day-to-day price on the cattle entering into market by the sheer volume of their purchases. It is taken for granted, but nonetheless remarkable, that the controlling influence on cattle prices is not the seller, a farmer whose only choice is to sell or not to sell, but the packing-house buyer who has a big stake in maintaining a downward trend on prices.

Once the animals are purchased they are either slaughtered and sold as dressed beef in bulk to supermarket chains, or trimmed and ground for canned meats and sausages, or sold as boneless frozen beef for institutional use.

The end use of the beef depends primarily on the grade and weight of the live animal. A-1 and A-2 beef is the top grade used for prime beef cuts and makes up 60 per cent of the commercial trade. A-3, and A-4 along with B-grades, are poorer finished animals which are also sold in bulk carcass form and make up about 15 per cent of the market. The remainder of the commercial market consists of older culled cows and bulls which are boned and frozen, canned, or used in sausages and weiners as low grade beef. In addition to domestic supplies of this lower grade beef, there has been a growing pattern of imported 'cow beef' from Australia and New Zealand.

The dominant market of choice steers breaks down as follows, from the time the live steer is brought to slaughter (see chart). A 1,000 pound animal produces a carcass of 570 pounds. The remaining weight consists of 170 pounds of animal waste and 260 pounds of commercial by-products. The salvagable by-products include the hide (65 pounds), inedible products such as tallow, skull and so on (105 pounds) and 90 pounds of edible products such as heart, liver, kidneys, and tongue.

The carcass itself, which is sold intact to supermarkets, breaks down into 103 pounds of steaks, 187 pounds of roasts, 138 pounds of ground and stewing beef, and 142 pounds of bones, fat, and shrinkage. From an original 1,000 pound choice steer the actual food commodity consists of 518 pounds, including such specialty markets as heart, liver, and tongue.[2]

Often bulk carcasses are frozen in warehouse storage for later sales. The ability to maintain frozen inventory gives the large packing plants an advantage in overcoming market irregularities. They can neutralize the effect of short-term shortages or surpluses of cattle by reducing or expanding their warehouse stocks of frozen beef.

The formal organizational voice of the packing plants is the Meat Packers Council, a national lobby dominated by the larger firms. The major packers work as a single unit in labour contract bargaining with the Canadian Food and Allied Workers Union as demonstrated by the lock-out strategy used by Burns, Swift, and Canada Packers against their Alberta workers in 1974.

In addition to their collective powers relative to producers and their unionized workers, the three biggest national companies have considerable individual powers relative to retail distributors. As large-volume suppliers of 'nationally advertised brands' they are in a position to demand preferred treatment from supermarkets which is denied to smaller packing plants. This power is further enhanced in the case of Canada Packers, which has a rising proportion of Dominion Store meat sales and is a major shareholder in that chain.

Retail distribution of meat products is done primarily through the national supermarket chains who make their purchases directly from packing plants which serve as wholesale distributors in urban centres. Beef is purchased as dressed beef and butchered in the supermarket directly for fresh cuts. Smaller retail outlets must buy more expensive

FIGURE 11
APPROXIMATE DISPOSITION OF A FED BEEF STEER

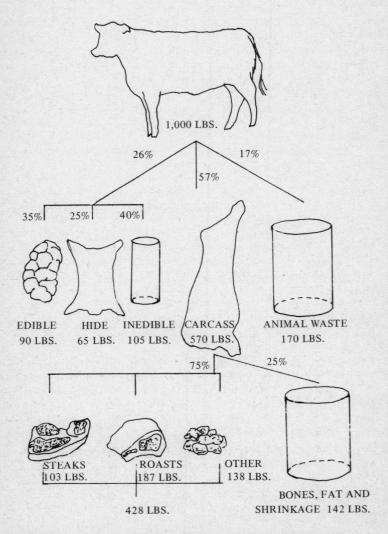

SOURCE: *FOOD PRICES REVIEW BOARD*, BEEF PRICING, *JUNE, 1974*

packaged fresh meats from packers at higher prices. The price advantage of the major retail chains over smaller stores comes in their ability to purchase carload lots in bulk form as opposed to packaged meats. The mark-up in beef products in supermarkets is roughly 30 per cent.

Supermarket purchasing and marketing of prime beef cuts from choice A-1 and A-2 steers is relatively straightforward. Excessive mark-ups are simple to calculate in relation to the market price of cattle.[3] But ground beef is often a blend of high grade beef and cow-beef. The cow-beef is not only a cheaper source of supply to supermarkets but it has a lower fat content than pure 'hamburger' from steers. Blending is good economics for the supermarkets and it allows the finished product to meet federal restrictions on the fat content limits for ground beef. Federal regulations place a 30-per-cent fat limit on hamburger, but certain ground beef can be classified as sausage meat and allowed up to 40-per-cent fat content.

Ground beef rip-offs have been contentious at the supermarket level. Both over-fat beef and beef containing severe amounts of bacteria have been found by both federal inspectors and independent researchers. From March 1972 to March 1973, the Department of Consumer and Corporate Affairs inspected 609 samples of ground beef and 147 samples of sausages. They found 25 per cent of the ground beef was unsatisfactory and 31 per cent of the sausages. There were eleven prosecutions for ground beef violations and sixteen for sausages, with fines to retailers from $50 to $1,000. 1973-74 figures were similar, with seventeen prosecutions for ground beef and seven for sausages. The small number of prosecutions is a reflection of the small number of samples gathered, while the apparent percentage of illegally marketed beef is astounding.

In addition, the Health Protection Branch of Health and Welfare Canada was forced to research more aggressively the bacteria counts in beef after CBC's "Marketplace" exposed dangerous bacteria levels in several southern Ontario supermarkets tested. Even before the Marketplace scare a small number of samples for bacteria (105) produced a conviction in 1973.[4]

Price Movements on the Open Market

Much as Canadians had reason to be concerned about the quality of supermarket meat products, the real impact of industry policies and practices was still the economic one. The livestock-beef industry had long boasted the status of the open market as the great strength and protection of consumers. The absence of marketing boards, price regulations, and trade restrictions was in sharp contrast to the dairy, poultry, and cereal commodities, all of which had some degree of government regulation. Critics of marketing in these other commodities were calling for precisely the approach to marketing which characterized cattle and beef. But milk, egg, and bread prices were all more stable than beef, even if most observers felt they were too high.

Since 1972 the market for both cattle and beef has been chaotic beyond precedent. Supporters of the open market suggest that the condition in the beef industry during this time was not an indictment of the open market so much as a result of the unwarranted intrusion of government policies which disturbed normal market patterns. This was roughly the analysis of the Canadian Cattlemen's Association. On the other hand, supporters of regulated markets said that the conditions of the open market were primarily responsible for the destructive trends in the market. The National Farmers Union took this position, although they too were critical of government intervention on the grounds that it was half-hearted and ineffective and had failed to develop orderly marketing as an alternative to the open market.

Regardless of the interpretation placed on the situation, or on the specific role of government after 1972, it was clear by 1975 that neither the traditional open market based on continental free trade nor a publicly controlled domestic and export marketing mechanism were in existence. Almost none of the nation's 100,000-or-so cattlemen were content with what existed by 1975, although they held widely differing attitudes towards marketing. Caught in the middle were the federal cabinet, and specifically Eugene Whelan.

The obvious beginning to the confusion and chaos in the livestock-beef industry was the sharp rise in cattle prices in August 1973. It set off a chain reaction of price rises through the industry. But the contributing factors to beef industry problems began earlier still.

The first disturbing development in a fluctuating but generally healthy beef industry was the rise in world prices for grain and protein commodities. Faced with potential world shortages in fall 1972, the Chicago and Winnipeg commodity exchanges bid up the price of North American protein crops (soybeans and rapeseed) and all grains including oats, barley, and corn used for livestock feeding. Soybean meal (used as supplement in cattle feed) was bid up from $104 per ton in fall 1972 to $430 by June 1973. Wheat, barley and corn prices all more than doubled. These price hikes were artificial in the sense that they bore no relationship to costs of production or returns to grain producers. But the impact they had on the livestock industry was very real. The accompanying graph tracing the commercial price of barley relative to cattle prices makes the point quite well. Average

FIGURE 12

COMPARISON OF FEED GRAIN PRICES PAID BY FARMERS WITH CATTLE SELLING PRICE NOV. 1972–FEB. 1975

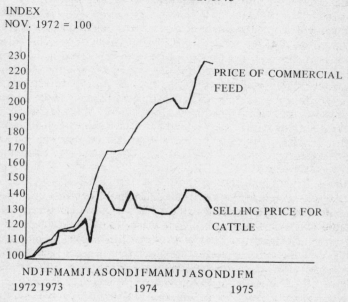

INDEX
NOV. 1972 = 100

Canadian feed barley prices jumped over 100 per cent from January 1973 to January 1975 while selling price for cattle was up 10 per cent.

When these price jumps for feed began in fall 1972, the returns to cattle-feed-lot operators for finished beef stood at about 35¢ per pound. They had reason to expect still higher grain prices in the spring on the basis of futures trading in soybeans and feed grains on the commodity markets.[5] Yet there was no assurance cattle prices would rise. The reaction of cattlemen in both Canada and the United States was first of all to sell their cattle at lighter than market weight in spring 1973 to cut down on feed purchases and avoid certain losses. Above-average marketings occurred from mid-January to mid-March 1973 as more but lighter animals were sent to slaughter. This was followed naturally by a 6 per cent decline in slaughterings in April and fewer than average slaughterings until mid-June.[6] By July and August the effects of cattlemen's actions were beginning to be felt, with growing evidence of a meat shortage in both the United States and Canada. Price offerings for cattle began to push upwards, and consumers were first notified of a potential beef shortage.

To add to the problem, U.S. cattle producers were withholding their cattle from the market in response to a Nixon-imposed price freeze on beef which was holding U.S. cattle prices down. This added to the beef shortage, raising it to a crisis phenomenon in the urban United States. Nixon's price ceiling on cattle came at a time of rising corn and soybean prices in the U.S. and it placed American cattle producers in a devastating cost-price squeeze. Since the freeze was scheduled to be lifted September 12, 1973, most producers chose to hold their cattle rather than sell them at a loss at normal market weight. As the reserves of frozen beef stocks disappeared, and the barbecue season reached its peak, panic buying set in among consumers by August 1973.

The U.S. developments in the market in July and August 1973 caused serious repercussions in Canada. The multiple effect of Nixon's price freeze and the producer withholding action was an acceleration in the demand for the export of Canadian cattle into the U.S. market, a resulting shortage of cattle for the Canadian market, and a sharp increase in the price of cattle slaughtered in Canada as Canadian packers were forced to compete with U.S. buyers for the Canadian supply of finished cattle.

These developments were unusual and unprecedented because although the Canada-U.S. boundary has been an open gate for the North American cattle economy, the traditional flow has involved the *export* of calves and feeder cattle to the U.S. and the *import* of finished animals and dressed beef to Canada. What happened in the summer of 1973, with a serious market shortage in the U.S. for finished beef, was that the open border became an invitation to 'raid' Canadian supplies of finished beef. This disturbed our normal marketing pattern. Canadian exports to the U.S. in July and August rose by more than 100 per cent over the levels of 1972.

The price for cattle in Canada was bid up to a peak of 62¢ in August, 15¢ per pound better than the average for the year. For Canadian cattlemen this was a brief moment of glory, causing them to rejoice in the virtues of the open market system and forget temporarily the problems of high feed grain prices.

But the one-month jump in cattle prices in August 1973 had little to do directly with recognition of the higher feed costs to producers or to conditions in the Canadian livestock beef market. It was purely a reaction to American demand at a time when the U.S. markets for cattle were being temporarily boycotted by their own producers. Yet in retrospect it appears that the impact of this price jump for cattle, which lasted only three weeks, was to set a permanent pattern for retail beef prices in Canada, and lead Canadian cattlemen into disaster. Two unusual developments occurred in livestock production on the basis of confidence over the high prices for finished cattle. Feed-lot operators were prepared to bid aggressively for feeder replacement cattle purchased from cow-calf operators in fall 1973. Their aggressive bidding for calf and yearling supplies pushed the price up to as high as 75¢ per pound, almost double the normal market price. Secondly, cow-calf operators encouraged by the high market price for their calves kept back a larger than usual number of yearling heifers and heifer calves in order to build up the capacity of their breeding herd. This added directly to the short-term shortage of animals to feed-lots, adding to the pressure for high prices on feeders. In other words the optimism based on a temporary peak in finished cattle prices, which was directly caused by an artificially created market shortage in the United States, resulted in a future-based gamble by Canadian cattlemen. It was a gamble which in retrospect we can see did not allow for the continued upward spiral of grain prices, nor did it allow for the drop in per-capita consumption of beef which was to overtake the acceleration in beef production and cause an international glut.

Government Intervention: Too Little or Not Enough

Back in August 1973 the concerns of the industry and government were more immediately focussed. Politically the minority Liberal government was under increasing pressure from consumer groups and the packing plants in Canada. Prime roasts and steaks peaked at well over $3.00 per pound, and consumers began to look elsewhere, to poultry, cheese, and vegetables as the source of protein. The industry in Canada did not like having to raise its price offerings to cattlemen in competition with U.S. buyers, and undoubtedly feared the inevitable drop-off in per-capita consumption. They allowed their freezer stocks in beef to reach 34 million pounds, the lowest point in several years.

The federal cabinet met in Ottawa on August 12 to produce a solution. They responded to uncontrolled exports and runaway domestic prices by restricting further exports of beef and pork to the United States. Trade Minister Allistair Gillespie assured consumers that this move would ease the price spiral on beef products. Allowing it might take "a week or so," he was confident after talks with the packers that there would be "an easing of prices in the near future." Gillespie was wrong; so was Beryl Plumptre, who made the same prediction. Prices were up in August and again in September. The cabinet had gambled that the packers and supermarkets would respond to textbook theories of supply and demand, cutting their prices back as the supply of cattle and beef returned to normal. But the price margin from farm to retail widened, with no relief for consumers.

The Canadian Cattlemen's Association were not amused by the federal experiment. Terming the export control measure "a ridiculous example of two-faced political manouvering," they accused the federal cabinet of attempting to cut Canadian producers off from the riches of the world market. The Cattlemen knew that even if the textbook logic of supply and demand didn't affect the oligopoly pricing of wholesale and retail prices, it would affect the producer. They watched cattle prices cascade from their August high of 62¢ to 44¢ by the first week in October.

Gillespie was a two-fold loser, having alienated the Cattlemen while failing to make the anticipated gains with consumers. In an attempt to justify the position, he later argued that "there was every indication that a major raid on Canadian supplies was in progress or about to get underway." The necessity was to "prevent a shortage in Canada." Despite the failure of his solution in terms of influencing prices downward, Gillespie argued that the export restrictions were necessary and justified to protect the Canadian resource.

But if cattle prices went down to pre-August levels how was the industry able to avoid wholesale and retail price adjustments of the same magnitude? The reason was simple, and an Edmonton general manager for Burns Foods let it slip during an August news conference. He pointed out that the market demand for beef was continuing high and keeping prices up *after* the export controls were imposed because consumers were filling their freezers in a panic-buying spree to hedge against future increases. "I suppose you could include us in that as well," added the packing-house spokesman. In other words Burns and the other major packers were keeping the flow of meat to retail markets in line with demand after August 12 by beginning to fill their half-empty freezer warehouses. They were speculating on their ability to keep prices up.

After September 21, when the Nixon price freeze on beef was lifted and American cattle began to glut the market on both sides of the border, the Canadian packers continued to stock their warehouses with beef and pork at prices depressed to the producers. The 34 million pounds of frozen beef stock in August became 50 million pounds by December 1973 and 62 million pounds by March 1974. By filling warehouses the packers prevented some of the potential surplus from affecting retail prices. They took advantage of an over-supply of cheap Canadian and U.S. cattle to build up reserves without dumping the lower priced products on the retail market, and so managed to keep retail beef prices high while they paid depressed prices to producers.

The federal government had scarcely recovered from the failure of their August 12 restrictions on the flow of exports from Canada to the U.S. when they were faced with the opposite problem. As September 12 came and went the flow of cattle was reversed. U.S. producers began dumping their overfed cattle onto the continental market. Their hopes for a price increase after the freeze was lifted were quickly dashed in the wake of a market glut. Prices dropped in both the U.S. and Canada. Suddenly Canada was faced with a market surplus created by a ten-fold increase in the rate of imports of live cattle from the United States. The politics of the situation was also reversed. Now the 'continental free market' had a bias potentially favouring consumers. It was the livestock producers who were in difficulty unless measures were taken to constrain the 'free market.'

The federal cabinet again intervened in November 1973. This time Gillespie announced a tariff surcharge on all American imports of six cents per pound on dressed beef and three cents per pound on live cattle. The idea was to discourage U.S. sellers from pursuing the Canadian market by enforcing a 3¢ lower return. But the industry itself created and maintained a 3-4¢ differential between price offerings in Toronto and Kansas City, so that the price differential was non-existent for U.S. cattlemen. The surcharge became a token subsidy to the federal government in lieu of higher cattle prices in Canada. The onslaught of imports continued through December and January and up to April 1974.

If the surcharge failed to curb imports from the U.S. it did manage to alienate U.S. Trade and Agriculture officials who launched the first of many official protests. Claiming the move was a violation of the General Agreement on Tariffs and Trade (GATT), the U.S. government cited the drop in cattle prices in Kansas City as evidence of losses incurred. They spent over a year trying to collect damages in the amount of the revenue the Canadian government collected while the surcharge was in effect. The surcharge itself was quietly and unceremoniously withdrawn by the federal government in February 1974.

But the problems for Canadian cattle producers were going from bad to worse. By January and February 1974 the number of U.S. cattle and dressed beef imported into Canada had increased 15-fold over the same period in 1973. Prices for Canadian cattle dropped 35 per cent from August to March. And feed grain prices continued to advance in all regions. Reports of malnutrition among cattle, liquidation of herds and bankruptcy of feed-lots became common. Operators who had paid up to 75¢ for replacement feeders in August and September 1973 were selling them finished for 35¢ to 40¢ per pound. Canadian Cattlemen's Association President Gordon Parke claimed in March 1974 that "our feed-lot men are losing between $85 and $100 per head and if this continues many will go out of business."[7]

The Cattlemen's Association had by this time abandoned strict adherence to continental free-flow policies and were themselves calling for import restrictions. They proposed that a quota be placed on American imports into Canada at one-tenth the number of Canadian cattle shipped to the U.S. (Based on roughly 400,000 annual exports this would mean 40,000 total imports.) In 1973 there were 208,000 imports, five times the proposed quota, and in 1974 the 40,000 figure was surpassed before the end of February. Eugene Whelan, while sympathetic to the intent of the cattlemen's proposal, was not yet prepared to carry it into action. He had landed, unhappily, on a solution which pleased almost no one. On March 15, after weeks of producer insistence that "something had to be done," Whelan unveiled a federal subsidy to the beef industry of $2.75 million per week. The subsidy was ostensibly aimed at producers, and amounted initially to 7¢ per pound on the four top grades of cattle. The 7¢ amount was judged to be the difference between the price of cattle in the Toronto market in March (43¢) and the estimated break-even price of 50¢. According to Whelan's announcement of the subsidy, consumers would also benefit from the nearly $3 million per week they were transferring in tax monies to the beef industry because the subsidy would keep retail beef prices from rising. This promise of price relief was becoming familiar and lacked somewhat in credibility.

Unfortunately the government chose to have its subsidy paid to producers by the packing plants who would then be reimbursed by the federal treasury. What happened was predictable. The packing plants took advantage of the subsidy. They reduced their purchase price offerings to producers for cattle by roughly the amount of the subsidy. Immediately following the subsidy announcement, the price for cattle dropped by 5¢ per pound and the $2.75 million a week went toward sweetening the profits of the industry.

The response of the Cattlemen's Association was swift and furious. Colin Thatcher, a Cattlemen's Association board member, son of a former Saskatchewan premier and himself a Liberal candidate, described Whelan's subsidy as "a fraud and a hoax on both cattle producers and the taxpayers of this country." Cattlemen were insulted by the 'welfare' aspect of the program, but also saw clearly that it wasn't working. Producers ended up with the same low cattle prices (38-40¢) for another month after the program came into effect.

Consumers had even less to be pleased about. They were forced to use tax spending to reduce grocery spending, but unsuccessfully, since meat prices failed to decline in the wake of the subsidy.

The only clear winners were the packing plants, but even they were complaining because the handling of the subsidy meant extra administration, and because they could collect no interest on their pay-out to producers while waiting for reimbursement from the federal treasury.

Whelan's first response to the drastic cut in cattle prices by the packers (thereby nullifying the subsidy to producers and keeping it for themselves) was one of pretended disillusionment over the lack of integrity of the companies in question. "If that's what you call good corporate citizenship, I don't appreciate it," he announced to his colleagues in the Commons Agriculture Committee. He criticized the packing industry for refusing to "play fair ball," adding that the government had wanted a system where the subsidy could have been paid directly to farmers but it would have taken longer.

Whelan's subsidy continued through the summer and fall of 1974, being reduced first to 5¢ and later to 3¢ as market prices gained some stability. Finally it was replaced by a floor price on cattle of $47.50 per cwt. which would be activated in the event of a total price collapse. Before the beef subsidy was concluded it cost the federal treasury roughly $50 million in 1974.

By April 1974, the federal government's handling of the beef issue had produced little more than headaches. Retail prices were higher for beef and market prices were lower for cattle than they had been when the cabinet took the matter in hand. Finally they arrived at a more successful choice of tactics. The problem still was one of reducing the flow of U.S. cattle and stabilizing Canadian prices for producers. Consumers appeared out of luck, however, as Eugene Whelan was quoted as saying in April 1974 that beef prices to consumers might have to go up 20¢ to 30¢ in order to improve farm prices.

The solution ultimately arrived at for blocking imports was politically sound on all fronts. The cabinet declared on April 10 that cattle and beef coming into Canada from the U.S. had to be certified free of a growth-promoting drug, diethylstilbestoral, or DES. This effectively halted border crossings beginning in mid-April because U.S. officials were neither willing nor able to co-operate.

The story behind DES, a drug which is fed to cattle to stimulate growth hormones and accelerate fattening, began with medical evidence in the United States that its presence in meat for human consumption was a contributing cause of a form of vaginal cancer.

This discovery came after years of popular and widespread use of the drug in North American feed-lots. The DES link with cancer caused a considerable stir and raised questions about the adequacy of testing and inspection mechanisms used on all chemical food additives. With the combined pressure of health officials and consumer groups, DES was banned by U.S. courts from being used in animal feeding. That was in 1972. A similar ban was instituted in Canada by the federal Department of Agriculture, effective January 1, 1973. This ban on animal feeding in Canada was followed by a ban on the sale of meat products containing DES, effective August 10, 1973.

The original U.S. ban and the Canadian ban had been bitterly fought by the livestock industry. Their position was one of pure economic self-interest based on the knowledge that animals make 12-15 per cent higher weight gains in the same feeding time when adding DES to feed. A spokesman for the Canadian Cattlemen's Association as recently as April 1974 described DES as "a safe and useful product."

It was this opposition from the industry which was successful in reversing the U.S. ban through an appeal court decision in early 1974. The basis of appeal was that improper legal and technical procedures were used in the original suspension. The medical evidence was never successfully disproven or contradicted, yet the drug was once again being used legally by U.S. cattle feeders.

The decision of the federal cabinet, then, to ban U.S. animals which weren't fully and officially cleared of DES was only right and proper. But there was a good deal of hypocrisy and sheer opportunism motivating the decision. One week before the DES ban, Eugene Whelan was setting out his options to the House of Commons for dealing with the effects of the flood of American import cattle. They included 1) extending the subsidy, 2) restrictions on U.S. cattle fattened with DES, 3) *reinstitution of DES for domestic use*, 4) a formula of import quotas, and 5) high surtaxes on imports.

With concern for all the political consequences involved in the options as seen by Whelan, the DES ban was clearly the most politically wise. The subsidy had already failed and was opposed by the producers themselves, while import restrictions by way of quotas or surtaxes would invite U.S. trade retaliation. But the fact that reinstituting DES was a live option (as a way of making Canadian cattlemen more competitive) showed the limited depth of Whelan's concern over consumer health.

The result of the DES ban was to improve temporarily the market price for Canadian cattle as more western-fed cattle were moved into Toronto and Montreal markets to replace the flow of imports. Prices for cattle rose 5¢ in the first two weeks or so after the ban. Although the government was clearly contributing once again to higher consumer beef prices, it was immune to attack from the Consumers Association and other groups. It was, after all, instituting a protective health measure which the CAC had itself insisted on. They supported the ban on use of DES in Canada when it was proclaimed a year earlier. The Cattlemen's Association were also pleased with the effect of the ban although they would have preferred a decision which imposed permanent import quotas.

The pressure on the federal government to lift their restrictions continued from top levels of the U.S. government. Agriculture Secretary Earl Butz threatened retaliatory measures in June 1974 while Eugene Whelan and his cabinet colleagues were in the midst of a federal election. Whelan held firm, refusing to be bullied into submission, at least until after the Liberals were safely installed with a majority government on July 8.

Within a month of the federal election the Liberal cabinet backed off on its tough no-compromise position and reopened the border. They still required declarations that animals were free from DES, but were prepared to take U.S. suggestions on how such an inspection system would be administered. By September, border crossings were again operating normally. But the Canadian government then set maximum quotas on the number of annual imports based on the average of the previous five years. U.S. officials were as unhappy with permanent quotas as they had been with the DES ban. They retaliated in November with their own set of quotas against exports of Canadian live cattle and beef into the United States. The U.S. quotas against Canadian exports were much more narrowly defined, allowing for 17,000 animals, less than ten per cent of the volume totals of 1973 and 1974.

The Packers' Lock-out: Summer '74

Overshadowing the international trade dispute in beef during the spring and summer of 1974 was an internal domestic struggle in the industry between the major national packers and their unionized workers. Both cattle producers and the consuming public were more than casual observers. It became clear long before the threat of a June lock-out against the union by Burns, Swift, and Canada Packers that the companies had much more in mind than just another anti-union manoeuvre. Their dispute with the Canadian Food and Allied Workers (CFAW) capped off a year of unusual developments in the industry which now made a lock-out of their workers not only attractive to bargaining strategy but useful for their own price manoeuvring and potential profits. The union was in a sense trapped by larger events.

A threatened national lock-out of the packing industry was intended to perform three purposes. It would enable the national companies to unload their share of the 125 million pounds of frozen meat they had built up in warehouse freezers over the winter months.[8] These freezer stocks, built up during the flood of U.S. cattle and hogs between October 1973 and April 1974, were only an asset to the companies if they could be unloaded onto the retail market without creating a surplus and a decline in prices. Secondly, the lock-out would cause a build-up of the supply of market weight cattle and hogs on farms. This would tend to depress producer prices in the period following a lock-out, enabling the packers once again to replenish their frozen stocks at firesale prices. Finally, the lock-out might intimidate the CFAW and reduce its ability to sustain support among rank-and-file workers for wage demands of 40 per cent over 26 months.

The failure of the companies' strategy to materialize fully was a tribute both to the strength of union resistance and the critical support of a sector of the farming community represented by the National Farmers Union in Alberta. The whole dispute was an exercise in the politics of oligopoly, in this case the packing house oligopoly of Burns, Swift, and Canada Packers.

Representing the nation's packing-house employees, the CFAW went into bargaining in early 1974 for a new contract covering 26 months effective April 1. The union leadership knew that inflation demanded a 'catch-up' contract and that the rank and file were anxious for a healthy settlement. At the outset the union was prepared for a national strike — an option quickly reinforced by delays and provocation of company negotiators.

As the old contract expired and agitation grew for a settlement, the national policy conference of the union, made up of elected representatives from each major local and charged with planning and recommending bargaining strategy to the union membership, announced its strategy. On the basis of past experience the union chose the tactic of isolating one company as a strike target. In 1947 packing-house workers had shut down the entire national industry for nine weeks in a bitter strike, only to discover that the build-up of livestock had provided a windfall advantage to the companies. Purchase of cattle and hogs at depressed prices gave the companies a profit position in 1947 that union officials describe as "breaking all records." A second national strike in 1966 which singled out Canada Packers was extremely successful from the workers' point of view in producing a strong no-compromise settlement. Canada Packers just couldn't afford to sustain loss of markets to its rivals, and settled on terms which then set the pattern for the entire industry.

In May 1974, CFAW served notice that Swift would be the target company and the strike would be initiated in Alberta where Swift's two large-volume plants are located. Swift was chosen in part because it had better contract terms for pensions and would serve as a better model for bargaining with the other companies. A strike deadline was set for June after a vote of members rejected the final company offer.

At this point the companies retaliated by announcing they had formed their own "union," an amalgamation of Swift, Burns and Canada Packers. Bargaining as a single unit, they made it clear they would not tolerate a strike of one company as announced by the union and that they would invoke a national lock-out at all their plants. The formalizing in a public way of common strategy among the companies was a reflection of co-operation among competitors evidenced not only in bargaining with unions but in other areas as well. The union dubbed the new formation of the big three "the millionaires' club."

With the union setting a strike deadline of June 5 and the companies retaliating with the threat of a national lock-out, Alberta and Ontario government mediators went into high gear to try for a compromise. (These two provinces had about 75 per cent of the CFAW membership between them.) A last-minute mediation proposal was set forth in the first week in June offering the union a 29 per cent increase over 26 months. At this point settlement without either strike or lock-out should have been a good possibility. But the companies were not about to settle. They were pressing for a lock-out for reasons of their own.

The CFAW national policy conference met on June 3 and 4 to consider the mediation offer. They were told by a government mediator that the offer was agreeable to the companies. This meant the companies would postpone a lock-out until a ratification vote was taken among union members on the proposed settlement. The CFAW in turn suspended the June 5 strike deadline and recommended acceptance of the mediation offer to the membership.

While the union's national policy group was meeting to consider its position, the millionaire's club was also meeting in Calgary under the leadership of Burns president Art Child. Despite assurances they had given the government mediator and an exchange of letters with the union agreeing to suspend further actions, the companies pulled a double-cross. They waited for the union to lift its strike deadline and then announced a lock-out of Alberta plants effective June 5 and 6. A national lock-out would follow on June 12, they said, if union members failed to accept the mediation offer.

The union claimed it was double-crossed by the companies because they originally threatened a lock-out of Burns and Canada Packers *only* if Swift was struck. In the view of the union the national packers were determined to get a national lock-out regardless of what the union did. Child, as the company spokesman, said the lock-out was essential to protect company interests until it was clear the union members were prepared to accept the mediation offer.

On June 5, 2,500 Alberta packing-house workers were locked out without pay, before they had a chance to consider the latest mediation offer. They demonstrated their anger by overwhelmingly rejecting the settlement they might otherwise have accepted. Rejection by Alberta and B.C. members swung the national vote narrowly against the settlement recommended by CFAW leadership. The union was left in a state of confusion. It had become clear that management simply wasn't interested in an early settlement. The union had no choice but to continue bargaining for higher stakes while the companies' scenario unfolded.

After mid-June, despite the earlier threat of a national lock-out in the event the union failed to endorse contract offers, it became apparent that the companies' shutdown would remain restricted to Alberta. This narrowed the possibility for success in the companies' overall objectives. With plants operating in other provinces and near-normal marketings of cattle and hogs at a national level, the reduction of frozen meat stocks was somewhat difficult. (Nevertheless stocks of pork and beef in frozen storage *were* reduced by 30 per cent in Canada during the months of June and July when the lock-out was on.) But the Alberta lock-out failed to provide the intended build-up of live cattle and hogs to depress prices in the immediate period of time after a lock-out occurred. Prices for live animals recovered quickly in Alberta after the July settlement of the lock-out.

Why the millionaires' club abandoned the national lock-out strategy is a matter of speculation. Two explanations seem plausible. One is that the companies feared the political climate of a federal election might lead to an early arbitrated settlement, and an Alberta lock-out was better than none at all. Federal arbitration had been generous to railway workers and the vote-starved Liberals could have used the friendship of the 2,500 Alberta packing-house workers. There was even the remote possibility that the federal government might have taken the industry into trusteeship.

Another possible factor in the companies' thinking was the Alberta workers' overwhelming rejection of a recommended mediation compromise after they had been locked out. A national lock-out might similarly have created a militant and uncompromising rank and file across the country replacing the otherwise moderate CFAW membership. Alberta workers had shown that a kick in the teeth produces a fighter. The companies wanted a national lock-out of limited duration but they didn't want a long hard struggle which could deny them access to the summer barbecue market and erode company profits.

When 1,000 NFU members from Alberta marched on the Legislature in Edmonton on July 3 with demands that Burns, Swift, and Canada Packers be taken under government trusteeship, they were met by a smiling Peter Lougheed. He assured the rally that the situation was well in hand and that the companies had agreed to end their lock-out on July 8 so things could return to normal. But CFAW leaders who attended the farmers' rally and spoke made it clear that they had been excluded from back-room dealing to end the lock-out. They weren't about to go back empty-handed, their contract having expired April 1. The NFU indicated strong support for the union cause, indicating they were interested in an end to the lock-out only on terms which would prove satisfactory to CFAW. With NFU support, the July 8 "return to normal" didn't occur, and the shutdown of plant operations continued until a new basis of settlement was reached on July 12.

The CFAW membership ratified the agreement and plants reopened July 18. The companies had clearly been licked by the clumsiness of their own tactics. They ended up agreeing to an overall increase in wages of 34½ per cent, 5½ per cent better than the mediation offer the union might have been prepared to accept if they hadn't been locked out.

Freezer stocks for the national industry were reduced during the lock-out but cattle and hog prices returned to normal. The companies gained nothing, but they didn't lose much either. Had they been competitive in the situation instead of functioning as an oligopoly, Swift as the target company could have been seriously damaged in its Canadian operations.[9]

Cow-Calf Chaos

The conditions in the cattle industry by fall 1974 were a far cry from the extreme optimism and confidence of a year earlier. Feed-lot operators who had been burned by losses in the winter and spring of 1974 were more cautious in their purchases of feeder replacement stock. U.S. buyers faced with their own conditions of surplus beef were not inclined to buy the usual volume of Canadian live cattle and calves for feed-lots and were prevented from doing so by quota restrictions after November 1974. In general, market conditions were extremely poor for cow-calf men attempting to sell their annual crop of calves. The price of 75¢ per pound in 1973 was suddenly more like 35-40¢ in 1974.

By October, conditions had reached the point where industry

spokesmen and government were becoming alarmed about the possibility of widespread liquidation of herds among cow-calf men who were losing their shirts. The productive capacity of Canadian beef herds which had been built up systematically from 1969 to 1974 was threatened with rapid destruction. This in turn could mean more of the familiar 'Higher Beef Prices' headlines.

The immediate problem for the cow-calf man was that it cost him at least $150 to keep a cow for a year. For that investment the cow usually (but not always) produced a calf each spring which could be sold in the late fall. In 1973 the cow-calf operator sold his calves for an average $150 to $200 and made out fine. In 1974 he was selling calves for as little as $50 and losing money. His response was often to sell not only his calves but a good proportion of his cows, rather than face the costs of wintering them over.

The glut of cows on the market meant cheap supplies of low-grade beef to the packers. There was even some limited and temporary reduction of the price of ground beef to consumers. But the longer-term danger was that two years after cows were sold there would be a beef shortage because the calves to which they would normally have given birth in 1975 wouldn't be coming to market.

The seeds of the problem of cow-calf operators are contained in the recommendations of the federal government's Task Force on Agriculture. That document placed a major emphasis on expanding beef production by cutting back on wheat and dairy products and building up beef herds. From 1970 to 1974, federal and provincial governments encouraged this trend by investing public funds toward diversification on the part of wheat and dairy farmers into livestock. Low-interest government loans and grants were available from all major agricultural provinces and the federal government. From 1969 to 1975, the population of breeding herds expanded by 40 per cent from 11½ to 16 million head.

But one of the consequences of rapid expansion of herds was the holding back of female stock from the beef market. In fall 1973, this withholding of large numbers of female stock for breeding was encouraged by the high market prices for both calves and finished beef. The unusual acceleration in breeding herds contributed to a temporary shortage of beef on the consumer market because both older 'cull' cows and heifers for veal were kept on the range. The beef shortage in 1973 allowed prices to go up sharply, especially on cheaper cuts, which in turn caused a drop in per-capita beef consumption. Finally, in fall 1974, the combination of five years of expanding beef production and a leveling off of consumption led to a market glut in North America and around the world. Cow-calf operators in western Canada were faced with a depressed market.

Normally producers would weather a depressed market for calves and hope for better luck next year. But with record costs for feed they couldn't afford to keep their basic herds over winter. Many sold them. The selling of cows onto the market created a glut of its own accord, added to by the growing proportion of cheap import beef from Australia and New Zealand.

The prairie governments responded to the crisis affecting cow-calf operators by providing a system of cash advances to producers who maintained their herds and wintered their calves over 1974-75. This may not have been consistent with a solution depending on the market capacity for beef another year. What it did was buy time for the producers to assess future market potential while avoiding the firesale prices of October-November 1974.

The National Farmers Union called on the federal government to introduce a national beef authority to set market quotas and guarantee prices on beef so that the constant boom-and-bust condition of cattlemen could be eliminated. The Canadian Cattlemen's Association attacked the NFU proposal and called instead on a total withdrawal of government from the livestock-beef industry, citing government interference as a major problem in creating bad market conditions. The federal government for its part was intensively involved in discussions around the cow-calf crisis and various policy options. But their involvement was strictly from the sidelines. Two separate, parallel and competitive sets of inquiries were being carried out simultaneously into the livestock-beef industry. The first involved a series of investigations and reports from the Food Price Review Board, released throughout the winter of 1974-75. The second involved a special Commons inquiry set up by Eugene Whelan and the federal cabinet after a special debate about the beef crisis in November 1974. At that time Quebec farmers had protested low calf prices by a mass slaughter of calves buried in open pits before the watchful cameras of the CBC. A special emergency debate produced confusion and a promise of a special inquiry. When Mrs. Plumptre released the Prices Review Board's major report on the beef industry the very next day, Whelan admitted that he hadn't bothered to read it before calling another separate investigation. Mrs. Plumptre called the Commons inquiry "politically motivated" and a waste of the taxpayers' money.

The Prices Review Board's Reports were generally uncritical of the domestic livestock-beef industry. No one was ripping off anyone, they said, and industry problems stemmed from the impact of higher world grain prices and unstable trading patterns with the United States. They made no major recommendations concerning marketing controls or adjustments to the 'free market' pricing mechanism. The one specific criticism of industry practices was revealed in the Board's

January report released in Saskatoon. This had to do with the price differential between industry price offerings to farmers for steers and heifers which did not show up as consumer savings. The price difference between market-weight steers and heifers varied from 4¢ to 12¢ per pound. This spread at a level of about 4¢ has always existed, but it persisted in 1974 at 10-12¢ per pound although everyone agrees there was no difference in the quality of meat. And more significantly the price spread is not passed on to consumers. In fact the existence or choice between 'steer beef' and 'heifer beef' is not even a question at the retail level because neither is identified by sex.[10] Yet on the basis of the price differential on livestock the retail price differential between the two types of beef should be 25-30¢ per pound. This extra mark-up on heifer beef is pure profit for the processors and supermarkets.

Aside from this important critical observation by the Review Board there was nothing in its extensive reports which could lend optimism to future prospects. The ideological bias of Mrs. Plumptre toward the continued open marketing of livestock was clear.

Eugene Whelan and the cabinet proceeded with a separate inquiry on beef appointed in January 1975 to conduct extensive hearings.[11] One possible interpretation of this move is that Whelan as an advocate of supply management approaches to farm production and marketing differs with the conclusions of his arch-rival Mrs. Plumptre on the specific question of a national beef marketing board as proposed by the National Farmers Union and opposed by the Canadian Cattlemen's Association. Mrs. Plumptre is unreservedly opposed, while Whelan is open to national beef marketing proposals. As a recommendation by a Commons investigation into the industry, the idea could perhaps gain prominence. The 'anti-marketing board' bias of the Review Board could be cancelled out, and federal strategy toward farm product price stability moved closer to reality. Such a scenario is possible but not altogether likely by 1976.[12]

Beef Production and International Trade

Despite a 40 per cent increase in beef productive capacity from 1969 to 1974 and what appeared as a serious surplus in 1974, Canada remained a net-importer of beef products. Our production and trade position in beef reflected not our incapacity to meet our own needs but our planned role as a resource colony of the United States. Our import-export role in beef has been to supply the raw material and accept the finished product while the job and revenue advantages of processing go elsewhere. For example in 1972 we exported 225,000 cattle, roughly 10 per cent of our total production. Almost all of these animals went to the United States. These were not finished cattle for slaughter in American packing plants, but primarily range calves or yearlings under 700 pounds, being sold to U.S. feed-lots. In contrast the live cattle imported from the U.S. into Canada have been fewer in number (up until 1973), and they have nearly all been for immediate slaughter. The expanded Canadian cow-calf operations over the past decade have been serving as a raw material supply base for U.S. feed-lots and packing plants. In contrast, their live cattle shipments amount to periodic dumping of the finished product in competition with Canadian feed-lots. This was especially true in late 1973 and early 1974.

The trade in dressed beef and veal completes the picture. In these products Canada has been a net-importer since 1968. The bulk of our imports come from Australia and New Zealand for sale as ground beef. We also import some canned beef from Brazil and Argentina. But a substantial growth in high grade beef cuts was from the United States. U.S. beef imports jumped from 15.4 million pounds in 1970 to 38.3 million in 1973, primarily due to the restaurant-hotel specialty cuts. The U.S. made up 35 per cent of the total value of beef imports by 1972.

To summarize, we expanded our domestic capacity for beef production since 1969 in part to meet an expanded consumer demand, but primarily to fill an export market for live cattle and calves in the U.S. Increasingly we developed a pattern of shipping young stock from western Canadian ranches into the U.S., while relying on finished imported cattle from the U.S. into eastern Canada, as well as dressed beef and veal to fill out our consumer demand.

Then came 1973 and the series of disruptions connected to the rise in world grain and protein prices. Briefly what happened was a rise in grain prices, a rise in beef prices and then a levelling off of consumer demand for beef. This coincided with the accelerated build-up of cattle herds in all beef-producing nations. Suddenly, in the developed countries of Europe and North America, the supply of beef had overtaken the demand. Normally such a glut of beef would have led to a drop in prices. But the impact of higher grain prices had already narrowed the profit margins of beef producers. If prices for cattle fell, operators would go out of business quickly, something the governments of these countries couldn't allow to happen. Many countries therefore began to protect their own markets and producers against world trends. They began to subsidize prices for cattle sold for slaughter and they restricted competitive imports from other countries. (European countries especially pursued these tactics first, as did Canada, eventually, and the United States.) This development left the few countries which were major beef *exporters*, like Australia, in the desparate position of having no access to some of their traditional markets. They began to dump increasing volumes of frozen boneless beef on the markets which were still open, including the United States and Canada.

Canada's beef industry was affected in two ways by these world trends to which our government and meat-packing industry had contributed. First, we faced a sharp increase in the volume of cheap imported beef from Australia. Our total beef imports were up to $134 million in 1973 from $89 million in 1972. Secondly, we had a substantial shift in trading patterns and eventually a trade dispute with the U.S. over beef. On the one hand the U.S. was anxious to expand its marketing of finished cattle onto the Canadian market to relieve its own glut and prevent a price collapse. The Americans increased their exports of live cattle from 66,000 in 1972 to 214,000 in 1973 despite a Canadian import surcharge imposed in November 1973. On the other hand they were less anxious to buy Canadian calves and feeder cattle by 1974. Inevitably both Canada and the U.S. applied import and export quotas in 1974 to restrict the movement of what had come to be regarded as 'surplus' cattle onto the other country's market. The traditional 'continental free market' was quickly disappearing, and *all* major producing countries were looking more and more to a strategy of self-sufficiency and protected markets.

A strategy of national self-sufficiency could be of benefit to the Canadian livestock industry and the nation. Unfortunately, events unfolding up to 1975 often contradicted this objective. The creation of import-export restrictions with the United States might have altered the pattern of continental marketing of livestock and meat products. But in reality it failed to consolidate the Canadian market for Canadian producers. The restriction on the export of finished cattle and dressed beef from the United States into Canada imposed no serious change on the Americans because it was a quota based on the previous five-year average of imports. What it did do was prevent excessive dumping of American products which would have been sure to further depress Canadian cattle prices. In contrast to these Canadian restrictions, which enabled a normal flow of U.S. beef into Ontario and Quebec, the U.S. restrictions cut the traditional market of live feeder cattle and hogs from Canada to the U.S. to a mere trickle, less than 10 per cent of the previous five-year average.

In 1975 the potential for national market self-sufficiency was great. Western cattlemen who lost their market of live cattle exports to the U.S. should have been able to market into eastern Canadian feed-lots or expand feed-lot operations themselves and market dressed beef into the east. But this assumes that the flow of U.S. finished cattle and dressed beef into Canada had been substantially arrested.

Unfortunately, as of spring 1975, the flow of U.S. imports continued, under control but unabated. Instead of self-sufficiency and a stronger national market, the double standard of trading policy between Canada and the United States was encouraging continued dumping of American products. There was nowhere for calves to be marketed from western Canada, and the investment by both levels of government in expanding beef production capacity was threatened. And federal politicians appeared afraid to once again cut off U.S. dumping of agricultural products as they had for a few months under the DES restrictions in 1974.

A further aggravation to the development of national trading patterns was the 30-per-cent across-the-board freight rate increase announced by the national railways in January 1975.[13] This influenced more commodities than just beef, but it was a particular blow to both western cattlemen and to the Alberta-based packing-house industry which relied on competitive access to the eastern Canadian market by rail. The higher freight rates stood either to further expand livestock feeding in Ontario on corn imported from the United States, or else encourage more beef to be imported directly from the U.S. The general slowdown in western meat-packing reflected in the closure of Burns processing operations in Prince Albert may have been partly a result of the projected loss of eastern markets.

The Winners

Despite the 1975 slowdown in all levels of the livestock-beef industry, it is clear in retrospect that the packing plants and retail supermarkets emerged as winners from the period of uncontrolled prices and markets beginning in mid-1973. The three national packers all had excessive profits in 1973, in a range of 12-per-cent return on capital investment. In 1974 they again managed to increase profits, despite the dislocations involved in a seven-week lock-out at their Alberta plants. And in terms of prices up until February 1975 the packing plants managed to keep prices on average 7.2 per cent above the June 1973 price, while farmers had an average price gain over 1973 of 3.9 per cent. Retailers managed to up *their* prices by an average of 9.3 per cent over June 1973.

Canada Packers' status, as reported by the *Financial Post Corporation Service*, put the question of what was happening during 1973-74 in context:

Net income from operations, before extraordinary items, for the fiscal year ended March 30th 1974 rose 34 per cent while sales increased 32 per cent over the previous fiscal year.

The net profit represents 1.3 per cent of sales and *13.4 per cent* of shareholders' investment in fiscal 1974 compared with 1.27 per cent and 10.9 per cent respectively in 1973. — Annual Report, June 11 1974 [emphasis added]

Solutions to the problems in the beef industry await a substantial redistribution of power, beginning with a regulating mechanism for prices and markets which is less purely and obviously controlled by the oligopolies.

Notes to Chapter 5

1. Per-capita consumption feel in the United States from a 1972 high of 116 pounds to 109.3 pounds in 1973 and an initially estimated 105 pounds in 1974. Canadian consumption fell from 92.5 to 91.8 in 1973 and an initial estimate of 91 in 1974. The drop in consumption affected not just the market for cattle, especially in the United States, but also the operating levels of beef processing plants. This decline in volume of production of beef coupled with declines in pork production in 1974 contributed to both closures and lay-offs at packing plants in both Canada and the United States by early 1975. There were parallels to what was happening in the auto industry.

2. On the basis of the breakdown of steer beef to carcass and other edible and inedible by-products, the Food Prices Review Board calculates in its special report on beef pricing that wholesale beef prices should average 1.75 times the farm price of beef and retail beef prices and 2.34 times the price to farmers. This calculation enabled the Board to claim that no one was out of line in the pricing of beef products, including retail stores. They admitted that the winter and spring of 1973-1974 had seen a price-spread expansion, but felt this was temporary and a product of unstable markets. (Food Prices Review Board, *Report on Beef Pricing, June 1974.*)

3. The Canadian Cattlemen's Association monitors retail prices to enable them to make comment on excessive price spreads. On several occasions from November 1973 to February 1975 the CCA observed that retail prices had moved out of line.

4. Food Prices Review Board's *Report on Ground Beef*, June 1974.

5. "Futures markets are a major indication of forward prices. . . . A substantial move up in soybean meal prices forces the livestock producer to do one of several things: cut back the amount fed to cattle and hogs, make no expansion plans, and market the animals faster without waiting for marginal gains." (Federal economist Douglas Hedley, in *Financial Post*, September 1973.)

6. Agriculture Canada, *Livestock and Meat Trade Report.*

7. Loss claims by cattlemen were substantiated by the findings of the Food Prices Review Board in their *Report on Feed Grain Prices* June 1974. They broke down the costs as follows:

Average cost of feeders during autumn at $58/cwt. x 550 lbs.: $319.00

Average feed costs (based on prepared feeds at 4.5¢ per lb. x 500 lbs. gained x 8.5)*: $191.25

Non-feeder costs: $ 60.00

(Total) $570.25

*(The 8.5 represents the ratio of grain to weight gained. It takes 8 1/2 pounds of grain to gain 1 pound of animal weight.)

The break-even price for a 1,050 pound steer given the above costs would be $54.31. The price for steers in February and March 1974 averaged about $45 per cwt. for a net loss of $94.46 on every animal sold.

8. Burns Food Limited spokesmen claimed later they had no amount of beef to unload from freezer stocks and the claims that they could use the lock-out to advantage in this way were false. It is impossible to dispute this claim since warehouse freezer stocks as released by Statistics Canada in monthly bulletins are not broken down by company. It is conceivable, but highly unlikely, that the three national companies were in contradiction to the rest of the industry. What is clear is that freezer stocks were built up prior to the major companies' lock-out and that they decreased substantially, by about 20 per cent, while the lock-out was on. (Statistics Canada, *Report on Frozen Stocks of Meat in Canada.*)

9. Observations on the packing-house lock-out were based on interviews with Art Child, Burns's president, and Clarence Lyons, employed by the Canadian Food and Allied Workers Union, both in July 1974.

10. The problem of heifer-versus steer-beef as analyzed by the Food Prices Review Board, *Market For Heifer Beef in Canada* (January 1975), was two-fold. First there was a problem in the buying practices of the major retail chains who often bought only steer beef A-1 and A-2 choice and never even considered the lighter-weight but equal-quality and cheaper-priced heifer beef, thereby denying access to consumers. Secondly, those stores which did buy heifer beef at a saving failed to distinguish it on the counter and simply made windfall gains when they priced it equal to steer beef. The Board recommended special efforts to market and advertise heifer beef as a consumer bargain. The problem for producers who pay as much to

feed heifers as they do steers was not dealt with, and it was assumed apparently that the price differential would continue.

11. The Whelan inquiry included a prominent Alberta Liberal, Hu Harries, and a former Steinberg's official. Producer organizations like the National Farmers Union were openly skeptical about the results which could be expected.

12. One factor which supports the possibility of a public marketing authority is the growing evidence of unrest among producers outside the hard core of the Canadian Cattlemen's Association leadership. In addition to the mass rallies of the National Farmers Union in support of a national beef marketing authority in November 1974, Ontario producers at a convention in February 1975 voted to have the federal government investigate the possibility of public marketing.

13. The freight rate increases first announced in January 1975 were challenged by the Canadian Transport Commission which would grant only one-half the increase until further discussions and revelation of cost figures for the railways were revealed. This decision was successfully challenged by the railways in court as being beyond the powers of CTC. The rate increase proceeded while provincial governments in western Canada appealed the court ruling.

VI

Milk, Butter and Cheese

The dairy industry in Canada is viewed by critics as a bureaucrat's nightmare from cow's udder to breakfast table. It is clearly the most legislated and regulated area of agriculture and food, and has been since the 1930s. There are tariffs and subsidies, production quotas, licences, inspection standards, and pricing and marketing agencies at both provincial and federal levels. The degree of government intervention through laws and regulatory agencies reflects both the strength and the weakness of the industry. Its strength is in its stability of price and security of markets for producers. The *level* of prices established has been generally depressed to producers and the subject of repeated bitter challenges. But the *concept* of a guaranteed price and market has enabled producers to plan their operations. Unlike those engaged in the week-to-week gamble in other commodities such as beef, they have generally known where they would stand six months or a year hence. The boom-and-bust extremities were cushioned.

The weakness, though, of this form of state intervention has been that although it guarantees price per unit of sale to producers it does not guarantee net income. There is no protection against the cost-price squeeze. It does the farmer no good to know that the price of industrial milk will stay steady for a year at $9.50 per hundred pounds if the price of feed for his cows is increasing five per cent per month. The second weakness of state intervention from the consumer perspective has been that it fails to curb profit-taking by corporate agribusiness. On the contrary, the combined price and market guarantees on *farm milk* coupled with subsidies make the diary processing industry among the most profitable. There is in general no control over prices of milk products at the *retail* level. Kraft Foods, Canada's major user of industrial milk for processing, hauled in 1973 profit earnings of 18.3 per cent return on investment, the highest of all food manufacturing companies.

The trends gripping the dairy industry are not unique. They exist in other sectors of agriculture and agribusiness. But in the dairy industry they come in an extreme form and include: an exaggerated rate of inflation in all milk products (if subsidies are included in calculations), a production shortage in milk caused by a mass exodus of farmers out of production, concentration of ownership and control of the dairy manufacturing and distribution sectors among a few super food corporations, and a decline in the work-force in dairy processing coupled with industry wage levels well below the average for manufacturing in Canada.

Each of these trends warrants brief elaboration before examining the character of the industry, the development of government dairy policies in Canada, and the politics surrounding inflation and price movements from 1973-75.

The rate of inflation in fluid milk prices is modest if measured in terms of retail prices alone. From August 1972 to August 1974 milk prices increased only 23 per cent, little more than half the increase in beef prices and much below that of bread. But this increase came despite an additional 'five-cent-a-quart' subsidy paid out by the federal government from September 1973 to October 1974 at an estimated cost of $108 million. Similarly industrial milk products like ice cream, butter and cheese had their price levels cushioned by direct subsidies to industrial milk producers which totalled $250 million by 1974. There were also export subsidies on powdered skim milk as part of Canadian food aid programs. If subsidies were included in a calculation of consumer price levels the rate of inflation from 1972 to 1974 would have been roughly equal to that of beef, which totalled 40 per cent.

There was a 20 per cent decline in total milk production from 1967 to 1974. This occurred at a time of rapid growth in population, and although consumption of milk on a per-capita basis declined as well in this period, supply shortages of milk had become severe by 1973. The biggest decline in milk production in a single year occurred in 1973 with a 4.7 per cent drop, and the Canadian market was forced to rely on substantial imports of milk products for the first time since the 1920s. Despite optimistic projections at the federal Department of Agriculture's annual 'Outlook Conference', which projected a recovery in 1974, there was another 3 per cent decline that year. The major factor in production decline has been the rate of attrition among dairy farmers who were abandoning production at a rate of 15,000 per year from 1966 to 1971 (when the last census was taken). The rate of out migration of dairy farmers is much higher than for farmers generally, suggesting some particular problems and policies not equally shared by other commodity groups.[1]

The trend toward concentration of ownership and control in dairy processing is consistent with the pattern of manufacturing generally, but again shows an extreme which reflects public policy initiatives in the way of industry incentives. From 1961 to 1971, the number of dairy processing plants declined from 1700 to 809 as a handful of agribusiness giants set out to swallow up the rest of the industry. In the Ontario fluid milk industry alone three major firms, Dominion Dairies, Silverwood, and Beatrice Foods bought up more than fifty independent dairies between 1961 and 1971. Similar developments were occurring among cheese factories and creameries.

Finally, in terms of the industrial work-force, the trend was to reduction in numbers and continued low pay and poor working conditions in comparison to other manufacturing, even within the food industries. The number of employees declined from 33,000 to 26,500 from 1966 to 1973 as an effect of the consolidation to centralized plants. Wage levels in dairy processing plants averaged $171 in 1974, 8 per cent less than manufacturing generally and 11 per cent less than the meat packing employees.[2] The relative position of dairy workers to the industrial work force generally was not nearly so favourable as the comparison of dairy industry profit margins to those of other industries.

Characteristics of the Industry

Basic Production: The romantic image of the farmer milking his cows after a hard day in the fields is slow to die. Somehow the pastoral setting of dairy farms with their neat green pastures, black and white Holsteins and brightly painted farm buildings gave assurance to the casual urban observer. Beyond the general notion of peace and tranquility, these enterprises seemed to be a wholesome and stable area of production. They were unspoiled by the excesses of industrial agriculture and food technology and they remained comfortably located on the outer edge of every city in Canada in open defiance of urban residential and industrial sprawl.

But the notion of the untroubled dairy farm with its cluster of contented cows is false. The cows may or may not be contented, but their owners are definitely unhappy. Overworked and underpaid dairy production is the most exploitive area of family farm enterprise remaining. For the small family dairy farm of the maritimes, Quebec, northern Ontario, and the prairie 'parklands', milk production has meant poverty income and a seven day work week year-round. The mass exodus of the 1960s was not surprising. It was also not unplanned.

Dairy farming is the oldest farming industry in Canada, predating the industrial agriculture of the twentieth century. Small dairy farms could function without technology or large scale mechanization. Even by 1966, only 54 per cent of industrial milk producers had electric milking machines (the remainder milking by hand), and only 37 per cent had refrigerated storage. Dairy farming is broadly based in all regions, and remains the most important source of farm income in Quebec, British Columbia, and Nova Scotia. It is the second source of income in Ontario and New Brunswick. Only on the prairies is dairy production a relatively minor sector within agriculture in comparison to cereals and livestock for red meats. In 1971, 35 per cent of all Canadian farmers sold milk or cream onto commercial markets, and cash receipts for dairy products were greater than for any other single commodity including wheat.

Dairy production is aimed at two distinct and important markets according to the final use of the milk. The most obvious and immediate market is the fresh or 'fluid' milk market through home delivery, retail outlets, and restaurants. The larger and less familiar market is the 'industrial' or 'manufacturing milk' market in which fluid milk is a raw material for processing into butter, ice cream, cheese, skim milk powder, canned milk, and so on. Producers are broadly distinguished according to which of these markets they are eligible or equipped to pursue. Of the 110,000 dairy farmers in Canada in 1973, 93,000 were tied into the industrial milk market through shipment of whole milk or cream. In general they were the smaller, less equipped dairy farms, often more remote from urban markets. In contrast, the roughly 17,000 fluid milk producers were larger, closer to urban markets and subject to legislated standards on refrigeration equipment, farm buildings and animal inspection.

The distinction between industrial and fluid milk in terms of producer incomes, political organization, and relationship between farmers and agribusiness has all been shaped by public policy and the divided jurisdiction between federal and provincial governments. The industrial milk market is subject to federal jurisdiction because it involves interprovincial trade and exports. Federal programs are aimed primarily but not exclusively at industrial milk producers. The Dairy Farmers of Canada, although nominally open to all milk producers, is primarily a federal lobby and concerned with the issues and policies of industrial milk producers. This is similarly true of the National Farmers Union, which includes dairy farmers among other commodity interests in its membership. Fluid milk shippers who are concerned more with provincial jurisdiction and provincial markets are primarily involved politically through Milk Producers Associations in each province. The public agency established to administer, co-ordinate and advise on federal policy is the Canadian Dairy Commission, appointed first in 1967. Provincially there are Milk Marketing Control Acts in each major producing province which spell out varying degrees of authority for Milk Marketing Boards (or Milk Control Boards or Milk Commissions). They are broadly empowered to set the pricing and marketing conditions of fresh milk marketing in which each province is virually self-sufficient. Some, as in Saskatchewan and Manitoba, control prices for milk to the retail level, others only control *farm* price of milk as in Ontario.

Although the federal and provincial division of both government agencies and producer organizations applies across Canada, there are some areas of overlap. The two central provinces of Ontario and Quebec have 90 per cent of the dairy processing activity and 80 per cent of the industrial milk producers. In these provinces, therefore, provincial agencies have shared authority with the Canadian Dairy Commission over production and marketing of industrial milk as well as controlling the marketing of fluid milk.

The separation between 'industrial' and 'fluid' milk in jurisdiction of public authority and the condition and politics of producers is critical. Despite the fact that both manufacturing milk and fresh milk are the same commodity, coming from the same source at the farm level, for other purposes they must be regarded as two distinct commodities.

The Industrial Milk Industry and Public Policy

In 1971 the 93,000 industrial milk producers registered with the Canadian Dairy Commission were about evenly divided between those shipping whole milk for processing into cheese, butter, skim milk powder, etc., and those shipping cream for the manufacture of butter. This distinction had mostly to do with their geographic relationship to processing plants. Outside of Ontario and Quebec the vast majority of industrial milk producers shipped cream while in Quebec and Ontario, areas close to cheese plants and powdered skim milk plants, most producers shipped whole milk. Regardless of their specialty, industrial milk shippers were rapidly disappearing from 1966 to 1971, with an overall decline of 40 per cent in numbers and roughly 20 per cent in total production. The reasons for the decline were related to public policies and the history of the industry. Summarized by recent studies on ex-dairy farmers, these reasons include "large capital requirements, age of operators, rising non-agricultural wages, increasing preference for leisure and improved old age security."[3] But the explanation goes back to federal policy initiatives beginning in the 1930s.

In the late 1920s, the Canadian market for butter both at home and through exports was threatened by the flow of dairy products from New Zealand. The Canadian advantage in supplying exports to the United States and United Kingdom had depended on geographic advantages which were rendered meaningless by improvements in transportation and refrigeration and the aggressive pursuit of export markets by both New Zealand and Australia. These countries and most of Europe could produce milk more cheaply and efficiently than Canada because of their more temperate climate. Seasonal extremes added costs to winter milk production in Canada. (Even in the 1970s late winter production of industrial milk runs at about one-sixth the volume of the peak production of late summer.)

The issue of whether to apply tariffs against the flood of dairy imports was central to the federal election of 1930. The manufacturers and producers were united in demanding tariff protections to allow the Canadian dairy industry to survive. The National Dairy Council, the manufacturers' lobby, made direct appeals to Mackenzie King while he was Prime Minister, but King maintained a 'free trade' position. His defeat by R.B. Bennett and the Conservative Party in July 1930 was aided by manufacturing interests and was followed almost immediately by an 8¢ per pound tariff on import butter. This effectively reduced imports and increased Canadian production by 62 million pounds a year in the five years from 1929 to 1934.

This policy initiative set a pattern and, from 1930 on, import restrictions and domestic self-sufficiency became permanent features of Canadian milk production and marketing. This policy meant that Canadian exports would be totally uncompetitive in world markets since the Canadian price, unless subsidized, would always be a few cents higher than the New Zealand price. But Canadian producers and manufacturers at least had guaranteed access to the growing Canadian market.

Further government intervention came in the 1935-36 dairy year in the way of federal dairy supports "to minimize price movements and give producers better returns." These subsidies, although temporary, set a precedent. They were introduced again under farmer pressure during the war and the immediate post-war years of the 1940s. The federal government was then trying to increase agricultural production without contributing to inflation in food product prices at the retail level. The Agricultural Prices Support Act in 1944 was aimed at "the support of the prices of agricultural products during the transition from war to peace." It was superseded in 1958 by the Agricultural Stabilization Act. Both of these acts provided for a system of floor prices which would be maintained for products by having a federal

Board purchase and store or export surpluses when the floor price was reached.

In 1949 the industrial milk market was again threatened, this time by a federal declaration legalizing the marketing and sale of margarine. This product, made from vegetable oils, was directly competitive with butter. It had been barred from the commercial market for a decade and was finally allowed over the objections of agricultural lobbyists. Colour restrictions were imposed at first, preventing margarine from being sold in the natural colour of butter. But the access to margarine as a less expensive substitute caused per-capita consumption of butter to drop from a war-time high of 25 pounds per year to 15.8 pounds in 1960 — a drop of 40 per cent. Since butter utilized 75 per cent of industrial milk production and 45 per cent of total milk production this decline was disastrous for dairy farmers.

One direct result of the drop in industrial milk consumption was a surplus of both butter and skim milk powder, and with it stagnating prices for industrial milk throughout the 1950s. Milk production was increasing because of new technology, improved animal breeding, and better feeds. Dairy farmers faced a cost-price squeeze as industrial milk remained at or near the floor price from 1950 to 1964. The federal government was forced to buy up surplus butter and skim milk powder to sell on export markets under subsidy or to give away as food aid. After 1951, import controls were rigidly applied on butter, cheese, canned milks, and dry milk powder. The controls went beyond maintenance of a tariff to prevention of *any* dumping of import dairy products at any price without application for a permit with the Department of Industry Trade and Commerce.

None of these measures alleviated the cost-price squeeze on dairy farmers, although they did protect their market within Canada. But the selling price of industrial milk remained virtually unchanged. Dairy processing plants enjoyed all the advantages of a buyer's market as the price of industrial milk, which was $2.81 per cwt. in 1957, was still only $2.77 in 1964 and then rose slightly to $3.08 by 1966. Cost of manufactured farm inputs in the same period had increased by roughly 40 per cent.[4]

Clearly the Agricultural Price Support Act (1944) and the Agriculture Stabilization Act (1958) by maintaining floor prices did nothing to encourage income adjustments for dairy producers. By keeping prices "within 80 per cent of the ten-year average", the Stabilization Act prevented the surplus in milk products from creating a total market collapse and bankrupting producers. The security of a floor price kept many small producers shipping milk for returns which although marginal were at least secure. However, by having a fixed floor price with no allowance for rising costs of production, dairy farmers were in effect asked to accept a steady reduction in disposable net-income.[5]

Finally in 1962 there was an effort by the federal government to stimulate demand for manufactured milk products by paying out to manufacturers a direct 12¢ per pound 'consumer subsidy' on butter. This brought the retail price of butter closer into line with the price of margarine (although the full 12¢ saving was not passed along to consumers), and per-capita consumption increased from 15.8 pounds per year in 1961 to 18.5 pounds in 1964. At the same time the Agricultural Stabilization Board raised the floor price or 'offer to purchase' price on both butter and cheese above the ten-year average.

The impact of federal intervention through the Agricultural Stabilization Board between 1958 and 1966 was one of stabilizing prices too low to encourage viable full-time dairy operations, but consistent enough to attract and maintain a large number of marginal dairy farms. These small operators, with twelve cows or less, tended to combine industrial milk or cream shipping with other commodity production. Since the Agricultural Stabilization Board bought up all surplus butter and skim milk powder, there was a constant demand in the market at a consistently low price.

The state of dairy production in the 1958-67 period was one of 'hanging-on' for a good many farmers. They knew returns were not adequate in relation to the work demands of milking a herd of cows seven days a week, but they also counted on the small cream cheque or milk cheque as a critical supplement to returns from less stable commodities such as hogs, cattle or grain.

It was only after about seven years, with no price changes in the farm value of milk, that militant farm protest began to develop in both Ontario and Quebec. These provinces, which contained 80 per cent of the nation's industrial milk shippers, were the scene of repeated demonstrations in the mid-1960s. Tractor demonstrations which rolled down the freeways to Toronto's Queen's park in 1966 were followed in 1967 by the largest demonstration ever to converge on Parliament Hill. In May 1967, an estimated 20,000 farmers marched to Parliament in support of a contingent of farm leaders who offered a brief to then Prime Minister Lester Pearson. Organized by the Ontario Farmers Union, the Ontario Federation of Agriculture and the Union Catholique des Cultivateurs de Québec, the farmers were demanding a farm price for industrial milk of $5.00 per cwt., instead of the $3.83 they were receiving.

The federal government was clumsy in its tactics of dealing with the mass delegation of farmers. First they took in some of the leadership core to a smaller meeting in the Commons committee rooms while the others waited outside. Pearson challenged farm leaders on the tone of the brief, saying ". . . I find it difficult not to resent the language." His Agriculture Minister, Joe Greene, noted for long-winded speeches, chose to talk out the clock and prevent farm leaders from developing their position: ". . . His long statement left no time for discussion on specific points of the brief" (*Globe and Mail*, May 25, 1967).

Later, outside, farmers reacted angrily after speeches and reports on the useless exchange between farm leaders and government leaders were summarized by Pearson's promise to "raise the matter with cabinet." The demonstration stormed the doors of the Commons centre block, smashing glass and forcing a waiting RCMP contingent to bolt the doors on the inside. Farmers eventually left, with tulips from the official government flower beds. The price was later set at a compromise of $4.40.

Coincident with this 'largest-ever' political protest was the beginning of a new stage of federal policy under the Canadian Dairy Commission which began full operations in April 1967. Motivated by the depressed dairy prices, production surpluses, and the growing farmer militancy of the mid-sixties, the federal government decided to streamline the entire system of marketing and pricing for industrial milk. They zeroed in first on the easiest and most vulnerable target, the marginal or part-time dairy farmer. The 1958-66 era of 'hanging on' in dairy production was replaced unofficially by the slogan 'shape up or ship out' and officially by the concept of supply-management. The task of the CDC was to eliminate milk surpluses, reduce levels of government subsidies, and discourage the marginal producer from continuing in operation. They succeeded marvelously in the first task, failed miserably in the second, and brilliantly executed the third.

The Pearson government had first initiated direct subsidy payments to industrial milk producers in 1965. These partly replaced the subsidy to dairy processors on butter which had been paid out since 1962. The new system increased the price received by farmers for their milk without imposing higher costs on dairy companies for their milk supplies. The government became a middleman paying 'something for nothing.' Consumers were presumed to benefit because the dairy processors would have no reason to advance prices.

The government's later concern with the direct payment subsidy was that it would encourage marginal dairy producers to stay in farming and try to expand their milking herds rather than shift to other commodities. This tendency, it was feared, would add to the problem of butter and skim milk surpluses.

The CDC was empowered to maintain and expand the direct payment subsidy program to industrial milk producers after 1967, but they had at the same time to discourage the marginal farmer from

---

TABLE 6

FARMS REPORTING MILK COWS 1961–1971

NO. COWS	1961	1966	1971	% CHANGE 1961–1971
1–2	65,350	47,240	34,000	−48
3–12	160,500	95,000	46,300	−70
13–32	74,400	64,100	45,500	−38
32–92	8,500	13,700	18,500	+117
over 93	192	330	567	+195
Total	308,980	221,850	145,318	−53

SOURCE: STATISTICS CANADA CENSUS

---

gaining its benefits. They succeeded, as evidenced by the decline in the number of farmers with twelve cows or less from 226,000 in 1961 to 80,000 in 1971.

The main weapon of the Dairy Commission in trimming down the 170,000 industrial milk shippers in 1967 was the "Subsidy Eligibility Quota." Beginning in the 1967-68 Dairy year, each shipper of industrial milk was allotted a quota equal to his 1966-67 production. On this amount of milk they would receive the federal subsidy over and above the market price. The subsidy level was then up to $1.10 per cwt. from the original subsidy of 20¢ in 1965. Any milk produced beyond the Subsidy Eligibility Quota would not be eligible for the federal subsidy. If the producer decided not to ship milk or ceased operations, his quota could not be sold or transferred to another producer. (Prior to the Subsidy Eligibility Quota the effect of subsidies was to encourage production rather than restrict it since there were no specific limits to the volume of production eligible for the subsidy.)

The curb on production was extended in 1968-69, when the Subsidy Eligibility Quota was allowed only to those producers whose previous year's deliveries exceeded 12,000 pounds of milk. Those too small to qualify were given a one-shot 'phasing out payment' equal to their quota in 1967-68. This policy generally cut off any producer who kept half a dozen or so milk cows from receiving a break-even price for his product.

The orchestration of smaller-scale milk shippers out of production was reinforced in 1969 by the research and recommendations of the federal government's Task Force on Agriculture. They called for tough measures by the CDC to eliminate the surplus in powdered skim milk still in evidence in 1969. The Task Force suggested gradual reduction in subsidy levels and further increases in the minimum production requirements for the Subsidy Eligibility Quota. They suggested the minimum be increased from 12,000 pounds per year to 30,000 pounds. This would have wiped out any farmer who didn't have at least twelve cows on a regular year-round basis. They also recommended a federal program to assist dairy producers to convert into beef production.

In reality the dairy farmers didn't need much further encouragement to give up milking cows. Two McGill economists in a March 1974 report on Dairy for the Prices Review Board summarized the choices and circumstances of those leaving dairy production in the 1960s. Their insights were based on a Department of Agriculture Survey of former dairy farmers in Ontario which revealed among other factors a resistance to the demands of a 365-day work requirement.

... For them the choice was to remain in a low-return dairy enterprise or give it up and take full time employment outside of agriculture. ... The extent of the financial incentive to shift employment is indicated by the fact that wages in agriculture at present run at 50 to 60 per cent of those prevailing in non-agricultural industries. In fact the average family income of the ex-dairy farmers referred to above was about 14 per cent higher in 1971 than it was in their last year as dairymen (1968).

The Department of Agriculture survey indicated that only 7.4 per cent of those *leaving* dairy operations had gross sales of over $10,000 per year. In 1971, 40 per cent of all dairy producers fell into the over-$10,000 gross sales category, indicating that the policies aimed at attrition among the 60 per cent of smaller producers was being successful since over 90 per cent of those leaving were from this group. 68 per cent of those who left had gross incomes of less than $6,000.

The smaller diversified farms who represented such a large proportion of Canada's industrial milk production were not part of the efficient mechanized agriculture of the 1970s. The Task Force in its report was appalled at the findings of the 1966 census in the dairy industry. 54 per cent of industrial milk shippers had no electric milking equipment, 37 per cent had no refrigerated storage, and 64 per cent earned a majority of their income from sources other than milk sales. Roughly half the milk shippers in 1966 had twelve cows or less and these were the real target of federal policies.

The 'success' of the federal policy initiatives after 1967 was to be measured in the fact of a 20 per cent production decline by 1973 and the shift from a 'surplus' to 'deficit' position in the market. But with a sudden dependence on imports reflecting a rising level of world prices federal politicians were no longer ecstatic about their achievements. Once the trend to other commodities was begun it was difficult to reverse and the number of dairy farmers continued to decline. A 6 per cent production decline in 1973 was followed by a further 3.7 per cent decline in 1974 and a projection of a 1.5 per cent decline in 1975 before the year even started. Chairman of the Dairy Farmers of Canada Ellard Powers in projecting a 1975 decline cited ". . . difficult production conditions, labour problems, a sharp increase in feed grain prices, and the reluctance of many farmers to work the seven day week. . . ."

By mid-1974 Eugene Whelan began to project the possibility of milk rationing unless serious adjustments could be made toward improving the lot of producers. Adjustments meant price increases, and Whelan faced dairy farmers during the 1974 federal election with a promise of substantial increases. The price of industrial milk was increased to the farmer from a 1973 price of $6.17 per cwt. to one of $9.41 in August 1974, with a further increase in 1975 to $10.02 per cwt. The relationship of these prices to rising costs of production and the relationship of higher subsidy payments to the price paid for milk by dairy processors are analyzed further below. But we need to clarify the position of 'fluid' milk producers in relationship to public policy and to the industrial milk market.

Fluid Milk and the Market Sharing Quota

Throughout the 1960s when industrial milk shippers were being obliterated and production surpluses brought under control, the situation of the fluid milk market was relatively stable. More tightly controlled by provincial marketing boards, the larger fluid milk dairy farms had better guarantees that their product would be used. Periodic price adjustments had consistently widened the gap between the farm price of fluid milk and that of industrial milk from the early 1950s until 1965 when the federal government began to add direct payment subsidies to industrial milk. By 1964 industrial milk producers were getting $2.77 per cwt. for milk, only about 60 per cent of

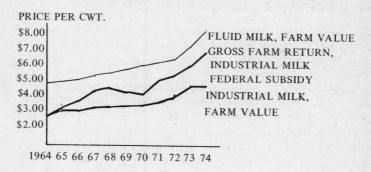

FIGURE 13

COMPARISON OF INDUSTRIAL AND FLUID MILK PRICES AND
FEDERAL SUBSIDY, 1964–1975

the $4.92 per cwt. being paid for fluid milk. In 1967 when the
industrial milk producers stormed Parliament Hill on a demand of
$5.00 per cwt. milk prices they were only receiving $3.83, including
their subsidy, while fluid milk producers had a price of $5.35.

There are obviously some higher cost factors that fluid milk
producers can point to as necessitating better prices. In each major
area of production costs, fluid producers faced some extra burden.
For example, feed requirements were of a higher standard for fluid
milk production, labour costs were higher because larger dairy farms
located near cities were forced to accept closer-to-average wages in
competition with the non-farm labour market. And, finally, land
prices in the areas surrounding cities were disproportionately high in
relation to the more remote farm locations more typical of the
industrial milk shippers. But no one, including fluid milk producers,
could justify a price difference of over $2.00 per cwt. when all of the
essential costs such as feed grains, labour, and land were similar if not
identical.

Farmer organizations, particularly the National Farmers Union,
demanded an end in the 1970s to the price, status, and income
discrimination between industrial and fluid milk producers. They
pointed out that despite the direct payment subsidy which had
increased to a 1974 level of $250 million, industrial milk producers

still faced depressed market prices in relationship to fluid milk producers. Fluid shippers were the aristocracy of the industry with incomes on average much higher than the industrial milk producers.[6] They had sufficient influence with the provincial marketing boards to pressure successfully for regular advances in prices for raw table milk. But the smaller and more diffused industrial shippers had difficulty making gains with the federal government and the Canadian Dairy Commission. They argued for a formula for annual increases based on a cost-of-production index. This would take the decision-making on prices, announced before the beginning of each Dairy year in April, out of the sensitive political arena. In January 1975, Eugene Whelan told dairy farmers in their annual convention that a formula proposal was being actively considered by cabinet.

The demands to integrate the two categories of producers were partly heeded in a 1971 decision to partially integrate fluid and industrial markets in the two major industrial milk producing provinces of Ontario and Quebec. But integration was on terms least favourable to industrial milk shippers and actually had the effect of widening the disparity. The Ontario and Quebec Milk Marketing Boards worked out with the Canadian Dairy Commission a system of market 'sharing.' The plan, jointly administered between the CDC and the provincial marketing boards, allowed fluid milk shippers to supply industrial milk if their production surpassed the needs of the fluid market. In other words, through the introduction of a 'Market Sharing Quota' the larger dairy farms had a better guarantee that all the milk they produced up to their quota limit would be purchased, if not as fresh milk, then as industrial milk for butter, cheese or ice cream. They would be eligible for the direct payment federal subsidy on milk sold for industrial uses on the same terms as industrial milk shippers. But the 'market sharing' was only one-way. The small dairy farms were not eligible to sell to the fluid milk market from their production. Many of them would not be able to meet legislated standards for fresh milk dairy farms. But even if they had met standards they would have to attempt to gain a quota for fluid milk production. With a decline in the consumption of fresh milk in Canada, few if any provincial marketing agencies were extending new quotas after 1971.

As well as further favouring large-scale dairy farms and closing off the industrial milk market for smaller producers, the market sharing system after 1971 also increased the direct authority of the provincial marketing boards in Ontario and Quebec. The regulation of price and supply of industrial milk to dairy processing plants was no longer a matter of direct dealing between farmers and the private companies who bought their products. Instead all sales were made through, for example, the Ontario Milk Marketing Board, which would then authorize delivery to one or other of the plants within the province. This might have been an arrangement advantageous to both producers and the smaller dairy plants but in fact it was to the advantage of neither. Producers had less choice about where to make deliveries, and felt they had no influence on price. They were governed not only by the Ontario Milk Marketing Board but also by a secondary government Milk Commission which could over-rule even the price of the OMMB. Market deliveries of farmers were shifted by the Marketing Boards away from the smaller plants and toward the larger firms like Kraft and Borden's. Government policy through the milk marketing boards was to assist the centralization of dairy plants, a key factor in the rapid rate of reduction of smaller cheese plants and creameries after 1970.

The Prices Crisis 1973-75

In dairy as in beef production, the major dislocation in the industry was a direct result of higher world grain prices in 1973. Between 1972 and 1975 dairy ration increased 250 per cent, from $3.91 per cwt. to $8.50, as the industry went from being the beneficiary of cheap surplus cereal grains in Canada to become victim of a world grain shortage and commodity price speculation. Feed costs made up 45 per cent of the total cost of dairy production in 1972, but the proportion increased as inflation in feed grain outstripped even manufactured dairy farm inputs like milking equipment, veterinary supplies, and farm machinery. As dairy operations moved sharply into the red in 1973, there were pressures to make price adjustments in the farm price of fluid and industrial milk. Fluid milk was increased an average of 14 per cent by provincial marketing boards in 1973 and the Canadian Dairy Commission raised the support price of industrial milk by 13 per cent. In 1974 further increases of 15-20 per cent were added for both categories of milk. But even while the Dairy Farmers of Canada made its appeal in the summer of 1974 for $10.00 per cwt. for industrial milk, the Ontario Federation of Agriculture was distributing the results of a survey which indicated costs of production for milk were up to $10.60 per cwt. The final adjustment of the price agreed to by the federal government in August 1974 was $9.41. The problem for dairy producers is graphically illustrated by contrasting price movements for dairy ration with that of farm milk prices for industrial milk.

Estimates by agricultural economists on the ratio of milk prices to feed costs suggest that a ratio of 1.6 to 1 has been the recent long-term average for farms in Canada up to 1972. In other words, the

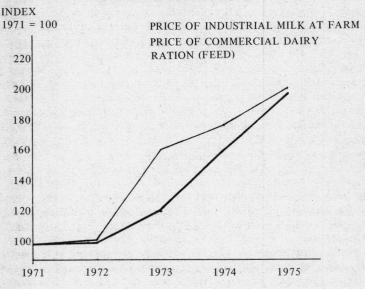

FIGURE 14

PRICE COMPARISON: INDUSTRIAL MILK
AND DAIRY RATION 1971-1975

INDEX
1971 = 100

PRICE OF INDUSTRIAL MILK AT FARM
PRICE OF COMMERCIAL DAIRY
RATION (FEED)

dairy ration price in mid-1974 of $7.00 per cwt. would require a return for milk in the area of $10.80 to meet the level of returns averaged in previous years. (Instead the price was $9.41.) With the dairy ration price in the area of $8.50 as in early 1975, the price for farm milk should have reached over $13. (Instead the price was $10.02.) If the normal milk:feed ratio had been attained, the retail price of milk products would be faced with yet another 20-30 per cent increase to keep pace. As it was, the dairy processing and distribution firms were only too anxious to pass along the more modest adjustments in farm level prices paid for milk.

The impact of higher farm milk prices on the consumer price of table milk and all manufactured milk products was fairly direct and immediate: up 23 per cent from August 1972 to August 1974 *plus* federal subsidies. Through subsidies of $250 million to industrial milk shippers in 1974, the government was paying 32 per cent of the farm price of industrial milk directly. On top of this continuing program and growing tax burden, the government added a $108 million one-year 5¢-per-quart subsidy on fluid milk to soften the impact on consumers. Some provincial governments added their own fluid milk subsidies. The subsidies on fluid milk, suggested and supported by the Food Prices Review Board, were aimed at maintaining consumption of milk by large and low-income families. The anticipated drop in consumption if price levels were fully passed on would create further problems and dislocations for the industry. While solving the problem of shortages in milk supply, a consumption drop would add to the income squeeze on dairy producers by forcing cutbacks in their quotas.

Despite all the arguments by both producers and consumer groups for maintaining the federal subsidy on fluid milk beyond the one year planned, the Liberal cabinet lifted the subsidy as planned beginning in October 1974 at a rate of 1¢ per month. Since the farm price was continuing to rise in this period as well, the lifting of the milk subsidy (which was paid to dairy processors) meant that retail prices had a double load of increase in 1974-75. The price of fluid milk jumped 7.3 per cent in a single month in November 1974. As the quart price of milk went beyond 50¢, decline in consumption was made inevitable.

Obviously if the grain price increases and the increase in prepared dairy ration were taken into account, much of the increase in the retail price of milk products had to be accepted. Even within the price movements of milk products, however, there is room for challenge to the role of both dairy agribusiness and government in determining and distributing the burden of higher prices.

The Butter and Cheese Disparity

In general dairy manufacturing firms have had the advantage of a highly subsidized arrangement on their primary raw material, i.e. industrial milk. They have paid farmers less for milk than the cost of producing it. In the ten years since 1965, the direct subsidy on farm milk increased from 20¢ per cwt. to $3.00. This meant that despite the inflationary pressures on dairy producers, and a 200 per cent increase in the farm value of industrial milk over ten years, the processers paid only a 100 per cent increase with most of that coming in 1974. The rest of the inflation was absorbed by government. This tremendous level of subsidy means in effect that the 'real' price of butter in spring 1974 was not 82¢ per pound as sold in supermarkets but $1.17 per pound, with 35¢ covered by government using tax revenue. The price of cheese at $1.30 per pound in the supermarket in spring 1974 had a real price of $1.70 per pound when the subsidy was added in.

Although both of these commodities increased substantially from 1961 to 1975 and both came from the same basic raw material at the same subsidized price, their price patterns are remarkably different. For example, the total increase in the price of butter including the value of subsidies was about 68 per cent up to 1974 from the price of butter in 1961. But the price of Canadian cheddar cheese from 1961 was up over 100 per cent if subsidies are included. The price of industrial milk, was the main cost factor in both of these commodities. The significant difference in price patterns between butter and cheese reflects the fact that the Canadian cheese market is controlled by a few large corporations who are able to use their market power to earn superprofits.

The explanation for the sharp differences in butter and cheese prices when the cost of raw materials, labour and packaging are roughly identical lies in the state of consumer demand. In the case of butter, per-capita consumption has been declining substantially despite subsidies to keep the consumer price down. Per-capita consumption of butter declined from 18.5 pounds in 1964 to 14.5 in 1972. In contrast, per-capita consumption of cheddar cheese has increased from 2.8 to 4.3 pounds from 1960 to 1972. Cheese has the greatest percentage increase in consumption of all Canadian dairy products. It is not just coincidence that cheese has also had the greatest price increase of all dairy products. Nor is it coincident that cheese manufacturing and marketing is more highly centralized in Canada and more profitable than the manufacture of butter, skim milk, and ice cream.

The Agribusiness Pattern: Industrial and Fluid

The dairy sector of agribusiness is divided somewhat along the lines of basic production, with industrial milk manufacturers having one set of marketing assumptions and policy guidelines and fluid milk processors and distributors having another. The two market areas are tied together through integrated ownership, but plant facilities are generally maintained separately. For example, Kraft Foods is active in all areas of dairy products manufacturing through its own major milk and cheese manufacturing plants and is active in fluid milk distribution as well through its subsidiary Dominion Dairies under the Sealtest label. Similarly, Beatrice Foods has subsidiaries in both industrial milk products manufacturing and fluid milk plants.

In manufactured milk products, the markets are national in scope and the large multinational firms have established near-monopoly conditions through ownership, brand-name advertising, and through influence over the marketing and pricing policies of public marketing agencies. Kraft Foods' role in the marketing of cheese products is the best illustration. Although the Kraft company reportedly manufactures less than 30 per cent of the cheese marketed in Canada, it sells well over 50 per cent of the cheese on a mark-up because of the strength of the Kraft label. In other words, through saturation advertising which forces retail distributors to concentrate on Kraft products, the company is able to force smaller plants to contract their supplies to be marketed through Kraft, for a price. Even the large Granby Co-operative plant, which is the largest cheese manufacturer in Quebec, markets its products under the Kraft label.

A story carried in the *Ottawa Citizen* in September 1973 outlined the frustration of just one small cheese plant in dealing with the market control of Kraft. The story described the closing of a cheese plant in Plantagenet, Ontario, with the lay-off of fifty employees. According to the plant owner, only about 10 per cent of the cheese his plant was producing was sold under the company label 'Tourelle.' The rest was shipped to Kraft as specialty cheese under contract. But then Kraft gave the plant notice that it was abandoning the contract because it discovered it could get its supply cheaper in Quebec. Without access to the Kraft label, the small plant folded.

Kraft and the other major firms have a close and apparently comfortable relationship with the milk marketing agencies in Ontario and Quebec. The allocation of quotas of available industrial milk to the processing plants is controlled by the Ontario and Quebec Milk Marketing Boards. These boards have the power to restrict the available supply to any size or category of supply. In line with a conclusion of the federal Task Force on Agriculture that "a great deal more consolidation is necessary . . ." (in dairy processing), the milk marketing boards have channeled an increased proportion of deliveries to the larger plants. The attrition rate among small cheese plants is comparable to that of farmers, and the OMMB states an open bias toward the larger 'multi-purpose processors.' Much of the admiration, of Kraft in particular, stems from its unquestioned power in retail markets. The gratitude felt by the Ontario Milk Board to Kraft was expressed in a memo refuting producer criticisms of Kraft from the National Farmers Union during their 'Kraft Boycott:'

> . . . a good part of this dramatic growth in the cheese market has been brought about by Kraft Foods' marketing expertise, including its packaging and promotion efforts, plus its close attention at all times to high and consistent quality.

The Ontario Milk Board apparently overlooked some of the recent challenges to Kraft 'miracle' products. In 1973 Kraft was forced to recall 2.2 million macaroni and cheese dinners after the U.S. Food and

FIGURE 15

THE KRAFT CONGLOMERATE

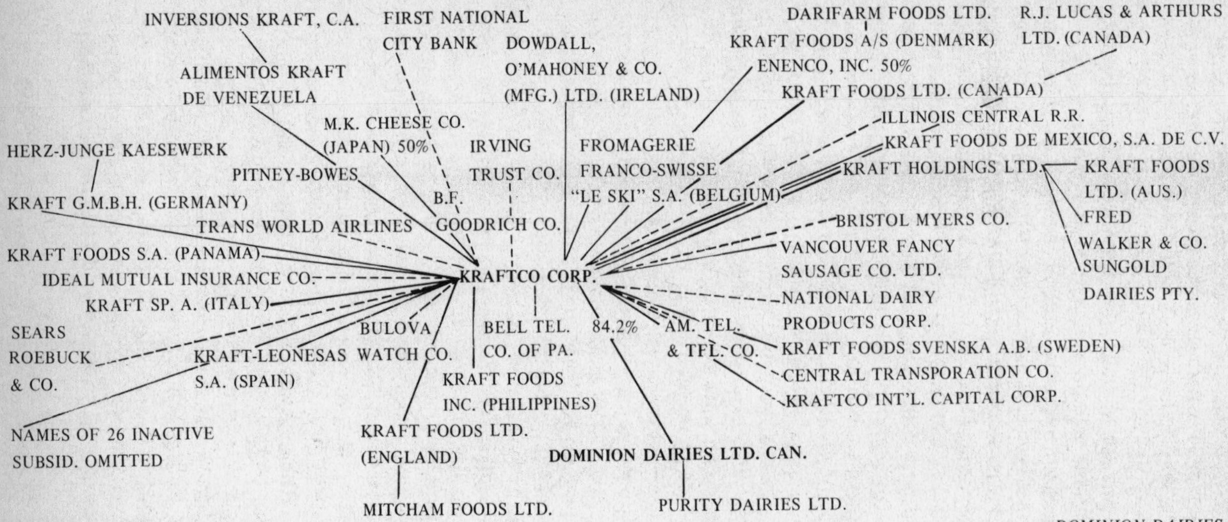

INVERSIONS KRAFT, C.A.

FIRST NATIONAL

DARIFARM FOODS LTD.

R.J. LUCAS & ARTHURS LTD. (CANADA)

ALIMENTOS KRAFT DE VENEZUELA

CITY BANK

DOWDALL, O'MAHONEY & CO. (MFG.) LTD. (IRELAND)

KRAFT FOODS A/S (DENMARK)

ENENCO, INC. 50%

KRAFT FOODS LTD. (CANADA)

HERZ-JUNGE KAESEWERK

M.K. CHEESE CO.

ILLINOIS CENTRAL R.R.

KRAFT FOODS DE MEXICO, S.A. DE C.V.

KRAFT G.M.B.H. (GERMANY)

PITNEY-BOWES

IRVING TRUST CO.

FROMAGERIE FRANCO-SWISSE

KRAFT HOLDINGS LTD.

TRANS WORLD AIRLINES

B.F. GOODRICH CO.

"LE SKI" S.A. (BELGIUM)

KRAFT FOODS

KRAFT FOODS S.A. (PANAMA)

KRAFTCO CORP.

BRISTOL MYERS CO.

LTD. (AUS)

IDEAL MUTUAL INSURANCE CO.

VANCOUVER FANCY SAUSAGE CO. LTD.

WALKER & CO.

KRAFT SP. A. (ITALY)

84.2%

AM. TEL. & TEL. CO.

NATIONAL DAIRY PRODUCTS CORP.

SUNGOLD

SEARS ROEBUCK & CO.

BULOVA WATCH CO.

BELL TEL. CO. OF PA.

KRAFT FOODS SVENSKA A.B. (SWEDEN)

DAIRIES PTY.

KRAFT-LEONESAS S.A. (SPAIN)

KRAFT FOODS INC. (PHILIPPINES)

CENTRAL TRANSPORATION CO.

KRAFTCO INT'L. CAPITAL CORP.

NAMES OF 26 INACTIVE SUBSID. OMITTED

KRAFT FOODS LTD. (ENGLAND)

DOMINION DAIRIES LTD. CAN.

MITCHAM FOODS LTD.

PURITY DAIRIES LTD.

KRAFTCO:
NET SALES: $2,959,635,000 (1971)
NET INCOME TO SURPLUS: $91,347,000

DOMINION DAIRIES
NET SALES: $77,621,193
NET INCOME: $1,979,988

Drug Administration (FDA) warned that the product contained traces of salmonella, a dangerous and occasionally fatal food poisoning bacteria. James Turner's *The Chemical Feast* pointed out also that FDA officials in the U.S. believe Kraft to be responsible for a major decline in the quality of cheese but feel powerless to act.[7]

As the arbitrator of prices for industrial milk for farmers, the OMMB's close affinity to Kraft is bad news for the dairy producer in Ontario. The OMMB takes the federal price proposal of the CDC as a 'target price' in its deliberations. Even if the influence of the OMMB, which has producer members, were to support price increases for farm milk, the provincial government-appointed Ontario Milk Commission can still veto the request. The lobby of Kraft and other agribusinesses can exercise its power at two levels. In January 1973 the OMMB announced increases to producers of 57¢ per cwt., a compromise between farmers and processers. This increase was reduced to 35¢ when reviewed by the OMC after further pressure was applied by the dairy manufacturers. This supervision over producer marketing boards by a higher appointed body made a farce out of the marketing board concept in Ontario and was the basis of the NFU demand for direct collective bargaining procedures with the companies. Failure of Kraft to even discuss collective bargaining with farmers in 1971 led the NFU organization to organize a consumer boycott of all Kraft products.

Kraft is an international giant with gross sales of roughly $4 billion in 1974. Its profit increase in the two years 1972-74, when inflation was pressing heavily on the economy, came to over 50 per cent. But Kraft, for all its tremendous size and reputation, is not the only international giant of prominence in Canada. Beatrice Foods, an American company with international sales of $3.5 billion, is involved in all aspects of dairy processing as well. Beatrice Foods was a major part of the consolidation process from 1969 to 1974 when, according to the Food Prices Review Board, the number of dairy processing plants decreased by 32 per cent in Ontario. Based originally in Chicago, Beatrice was restricted from further take-overs in the United States by a Federal Trade Practices Commission ruling in 1969. The ruling placed a ten-year freeze on further acquisition of milk and ice cream plants. The Beatrice strategy had long been one of buying up small successful food processing plants and maintaining them as decentralized subsidiaries retaining their original brand names, management personnel, and a good deal of independent decision-making. All Beatrice insisted on was that the operations make money and they called their growing network of local plants 'profit-centers.' (The cumulative profit increase for Beatrice from 1969 to 1974 was 130 per cent.)

The U.S. ruling against Beatrice take-overs brought the company

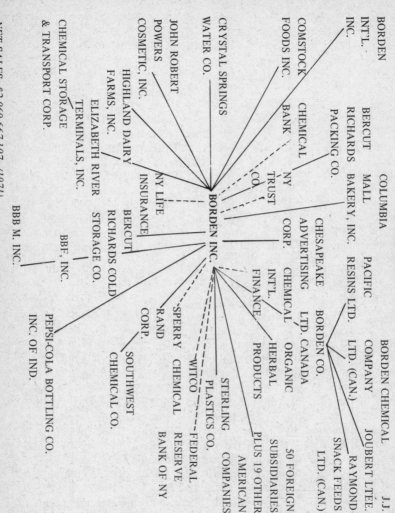

FIGURE 16
THE BORDEN GROUP

BORDEN INT'L., INC.

COLUMBIA MALL

PACIFIC COMPANY

BORDEN CHEMICAL LTD. (CAN.)

J.J. JOUBERT LTÉE.

RAYMOND

BERCUT RICHARDS BAKERY, INC.

RESINS LTD.

SNACK FEEDS LTD. (CAN.)

COMSTOCK FOODS INC.

CHEMICAL BANK

PACKING CO.

CHESAPEAKE

BORDEN CO.

50 FOREIGN SUBSIDIARIES

NY TRUST CO.

ADVERTISING

CHEMICAL

ORGANIC

CRYSTAL SPRINGS WATER CO.

CORP.

INT'L. FINANCE

HERBAL PRODUCTS

PLUS 19 OTHER AMERICAN COMPANIES

JOHN ROBERT POWERS COSMETIC, INC.

NY LIFE INSURANCE

BORDEN INC.

STERLING

HIGHLAND DAIRY FARMS, INC.

FINANCE CORP.

SPERRY RAND CORP.

PLASTICS CO.

ELIZABETH RIVER TERMINALS, INC.

BERCUT RICHARDS COLD STORAGE CO.

WITCO

FEDERAL RESERVE BANK OF NY

CHEMICAL STORAGE & TRANSPORT CORP.

BBF, INC.

SOUTHWEST CHEMICAL CO.

BBB M. INC.

PEPSI-COLA BOTTLING CO. INC. OF IND.

NET SALES: $2,069,667,107 (1971)
NET INCOME: $60,532,717

into Canada in a major way in 1969. With no restrictions on foreign take-overs, Beatrice purchased sixteen Canadian dairy operations in less than five years. The dairy 'profit centers,' along with grocery products manufacturing plants, and chemical plants, gave Beatrice 1973 sales of $160 million through Canadian subsidiaries. Consistent with the U.S. policy, the Canadian plants are given independence in management, and local identity through brand names, etc. This made the expansion pattern somewhat inconspicuous. But the flow of wealth was effectively centralized not only from Canada but the twenty-eight countries around the world in which Beatrice has developed a take-over strategy since 1960.

Borden Foods, though less spectacular in its expansion than Beatrice and less influential in the marketing of cheese and other manufactured milk products than Kraft, has a substantial empire in Canada with fifteen dairy processing plants in Canada to complement its U.S. operations. Borden was described by the Federal Task Force on Agriculture as one of the 'big three' in fluid milk distribution in Ontario along with Silverwood and Dominion Dairies, a subsidiary of Kraftco Corporation.

In 1964 Borden was required by a ruling of the U.S. Federal Restrictive Trade Practices Commission to divest of eight of its acquired dairy concerns. Like its rival Beatrice Foods, Borden responded to U.S. anti-combines measures by expanding its operations in Canada throughout the 1960s. They are substantially involved in the commercial baking industry, in addition to dairy manufacturing.

Silverwood Industries is engaged in both processing and distribution of dairy products with facilities and markets in Ontario and Western Canada. They have more recently expanded into the convenience store retail trade with the purchase of Mini-Mart stores in Ontario and the west. Silverwood is a major Canadian Corporation with assets of $60 million and sales of $172 million in 1972.

Dominion Dairies has been a subsidiary of Kraftco Limited since 1960 when Kraft purchased over 80 per cent of the outstanding shares. It engages in the manufacture and distribution of milk and milk products in Ontario and Quebec. The company has been in existence since 1926, formerly as Eastern Dairies Limited, and now has assets of $22 million and sales of $86 million.

George Weston Limited is a holding company primarily for food processing operations of all goods and commodities including dairy products. In addition to Eplett dairies, long a Weston subsidiary, Weston in May 1974 purchased a controlling interest in Clark Dairy, last of the independents in the Ottawa area. But Weston is small in terms of the fluid milk market in comparison to the others.

By 1961, what the Task Force described as the big three in

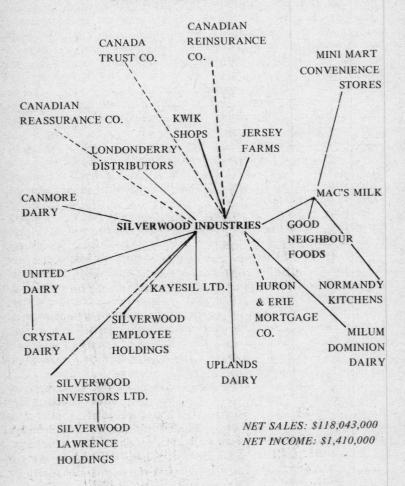

FIGURE 17
SILVERWOOD INDUSTRIES

CANADIAN REINSURANCE CO.

CANADA TRUST CO.

MINI MART CONVENIENCE STORES

CANADIAN REASSURANCE CO.

KWIK SHOPS

JERSEY FARMS

LONDONDERRY DISTRIBUTORS

MAC'S MILK

CANMORE DAIRY

SILVERWOOD INDUSTRIES

GOOD NEIGHBOUR FOODS

UNITED DAIRY

KAYESIL LTD.

HURON & ERIE MORTGAGE CO.

NORMANDY KITCHENS

CRYSTAL DAIRY

SILVERWOOD EMPLOYEE HOLDINGS

MILUM DOMINION DAIRY

UPLANDS DAIRY

SILVERWOOD INVESTORS LTD.

SILVERWOOD LAWRENCE HOLDINGS

NET SALES: $118,043,000
NET INCOME: $1,410,000

TABLE 7
THE DISAPPEARING SMALL DAIRIES

ONTARIO
PURCHASES BY
DOMINION DAIRIES, 1961–72

Roselawn Farm Dairies
(Toronto, 1962)

Peterborough Sunshine Dairy
Whitfield-Morrison Dairy
(Peterborough, 1965)

Alliance Dairy
(Toronto, 1966)

St. Thomas Dairy
(St. Thomas, 1966)

Rosedale Dairy
(Brampton, 1966)

Purity Dairies
(Windsor, 1967)

Kitchener Dairies
(Kitchener, 1967)

ONTARIO AND CANADIAN
PURCHASES BY
BEATRICE FOODS LTD.
1969–73 (PARTIAL LIST)

Brookside-Price's Dairy Ltd.
Holmes Dairy Ltd.
Ideal Dairy Products Ltd.
Lakeland Dairies Ltd.
Lakeview Pure Milk Dairy Ltd.
Maple Lane Dairy Ltd.
Modern Dairies Ltd.
Oxford Dairy (Woodstock) Ltd.
St. Boniface Creamery Ltd.
Sanna Dairies Ltd.
Smith's Dairy Ltd.
Standard Dairies Ltd.
Wilmot's Dairies Ltd.

ONTARIO
PURCHASES BY
SILVERWOOD INDUSTRIES,1961–72

Paulger's Dairy
(Toronto, 1961)

Mason's Dairy Products
(St. Catharines, 1962)

Lasalle Dairy
Kingsville Dairy
(Windsor, 1965)

Jeffrey's Dairy
(St. Catharines, 1965)

Campbell's Dairy Products
(Peterborough, 1965)

Dye Dairies
(Brockville, 1966)

United Dairies Ltd.
(Branches in several centres, 1966)

Findley Kemp Dairies
(Toronto,1967)(after merger of Findlay,
Kemp and Uplands Dairies in 1965)

Glover's Dairy
(Chatham, 1967)

Hurl's Dairy Ltd.
(Orillia, 1967)

United Dairy and Poultry
Co-operative (Ice-Cream)
(Renfrew, 1967)

Mark Ayre's Dairy Ltd.
(London, 1967)

Cooksville Dairy
Hamilton Dairyland
(Hamilton, 1968)

Mac's Milk Ltd.
(Toronto, 1968)

Londonderry Distributors
(Toronto, 1971)

Ontario's fluid milk processing industry had 35 per cent of the market. But along with Borden, Silverwood, and Dominion must be added Beatrice Foods, because of its role since 1969, and Weston Limited, which is not chiefly involved in dairy processing but has become an owner of some major 'independent' plants. These five companies appear to have amassed from 50-60 per cent of the fluid milk market in Ontario.[8] Much of the reduction in the number of processing plants since 1961 can be explained in terms of take-overs and centralized ownership patterns rather than plant shut-downs. There were obviously plant shut-downs as well. But a reduction from 1,700 to 800 is too great a phenomenon to have occurred without a concerted campaign of take-overs by the major firms. A partial listing of purchases by three of the major companies in Ontario — Dominion Dairies Limited, Silverwood Limited, and Beatrice Foods Limited — is provided as a sampling of the pattern. With this extent of concentration and reduced competition from smaller firms there was a coincident rise in both the profit-earning picture of the major companies and the retail price of fluid milk in Ontario. In the five-year period from 1968 to 1973, Dominion Dairies' sales went from $62.4 million to $97.5 million, an increase of 55 per cent. Their net profits rose from $1.4 million to $2.51 million, an increase of 79 per cent.

Silverwood Industries enjoyed the same healthy trend from 1968 to 1973 with an increase in sales of 40 per cent from $125 million to $190 million. Profit earnings were less strong over the five-year period because of capital expansion, but in 1973 Silverwood had a 72 per cent increase in profits over 1972.

Throughout this same period milk prices in Ontario increased an average of 50 per cent from 30¢ per quart in 1968 to 45¢ per quart in 1974. 1973 was the year when farmers, pressed by the escalation in feed costs, were finally granted substantial adjustments of 14 per cent in the farm price of milk. But this is also the year when the dairies showed their biggest profit jump in the decade since 1965. Obviously the increased costs of raw milk to them were more than passed on in the price to consumers.

In the six-year period from 1968 to 1974, the price spread from farm to retail widened by roughly 15 per cent. This margin went in substantial measure to improved net earnings but it tended to be described by the National Dairy Council as an increase in packaging and labour costs.[9] In comparing the cost breakdown of a quart of milk in 1961 and 1973 there was a fairly substantial shift from the basic cost of the raw material, i.e. the farm price of milk, toward packaging costs and profit earnings with a slight increase in labour.

The major distinction between corporate influence in the manu-

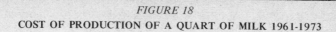

FIGURE 18

COST OF PRODUCTION OF A QUART OF MILK 1961-1973

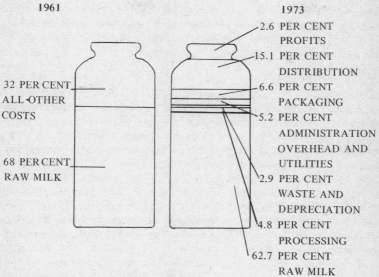

1961   1973

2.6 PER CENT
PROFITS

15.1 PER CENT
DISTRIBUTION

32 PER CENT
ALL OTHER
COSTS

6.6 PER CENT
PACKAGING

5.2 PER CENT
ADMINISTRATION
OVERHEAD AND
UTILITIES

68 PER CENT
RAW MILK

2.9 PER CENT
WASTE AND
DEPRECIATION

4.8 PER CENT
PROCESSING

62.7 PER CENT
RAW MILK

SOURCE: DAIRY STATISTICS ANNUAL

factured milk markets as opposed to fluid milk is that the latter are concentrated on a regional market basis while the former are concentrated on a national and continental basis. In illustrating the tremendous expansion and market concentration of the big three, Silverwood, Dominion (Kraft), and Borden in Ontario, a pattern is suggested for other regions. But in the final analysis each region is distinct in terms of the relative power and concentration of the dominant firms. The specific companies involved vary from one region to another. In Saskatchewan, for example, the dominant firm possessing a majority and near monopoly control of the fluid milk market is Saskatchewan Co-operative Creameries. Their major rival, Palm Dairies, a subsidiary of Burns Foods Limited, is not nearly so influential on provincial milk prices.

The regional character of fluid milk ownership and control patterns reflects the close proximity of markets to production. Once a processing plant has been established and has a working relationship with producers and consumers in an area it is difficult to displace through the usual technique of national brand advertising of an outside product. Fluid milk processing must be located close to its end market, and the major companies such as Kraft and Bordens seem unwilling to risk major investments in such scattered markets as the Atlantic region and prairies.

In Conclusion

The dilemma of public dairy policy in a period of high inflation has been how to avoid price increases in fluid and industrial milk which might cause consumer resistance, while at the same time ensuring enough adjustment in the price returns given farmers to protect them against inflation and discourage them from further cutbacks in production. The government is delicately balanced between milk price levels which might force large numbers of people out of milk consumption and lead once again to a market surplus in milk products and milk price levels which discourage producers and lead to serious shortages and a program of milk rationing. Their 'solution' repeatedly has been to increase prices marginally to producers through direct payment subsidies, thus avoiding undue pressure on the manufacturers to increase their prices. Consumers paid for milk increases indirectly and the processing companies profited handsomely from their ability to increase consumer prices gradually while maintaining cheap sources of supply.

But then came 1973-74, with a rise in dairy production costs which no realistic level of subsidy could possibly absorb. Compromise efforts satisfied neither the intention of avoiding market loss of low income consumers or the production loss of farmers discouraged by marginal returns for a seven day work week. The Whelan gymnastics in and around the federal cabinet couldn't overcome the contradictions facing producers and consumers. And despite the continued record profits of some dairy manufacturers in 1974, notably Kraft Foods, there was no suggestion of direct retail price control through trusteeship or take-over of the industry.

Despite the imperfections and difficulties in the industry which have resulted from public policies over the years, it remains within reach of political solutions for producers. National self-sufficient market protection and production and price controls through state agencies allow for adjustment in the priority of dairy production to encourage and reward producers. This has been something the federal government in particular has been unwilling to do, relegating industrial dairy farmers instead to a secondary status within the agricultural sector which itself is underdeveloped within the economy as a whole.

The consumption problem, that of class and income disparity, which in creating low income deprives people of essentials like adequate food, clothing, and shelter, cannot possibly be solved through dairy policy. It could be alleviated somewhat by more creative and selective forms of dairy subsidies toward school milk programs, rebates to people in regionally exploited consumer markets like northern Canada, and so on. But the present subsidy program, which allows for the protection and flourishing of the multinational agribusiness sector, can only add to the burden of low-income consumers. If it is not directly evident in retail price levels it must show up as taxes. A bloated, high profit manufacturing sector with all its junk foods, additives, expensive advertising, and wasteful packaging simply has to be paid for eventually.

In short, the rise of milk product prices, inevitable under present conditions, could be justified if it did not carry with it the excesses of the present food manufacturing and distribution system. The organized working class and the many people on fixed incomes will have to fight the consumption problem by demanding protections against inflation and declining income. Arresting the returns of producers in sensitive commodities like milk could only compound the problem of poverty.

Notes to Chapter 6

(General background on the dairy industry's history was obtained from the Special Report of the Food Prices Review Board on problems of the dairy industry by the articles of economist Vi McCormick in *Canadian Farm Economics*, and by the Dairy section of the Task Force Report on Agriculture.)

[1.] The staggering figures on the abandonment of dairy operations need qualification. Abandoning milking of cows as a part of farming operations, which is what the 77,000 figure represents over the five-year period from 1966 to 1971, does not mean that all or even most of these farmers went out of farming. Many simply shifted their labour and resources to other commodities because milking cows and shipping cream simply didn't pay for itself. Some of these farmers would only have been milking two or three cows and would not have been a significant factor in production.

[2.] Statistics Canada, *Employment, Earnings and Hours*, No. 72-002, August 1974.

3. Agriculture Canada, "Socio-Economic Study of Quebec Ex-dairy Farmers Whose Milk Quotas were Reallocated in 1967-68 through the Sale of Their Dairy Herd" (unpublished report, 1971).

4. *Dairy Review* (Statistics Canada monthly), No. 23-001.

5. The way these support prices were made operative was through the Agricultural Stabilization Board maintaining a standard 'offer to purchase' at the federal designated price. If the market price was above the designated price the Stabilization Board made no purchases, but if the price fell equal to the floor price the Board would purchase and store butter and cheese as frozen warehouse stocks. These stocks could then be moved back onto the market as prices improved or sold on the export market at a subsidized price.

6. Detailed comparisons of income between the two major categories of milk producers are made difficult by the fact that industrial milk shippers often have income from other sources.

7. James Turner, *The Chemical Feast*, a study into the Food and Drug Administration in the United States and the general decline in standards of food quality.

8. Estimates of concentration in fluid milk markets are made difficult by the extreme city-to-city variation in the number of competitors. What is unmistakeable is the trend toward consolidation through major company purchases of local plants.

9. The National Dairy Council cost claims are broken down in their 1973 submission to the Commons special committee on Trends in Food Prices.

VII

Federal Food Policy: Rotten Eggs and Supply Management

The political responses to the problems of Canadian agriculture and food price inflation have centred quite naturally on the federal government and all its agencies. In the turbulent inflationary period of the mid-1970s verbal confrontations between major sectors of the food industry or consumer groups and/or government are an almost daily occurrence. Co-options and compromises follow. Political parties present their measured differences in formal debate, and even cabinet ministers sometimes divide on aspects of agricultural policy or anti-inflation stop-gaps.

Much of the formal politics has been presented as a producers-vs-consumer polarization. It was therefore natural that Eugene Whelan and Beryl Plumptre should emerge as sometimes-conflicting public figures. Their public jostling came to acquire the air of a comic radio soap opera with regular weekly instalments and a surprisingly long run. Both the government and opposition parties faced internal tensions and splits over the issues at stake.

Behind the formal divisions around farm policy and inflation the reality of government strategy was to maintain a quiet consistency. The narrow role of the state in agriculture and food might expand slightly in response to substantial problems in the economy. But when it did it created shock waves in the system which reverberated back to Ottawa through the economic interest groups and industrial lobbies.

An apparent deviation from the accepted and traditional role of government in agriculture was the expansion of the power of marketing boards in the late 1960s and 1970s. This had the *short-term* effect, in conjunction with other programs, of improving the wealth and advantage of farmers slightly in relationship to agribusiness. This short-term consequence touched off formal political resistance on the part of some agribusiness interests. (The debate which raged around the 'Rotten Egg Scandal' contained elements of such resistance to the marketing board concept.) But in the *long term* this apparent deviation from the traditional role of 'non-intervention' by government could be shown to actually improve the power and wealth advantages of corporate agribusiness over farmers. The broader concept of 'supply management,' of which marketing boards were a part was outlined in the 1969 report of the federal Task Force on Agriculture. Supply management was a concept that included minor short-term irritations to agribusiness and long-term growth and security. For farmers it offered some short-term gains and stability — and long-term insecurity.

A cursory examination of the federal government's track record over the past half-century reveals a consistent pattern in relationship to both agriculture and agribusiness. In more recent years, since 1960, it is a pattern which tied directly into problems of high food prices, declining production, international food shortages, and the growth of monopoly in agribusiness. But the pattern applies to agriculture quite differently from the way it applies to agribusiness. (The relationship to agribusiness is examined in the next chapter.)

In agriculture, where production and ownership are still dominated by individual farmers, the role of government has been one of encouraging production efficiency while allowing 'free market forces' to set year-to-year conditions of product price, levels of farm income, farm production costs, and the decisions about what to produce. While the general role of government has not changed since the early development of an agricultural economy in pre-Confederation Canada, its specific character has altered substantially.

In the early stages of colonization and up to the settlement of western Canada, agriculture was an instrument of colonial policy. It took on importance in the developing political economy far beyond the purely functional role of providing a food staple. Economic historian Vernon Fowke has summarized the colonization role:

> ... first as a means of securing and defending new territory, secondly as a source of provisions for the activity of the great staple trades of fur, timber, and minerals, and finally as the provider of investment opportunities in the agricultural frontier.[1]

The ulterior purposes for agriculture extended beyond Confederation and became integral to John A. Macdonald's National Policy. The advent of mechanized farming in the late nineteenth century greatly improved the potential of agriculture as a provider of investment opportunities. Western settlement and the development of the wheat economy were essential to the success of the Pacific railway venture and to the concept of Confederation itself.

From 1880 to 1930, federal policies toward agriculture were aimed at fulfilling the objectives of national policy in general. The package of programs included the Dominion Land Act to provide free land to immigrant settlers in the northwest, as well as the development of agricultural research stations to discover new crop varieties and experiment with dry-land methods of farming. The federal government was prepared to help establish farmers, provide them with research and information to improve their production capacity, and regulate market conditions to the extent necessary to maintain political stability. The federal government established preferential freight rates on grain, provided for honest weights and measures legislation and so on. As has been pointed out in earlier chapters on dairy, beef, and cereals, this role of government as the 'arm's-length' regulator of production and marketing conditions has gradually been expanded, but never to the extent of totally removing the influence of free market forces on the price to farmers.

Settlement of the west and the creation of the grains economy was completed by about 1930. The overriding strategic objective of national agricultural policies was met. The jurisdiction of the land resource was turned over to the provinces and the federal government fell into a pattern of ad-hoc policies. Moving from crisis to crisis with the political winds, federal politicians operated in a boom-and-bust environment, always reacting to the conditions created by the free market economy. The situation from 1930 on was summarized in the Agricultural Institute of 1960:

> Canadian farm policy since 1930, with the single exception of a consistent effort to discover and promote improved technology in farm production, has been largely one of providing expedient measures to meet crises of depression, drought, war, inflation and surpluses. Farm policy objectives have not been clearly established or pursued. There is little evidence that Canada has had any overall national policy based on clear thinking and economic and sociological researched facts.

The existence of a national farm policy prior to 1930 was based on the importance of agricultural development to national economic priorities of trade, investment, and railway construction. It had nothing particularly to do with the welfare of farmers and their communities. The difference after 1930, then, involved no change of priorities toward farmers whose political influence had always been secondary. The real change was in terms of the relatively decreasing importance of agriculture to the rest of the economy. Basic food production was in a very real sense taken for granted.

The absence of consistent approaches to farm issues or an overall strategy did not mean that those policies which were adopted were unimportant. The impact of ad-hoc programs from 1930 to 1970 was overwhelming, particularly after World War II. The process of change arising from the cost-price squeeze on farming (discussed in Chapter 2), was encouraged and facilitated by federal programs. An example was the decision to extend low-interest farm credit through the creation of a Farm Credit Corporation in the 1950s. This encouraged the trend toward capitalization of agriculture through land and equipment purchases. In the absence of market stability, farmers were encouraged to produce more volume and accumulate debts for the sake of ultimate efficiency. The efficiency gains were then absorbed in the non-farm sector by banks, mortgage companies, and manufacturers of farm inputs.

The conscious decision to avoid certain policies was of equal significance in determining the direction and fate of rural society. For example, with the exception of the Canadian Wheat Board, there was avoidance of marketing policies at the national level. Land policies at both federal and provincial levels were restricted to special projects such as those of the Agriculture and Rural Development Act (ARDA) passed in 1961.

Government intervention in agriculture was parallel to the role of government generally in this period. The apparent but unstated assumption was that the acknowledged economic problems of a large number of farmers were caused by *individual* management failures and, on occasion, natural disasters. Government initiatives were reduced to a broad concept of welfare and rehabilitation. Programs such as the Prairie Farm Assistance Act (PFAA) and the Prairie Farm Rehibilitation Act (PFRA) were born in the depression of the 1930s. The PFAA provided minimum insurance against natural crop disaster, while the PFRA was a funding and development agency for land reclamation, irrigation, dams and dug-outs on farms. These programs, plus ARDA in 1961, typified government philosophy. ARDA aimed to shift land use patterns in marginal and subsistence farming areas by developing community pastures to displace small farms, and to encourage water conservation and soil improvement programs.

All of these programs were positive, but extremely limited in their overall impact. They assumed implicitly that unproductive land use or the threat of drought were the main enemies of the farmer. In reality, the long-term economic problems of farmers stemmed firstly from their specific market relationship to agribusiness and secondly from land tenure policies based on competitive private ownership.

ARDA, with its allocation of $25 million, could make little impact on the problems of low-income farmers no matter how creatively it was applied. It came under critical attack from agricultural economists for being hopelessly inadequate, yet it was the jewel of Diefenbaker agricultural policy. Agricultural economist Helen Buckley writes:

> The farm assistance policies advanced by ARDA are remarkable for their tendency to evade the question of what might constitute a solution for marginal farm units. . . . To a considerable degree ARDA project selection has been shaped by a widely held contention that improvements in land use and the development of soil and water resources are the appropriate measures for raising rural incomes. . . . Failure to devote attention to the labour, managerial and capital inputs of the farm business is critical. . . . The fragmented empirical evidence, as well as logical analysis, suggests that few of the ARDA investments in land and water would satisfy either the minimum criterion of economic efficiency or the goal of income redistribution in favour of the poor.[2]

The failure or conscious refusal to intervene in the conditions creating the cost-price squeeze brought the federal government under increasing criticism through the 1960s. The rapid accumulation of farm land and machinery debts, coupled with the collapse of the international grain market in the late 1960s, brought Trudeaumania skidding to a halt somewhere west of Winnipeg. By 1969, thousands of farmers in the prairies were taking to the highways in militant tractor-demonstrations. Trudeau was pelted with wheat as he spoke to mass rallies in Regina and Saskatoon in July 1969. Other regional focuses for protest involved dairy farmers in Ontario and potato farmers in Prince Edward Island, all caught in variations of the cost-price squeeze.

It was in this climate that the federal government unveiled a new phase of Canadian agricultural policy. It was not a new 'national policy' and it did not abandon the non-interventionist doctrine of free market capitalism. But it did set out some longer-term objectives for agricultural policy, and it introduced the concept of supply management. Supply management became the rationale for the exercise of government influence over production and markets.

The umbrella for new policy formation was provided by the report of a federal government Task Force. It produced a document entitled *Canadian Agriculture in the 70s* which became within weeks of its (1969) publication the most politically significant statement in the history of Canadian agriculture. It was to be discussed and debated by farmers, agribusiness management, and politicians throughout the next two years. It became the basis of most major agricultural policy since it was published and its assumptions and biases are critical to an understanding of the food crisis as it developed in the 1970s.

From the outset, the Task Force faced some heavy opposition

from farmers and their spokesmen. To begin with, producers were unhappy about the composition of the Commission, which consisted of four academics, a chartered accountant, and no farmers.[3] But the more basic political reaction was to the substance of the 460-page report. The assumptions of the Task Force were summarized in their Introductory section:

1) The surpluses must be controlled and reduced to manageable proportions by reducing production drastically if necessary. . . . Where alternative [market opportunities] cannot be found land and other resources must be retired.

2) Governments should provide assistance for crop switching and land retirement, necessary to cut production.

3) Agricultural subsidies and price supports should be phased out (where they are not achieving high priority objectives).

4) Younger non-viable farmers should be moved out of farming through temporary programs of welfare, education, and provision of jobs in other sectors, older farmers should be given assistance to ensure a "livable" standard of living.

5) Farm management skills should be improved through training programs etc.

6) Organizational structure of agriculture in government and private sector should be rationalized to incorporate program planning, cost-benefit analysis, etc.

Canadian Agriculture in the 70s was aimed at streamlining the agricultural sector only. It had no comment on the role or efficiency of non-farm agribusiness except to say that its general level of profits were fair at 10 per cent or less. Its authors failed to acknowledge any conflict between the objectives of farmers and agribusiness. They made no study of land tenure or the problems in the unrestricted private ownership of farmland. They did observe that government should avoid any curbs or interference in the encroachment of agribusiness directly into farming:

Agribusiness has a useful and legitimate role in securing the requirements of farmers and should be considered an integral part of the agricultural industry. . . . Translating this principle of non-interference to the question of vertical integration implies that governments would take no continuing action to promote or prohibit vertical integration by agribusiness.[4]

The Task Force in general reinforced the traditional role of the state under capitalist ownership, recommending only those adjustments necessary for improved efficiency. Their conclusions on farmers were contradictory. On the one hand, farmers were judged collectively inefficient because they failed to fully apply available technology. To become more efficient their numbers would have to be reduced. Yet in seeming contradiction the federal report also proposed curbs on production through supply management, thereby indicating in a real sense that farmers were too efficient.

The Task Force was telling the Canadian people in 1969 that Canada had too many farmers producing too much produce of the wrong kind. Task Force members were calling on government leadership to cut production, convert to new markets and retire some agricultural resources. They also advised government to refrain from direct involvement by way of subsidies and tariffs, preferring to let the forces of supply and demand take their necessary toll. The necessary toll, in the estimation of the Task Force, included reduction of farm population from 9 to 3 per cent of the Canadian total by 1990.

This projection and some others made the report a major political organizing focus for the National Farmers Union throughout 1970, 1971 and 1972. The battle cry of opposition was that the blueprint of federal farm policy called for elimination of two-thirds of the farmers from the land. The federal government tried to bury the more direct long-term projections of the Task Force and denied that the document was in any way official government policy. But the hapless Bud Olson, former minister of agriculture defeated in the 1972 election, was unsuccessful in disassociating himself from the report.

It wasn't easy for farmers or anyone else to avoid the conclusion that Task Force recommendations were indeed the blueprint of government policy. The major thrust of the Report's recommendations in grain, dairy, and livestock policy were identifiable from 1970 on in new federal programs. The recommendation for retirement of land from wheat production was followed in 1970 by the Lower Inventories for Tomorrow program (or LIFT). This program paid grants to farmers of $6 per acre to leave normally productive wheat land in fallow. The Task Force recommended conversion of cereal land to grass and the federal government adopted a grassland conversion program. The Task Force called for an end to subsidy-type programs which would enable producers to continue to produce wheat in times of surplus. The federal government obliged in 1971 by withdrawing the Temporary Wheat Reserves Act and the Prairie Farm Agricultural Assistance Act. (The TWRA had allowed for payments to farmers for wheat stocks which had been delivered to elevators but were not yet sold on the export market, while the PFAA was a protection against losses from total crop disasters through minimum acreage payments.)

The supply management concept, as proposed by *Canadian Agriculture in the 70s* and adopted by federal measures, applied to the national priorities of cutting back the 'surpluses' in dairy and wheat production after 1969. The success of federal initiatives has already been discussed in relation to each of grains, beef, and milk products in previous chapters. Their impact and consequence can be summarized briefly. In wheat production, acreage was reduced from a high of 30 million acres in 1966-67 to an average of less than 20 million in the four years from 68-69 to 72-73. This contributed to reduction in world wheat stocks in 1974-75 to their lowest point in twenty-five years. In dairy production, Canada moved from a surplus to a deficit between 1969 and 1973, importing butter substantially for the first time since the 1920s. In both of these commodities (dairy products and wheat), conversion to beef production was encouraged and the productive capacity of Canadian beef herds increased by 40 per cent from 1969 to 1974.

None of these planned shifts in production patterns was directly controlled by federal agencies. The basis of supply management was indirect, through incentive grants, subsidies, production and marketing quotas, and so on. But the results were dramatic, and closely linked to the problems which faced the agriculture and food system by the mid-1970s. The Task Force projections of a constantly expanding beef market and a falling market for cereal grains proved to be in serious error. The expansion of beef production, encouraged by federal and provincial governments, helped ensure a shortage in cereal grains as increasing acreage had to be converted to animal feed grains.

Some developments of the period from 1973 onwards could not have been fully anticipated by the Task Force authors or the government leaders who adopted their proposals. But the mathematics involved in red meat production, with its high energy costs vs. cereal production for human consumption, *were* known, even in 1969. Projections by the United Nations Food and Agricultural Organization (FAO), made in 1967 and referred to by the Task Force, suggested a world food shortage in the 1970s. They projected a shortage of wheat by 1975 would range from 18 million to 43 million tons. This was the difference between estimates for world wheat production (219 to 242.8 million tons) and world consumption (260.6 to 262.6 million tons).

Despite knowledge of projected world shortages of human cereals, the Task Force called for *less* cereal production in Canada and more cereal consumption through livestock feeding. The federal government accepted the recommendations. What was first charted up as a mathematical short-fall in world food needs became in reality a part of the formula for starvation in the Third World. The Task Force in 1969 raised this prospect as an academic consideration and then dismissed it, knowing that Third World markets couldn't be calculated as part of 'effective demand.'

It is tempting, but not useful, to moralize about the evil and insensitivity of bureaucrats and policy-makers who consciously direct vital food resources to the already overfed markets of Europe, North America and Japan. But for the Task Force authors, the relevant markets to be calculated in agricultural planning had no direct relationship to human need. The international food system, of which Canadian agriculture was and is a part, was organized for profit. 'Effective demand,' or the ability to pay cash or arrange trade, is the demand to which the market responds, and for which resources are planned. 'Human need' is an immeasurable market concept in profit terms and is left to the conscience and limited resources of international welfare agencies such as those attached to the United Nations.

The Whelan Package: Supply Management and the Marketing Board Concept 1970-75

A flexible interpretation of supply management allowed for a range of tactics by government. While the Task Force tended to de-emphasize the use of marketing boards or other such direct public agencies to influence production levels and prices, this was one area of supply management to which farmers generally lent their support. For some perishable commodities in which the market was primarily domestic, such as milk, eggs, and poultry, the need to co-ordinate production and markets between provinces was evident. Marketing boards had long existed at the provincial level, some dating back to the 1930s.

Eugene Whelan was able to take the concept of markeing boards and use it as the wedge to gain increasing farmer support for federal policies after 1972. Many of the Whelan-supported policies were in line with the original Task Force recommendations so strongly rejected by farmer organizations. But with a focus on marketing boards and a renewed prosperity in some sectors of agriculture, federal policies were more easily and painlessly swallowed after 1972.

Liberal election promises in 1972 and 1974 gave prominence to programs of farm-income stabilization, extension of marketing boards under the National Farm Products Marketing Act (NFPMA, passed in 1972), and cost of living adjustments. In general they pledged to ensure that farm product prices would be adjusted to cover inflation in areas where the government had set 'floor price' guarantees such as in dairy products.

Unfortunately for Whelan, as the main spokesman for the new supply management package, agriculture policies which corresponded in time to a galloping increase in the retail price of food products were likely to be criticized as central to the problem of inflation itself. (Conversely, this coincidence of new farm policy and rising prices on farm products went far to making Whelan's pronouncements and programs popular with farmers.) This fact shaped the character of discussion around the fledgling farm products marketing authorities set up for eggs and turkeys under the NFPMA.

The Whelan package enjoyed farmer support to a degree un-matched by Liberal policies since Agriculture minister Jimmy Gardiner dominated rural politics in the 1940s and early 1950s. The Liberals actually gained seats in 1974 in the Tory strongholds of rural Ontario and the prairie provinces, although they still held a minority in each. But the popularity of Whelan policy and rhetoric was counter-balanced by the bitter opposition of consumer groups, liberal 'free market' economists, and the Food Prices Review Board. These combined influences, along with the occasional agribusiness spokes-man, took aim on marketing boards as a central factor in rising food prices.

The theoretical basis of attack on marketing boards by economists was attached to an assumption about the competitive nature of the overall North American economy. They had an abhorrence for all monopolies, but only appeared to recognize those set up through legislation. One such critic, J.D. Forbes, a U.B.C. business economist, did a major report on the subject of Canadian agriculture policy for the Consumer Council of Canada. His major attack was reserved for marketing boards, which he said were costing consumers millions of dollars in inflated farm product prices.

The general attack on marketing boards appeared to ignore the double standard that exists between farmers and agribusiness. The farmer has no power over costs or income while agribusiness, organ-ized into oligopolies, administers its selling price and has strong influence over the cost it faces for raw material supplies. In these circumstances farmers require defensive protection of the minimum sort offered by marketing boards in order to survive. Larger farmers, like Whelan, who are fundamentally supporters of the capitalist system of ownership and production, look to marketing boards to provide them with the same market security and returns on capital investment as enjoyed by the non-farm monopolies. Smaller producers resent their erratic financial position and poor working conditions and tend to view marketing boards as their equivalent to trade unions.

But marketing boards, while necessary for farmer protection, are themselves inadequate to the task. They protect farmers on one side of the cost-price squeeze only. This means that the farm-supply sector could pass on unwarranted and exaggerated price increases for machinery and supplies with the safe knowledge that these costs to farmers would in turn be passed on by marketing boards in higher farm product prices. This was one of the observations made by J.D. Forbes and other economists in arguing that marketing boards result in constantly rising prices in farm products with no net gain to the farmer but highly inflated food prices. This argument recognizes that the farm supply oligopolies are capable of setting prices to farmers unrelated to their costs of manufacturing. But having recognized this tendency there is no conclusion that the major fault in the system lies with the unchallenged power of oligopolies in farm supply industries to administer their prices. Instead, farm product marketing boards are concluded to be the problem and the solution lies in a return to the 'free market.'

The difference between industrial oligopolies and marketing boards is that the oligopolies have no formal legal recognition for their collective pricing practices and are therefore unrecognized as being in contradiction to free market capitalism. But marketing boards are legislated and publicly accountable, and therefore fair game for critics.[5]

The essence of 'free market' criticism is that open market competition should be made to prevail among farmers so that only the largest and most efficient could survive. J.D. Forbes, like the Task Force economists, expressed the view that far too many farmers were being maintained on marginal units through subsidies or administered prices for milk, eggs, or cereal grains. The logic that eliminating farmers would cut down costs and improve efficiency rests on an assumption that 'pure competition' among farmers somehow weakens or discourages farm supply agencies from over-pricing their manufactured goods. There is no evidence that this has been the case. Oligopolies advance their prices whether or not farmers have marketing boards.

It is also not clear that the response of farmers who are unable to compete in the market because of their small size is to actually leave agriculture. Their response often is to retain their small holdings and await retirement. They continue in perpetual poverty but avoid the hostile environment and expense of a move into the city.

The key to analysis of the Whelan package lies in the separation of short-term and long-term implications. The short-term objective is one favourable to farmers but of less clear advantage to either agribusiness or consumers of food on the domestic and international markets. The short-term objective Whelan sets out is to eliminate the factor of underdevelopment characterized by depressed and erratic farm incomes, production declines and the wasteful conversion of farmland to other purposes. By stabilizing gross farm income through the techniques of supply management and guaranteed prices, the federal government hopes to guarantee future food supplies and stabilize consumer prices for food (albeit at a much higher price than characterized the 1960s). By integrating farmers as participants in the monopoly system of administered prices and markets, government strategists are clearly seeking a trade-off. They will tolerate the political consequences of higher food prices in return for the political advantages of future stability of supplies of food.

If Whelan were to succeed in developing more effective producer marketing boards, farmers would be able to float with the inflation imposed on them by rising costs of farm supplies. Rather than be trapped by the cost-price squeeze, they could continuously advance farm product prices through their power over marketing boards. For the first time in their history of relations with the organized market system of capitalism, farmers would potentially be in a position to enforce and enjoy profit return on capital invested equal to the non-farm sector.

Success in implementing of the short-term strategy remains in doubt. It has not advanced very far and is running into a strong resistance from two different quarters: agribusiness and consumer groups. From the point of view of some areas of agribusiness, the new strategy is an annoying disturbance in a relationship they have long enjoyed with producers. In the traditional relationship, *they* establish the price which farmers will receive; farmers accept it or quit farming. From the point of view of consumer groups and anti-poverty organizations, the development of farmer-controlled monopolies is just one more example of how they will be exploited through inflation. In attacking farmers they are aiming at the weakest and most movable part of the system. The larger system of monopoly capitalism remains intact no matter what happens to farmers' efforts at stability. By undermining farm marketing boards, consumer groups may achieve some savings for the system (not necessarily for themselves), but in the process they may help to destroy a group of small capitalists who are also productive workers in their own right.

Depending on the results of short-term strategy on marketing boards, the long-term implications are more profound. The politics surrounding the marketing board (or supply management) debate involves an unholy alliance between agribusiness and consumerists on the one hand and farmers on the other. Ironically, one of the longer-term effects of marketing boards may be to stabilize profits in agriculture sufficiently that it becomes more attractive for agribusiness to take over farming directly. From the capitalist point of view such a trend may not only be attractive but necessary in order to eliminate the farmer as an independent middleman who has become too powerful. The pattern is already well advanced in some commodities where a sizable proportion of production is done on vertically-integrated corporate farms.

The long-term dangers of marketing boards will not discourage farmers from supporting them in the immediate context as a progressive and necessary step. Ultimately the protection against monopoly encroachment into ownership of land and production facilities in farming will depend on collective, alternative approaches to farm production as discussed in Chapter 10.

The Rotten Egg Scandal

The debate around marketing boards became one of the livelier features of Ottawa politics in 1974. The focus of discussion became the Canadian Egg Marketing Agency (CEMA) which was the first national marketing authority established under the 1972 NFPMA. The CEMA debate served to illustrate the problems and relative powerlessness of marketing boards as allowed for by NFPMA, and the intensity of consumer feeling about food waste and inflation.

The issue of national egg marketing has been hotly contested since the mid-1960s through a series of 'chicken and egg wars' between the major producing provinces. Although all provinces had marketing boards which aimed at stabilizing production levels and prices within provincial markets, they tended to overlook the dumping by their producers of surplus eggs at lower prices into the markets of other provinces. Conflicts between provinces went to the Supreme Court, which ruled that no province had the power to restrict interprovincial trade from other provinces. A council of representatives from the marketing agencies from each province was established to mediate disputes and co-ordinate interprovincial trade. It was ineffective, usually unable to agree on conditions of trade and price, and always unable to enforce what it could agree on.

Finally, in June 1973, following hearings of producers, and under the conditions of the National Farm Products Marketing Act, CEMA was established. Its role was to set overall national quotas for eggs in conjunction with provincial marketing boards and to stabilize prices by maintaining a minimum floor price for eggs. CEMA would directly purchase any surplus eggs from provincial marketing boards at a price calculated to cover the costs of production. These eggs, generally *destined for processing*, would either be sold into other provincial markets, sold to egg processors directly, sold to export customers, or provided as food aid by the federal government.

The major problem for CEMA at the outset was that, while it could levy a producer quota based on calculations of the market, it had no power to enforce it. Provincial marketing boards administered quotas for egg producers and also set prices for the wholesale price of eggs within the province. This meant CEMA was faced with a variation in market prices across the country. More critically, it meant reliance for enforcement of quotas on provincial agencies which were not all prepared or willing to perform the task. In Ontario (the province most other provinces pointed to as a source of overproduction), there had been no quota applied prior to CEMA. With the knowledge that CEMA would mean quotas to regulate production, Ontario producers expanded their flocks in 1973 prior to CEMA starting. Statistics Canada figures indicate Ontario's population of laying hens increased by 130,000 in 1973 over 1972 while the country as a whole was down by 120,000. This contributed to a national surplus in 1974. The annual quota projection of 5.7 billion dozen eggs nationally was surpassed by 340 million.[6]

CEMA was faced with another problem within its first months of operation. With a sharp rise in feed grain prices, which went from $60 per ton in 1972 to $150 by late 1973, they were forced to sharply increase the offering price for eggs to keep ahead of costs of production. The higher price, combined with more surplus eggs than they expected, forced them to go into debt to the federal government first by $6 million, and (by fall 1974) $10 million. This cost would be repaid by a levy to producers which was increased to 6¢ per dozen by fall 1974.

Observers to the situation, notably the Food Prices Review Board, pointed out problems with CEMA from the consumer's standpoint. In January 1974 the Board reported that provinces were under-reporting their production to avoid quota restrictions when in reality production was accelerating, stimulated by the prices offered by CEMA for surplus eggs. Mrs. Plumptre recommended cuts in CEMA price offerings, greater control over the provinces to enforce quotas, and the inclusion of consumer representatives and processor representatives on the CEMA board. The same observations and recommendations were repeated in the August 1974 report of the FPRB when the issue had become more heated. By that time Eugene Whelan's response to Mrs. Plumptre minced no words: "Hogwash. . . . She has a lot to learn about the egg industry. . . . She had better get her facts straight or I will get out my axe," said Whelan.

Mrs. Plumptre was not the only vocal critic. In August 1974 Maryon Brechin, former president of the Consumers Association of Canada, described the strategy of CEMA as one of ". . . establishing a high price for eggs, keeping the prices high by restricting supply through quotas, and eliminating competition by banning lower-priced imports from the United States." (Her reference to imports arises from a decision of the federal government in May 1974 to restrict

U.S. imports under the Import and Export Permits Act. American egg prices were below Canada's and threatened to force down the Canadian price. The restriction aimed at maintaining imports at roughly the average of previous years, so that the U.S. could not engage in dumping practices. This policy was administered through the Department of Agriculture and had nothing directly to do with CEMA. It was in effect from May to September 1974 when it was lifted because of rising prices in the U.S. market. By early October the federal government announced controls on the export of eggs as a measure to prevent dumping of Canadian eggs into the U.S. This was seen as a consumer protection measure to avoid possible egg shortages and higher prices in Canada.)

All of the points and counter-points in the egg marketing debate went largely unnoticed by the Canadian media from January to August 1974. Then suddenly the issue, though essentially unchanged, caught fire in terms of publicity and held the nation's headlines for much of the next four months. The reason was the revelation in late August, confirmed ironically by CEMA's Toronto public relations firm, that CEMA had been forced to destroy 9 million eggs which had been kept in apple warehouses in Quebec until they had gone rotten. Then it was discovered another 3 million had been destroyed in Ontario and finally 28 million eggs was established as the extent of CEMA losses.

Rotten egg jokes came into vogue and a call went out for Eugene Whelan's resignation as the minister responsible. This demand was made by David Archer, president of the Ontario Federation of Labour, and echoed by opposition party spokesmen in Ottawa. Both Consumer and Corporate Affairs Minister André Ouellet and his ousted predecessor Herb Gray had criticism of CEMA management. They also criticized Whelan's uncritical defence of the agency. Newspaper editorials denounced the destruction of surplus eggs in a starving world.

Whelan's first response was to become belligerent. He lashed out at Beryl Plumptre and all the "instant experts" who had surfaced in the debate. He explained the egg over-production which CEMA had been facing was due to an "overnight" evaporation of the export market in the United States. He pointed out that the whole loss was less than one day's production and would be paid for out of producers' pockets. He said it wouldn't cost the Canadian tax-payer "a damn cent", unlike other industries like auto or steel where overproduction results in lay-offs which the public must support through the unemployment insurance fund. And finally Whelan argued that since the price had dropped six per cent between January and September the consumer had no business complaining. (Critics had been emphasizing the 37 per cent increase in 1973.) According to Whelan, the price of eggs to farmers was up only six cents a dozen since 1951. "If André Ouellet or anybody thinks he can lower the price of eggs any lower than they are at the present time we just won't have any eggs," said Whelan.

As the opposition and outrage continued throughout September, CEMA and Whelan combined began to construct a more positive image for the agency. They began with an announcement that $1.3 million worth of eggs (40 million dozen) would be forwarded to the World Food Plan as foreign aid. This brought the total foreign aid package to $2.5 million in eggs. But critics continued to press as new information was revealed. Jeffrey Rubenstein of Export Packers, largest egg processor in the country and an outspoken opponent of the marketing board concept, made a public estimate of egg losses as being up to 200 million. This was picked up, widely reported, and re-used in editorials, but never confirmed as having any substance in fact. A Toronto exporter, Rexim International, said CEMA should not have had to destroy 28 million eggs. They earlier had rejected Rexim's offer to purchase 50 million eggs for an order in Austria because the agency felt the price offered was too low. (Whelan later claimed the price offered was below cost and would have amounted to Canadian dumping of eggs on the international market contrary to the provisions of the General Agreement on Tariffs and Trade (GATT).) The long-standing demand for consumer representatives on national marketing boards was renewed by the Consumer Association, The Prices Review Board, and André Ouellet. There was also a demand for a parliamentary investigation into the whole issue.

By October, with the opening of Parliament, Whelan had begun to wilt under pressure. In the Throne Speech debate, he pleaded for the supply management concept, now threatened with extinction even in the limited and crude form which CEMA represented. First he tried to illustrate the practical problems of CEMA and egg producers, which were unlike those of any other industry. "Did you ever try to turn a chicken off? You just can't turn him off!" Then he tried to appeal to the sense of national purpose embodied in national marketing agencies which ". . . come closer to the spirit of Confederation than almost any other institution." And finally he compromised. He agreed now with the proposal for "consumer, labour," representation on national marketing agencies while expressing the hope that farmers would then sit on the CNR board, Air Canada, the CBC, and the Canadian Transport Commission. He also agreed with the Prime Minister's announcement of a full parliamentary inquiry on which he reflected, "I don't feel the truth has been told by hardly anyone at all."

Whelan had reason to be concerned about the attacks on the marketing board concept. As the hearings were initiated on CEMA by the parliamentary committee of fourteen, the opposition to marketing boards began to move in for the kill. The hearings began the last week in October and ran until early December. They revealed the obvious mismanagement and the frustration of a public agency with a large mandate and no power, and they revealed a few surprises. Whelan had been right that "hardly anyone at all" had been telling the truth and that included him. Early in the hearings the strategy seemed to be for CEMA officials to take the full blame and chalk it all up to growing pains. They were quick to deny that producers were to blame for over-producing (knowing they would need producer support). They placed the emphasis instead on international market conditions, particularly the U.S. market which was underpriced relative to Canada and difficult to sell to unless at a loss. Whelan said in testimony October 30 that he didn't know about the rotten eggs until July when they were discovered (though not made public until late August). He "was aware early in the spring that CEMA was building up heavy surpluses and debts." In later testimony on November 22, Whelan admitted that "early in the spring" was more like December 1973 when reports were made to him by the National Farm Products Marketing Board outlining the problems of CEMA in some detail. He said he instructed the Board to "try to do something about it." Clearly Whelan was negligent in responding to the problems which were dragging down CEMA, especially when he had so often proclaimed his commitment to the implementation of orderly marketing.

Aside from Whelan's personal failings, which he largely admitted on November 22, the significance of the hearings lay in the efforts of the agribusiness opponents of CEMA to discredit it. In this task they were aided by at least one of the provincial marketing boards (B.C.) as well as Herb Gray and Conservative members of the Commons committee which conducted the inquiry.

Max Rubenstein, president of Export Packers, testified that CEMA had tried to dump eggs, sight unseen, on major Canadian processors in July. He said CEMA called a meeting for July 19 in Ottawa to offer to processors 54 million eggs at 25-27¢ a dozen, well below the normal price of 40¢. He claimed that it was only when the processors insisted they be inspected under the requirements of interprovincial trade (the eggs were to move from Quebec to Ontario plants), that the original discovery of rotten eggs was made. Rubenstein implied by his testimony that CEMA officials were aware they had rotten eggs but tried to unload them anyway. He felt the processors had the last laugh because they got the remaining good eggs at bargain-basement prices.

Rubenstein's plants in Ontario and Manitoba produce 50-60 per cent of the 1.7 billion eggs processed annually into powdered eggs, shampoo and other products in Canada. He has a big stake in attaining cheap processing eggs as do the other members of the Canadian Egg and Poultry Council whom he was representing at the hearings in Ottawa.

In his testimony Rubenstein reported that CEMA had refused to sell him eggs earlier in the year even though they had a surplus building up. He had arranged to buy about $500,000 worth of eggs at 36¢ per dozen to be exported for powder in plants in Holland, Germany, and England. CEMA refused to sell to him because the domestic price was 42¢. He quipped, "I guess they were worried I would make a profit."

Rather than pay the going price as established by CEMA, a price 20¢ *below* the cost of production, Rubenstein chose to close down his Manitoba and Ontario plants a number of times. Eventually he said he bought eggs at a price of 44¢ because he didn't want to lose his workers. The attitude displayed by processers who assume that *they* should name the price even though they are buying rather than selling underlines the long-standing assumptions which agribusiness in all commodities holds toward producers. Clearly Rubenstein was pushing to smash even a weak marketing agency like CEMA because it violated the assumed rights of his company. For years he and other processors had profited from egg suppliers at whatever price they chose, usually less than half the costs of production to the farmer.

Another key witness at the hearings was J.D. Forbes, the UBC business economist who in 1974 presented a report to the Consumer Council of Canada. Consistent with the approach of his earlier report, Forbes attacked with enthusiasm the restrictions on pure competition implicit in marketing boards. He suggested if it were any group but farmers conducting monopoly pricing practices they would be thrown into jail for anti-combines practices. He pointed to his own province, where the B.C. Egg Marketing Board was enforcing a maximum farm size of 15,000 birds and argued that "larger" units would be more efficient and reduce costs. Apparently for Forbes the consolidation process is never-ending and will lead inevitably to the development of fully integrated factory farms as the dominant scale of production unit.

Forbes in his testimony did see CEMA for the pathetic half-creature that it was. He suggested it could only be saved if it had effective monopoly control over production and price *or* if it was disbanded in favour of open market competition among the provinces. Directly ruling out the extension of monopoly state powers he added that he "favoured as little government control as possible." There is little doubt that his views found support among the Liberal and Conservative committee members.

The final significant testimony was provided by the provincial marketing board spokesmen who were generally supportive of CEMA despite (or perhaps because of) their intense rivalry with each other. They suggested the problems that CEMA faced were not due to domestic over-production so much as the increased flow of American imports in the January-May 1974 period before federal restrictions were finally applied. Bob Rose of the Manitoba Egg Marketing Board claimed 52 million eggs were imported during the period when Canadian production exceeded demand. He claimed that Manitoba was actually 15 per cent below their allocated quota in 1973-74 but because of imports still had surplus eggs to ship to Alberta, Ontario, and Quebec.

If the provincial boards generally were well disposed toward CEMA they were far from unanimous. The B.C. Egg Marketing Board announced during the hearings that it had given notice of withdrawal from CEMA effective January 1976. (Provinces were required to give notice a year in advance of leaving.) As a major producing and consuming province, a split by B.C. seriously reduced the possibility of even a meek national marketing agency like CEMA surviving. The split occured despite the fact that the B.C. board's secretary manager was the full-time general manager of CEMA from January to August 1974. Ed Morgan, engaged with CEMA when all the trouble occurred, was openly hostile to CEMA during the hearings in November '74. Morgan also agreed under questioning that B.C. is opposed still as it has always been to CEMA and that it is "deliberately producing in excess" of allocated quotas and searching out foreign markets on its own. The B.C. egg board claims CEMA owes it more than $450,000 and is withholding its levy, from producer check-offs. (CEMA officials claim they only owe B.C. $25,000.) Mr. Morgan indicated the provincial body will probably take legal action against CEMA in an effort to end the dispute.

By the end of the hearings it was clear that CEMA had lost ground on its own behalf and on behalf of other commodity groups like turkey, chicken, and hog producers having or anticipating a national marketing authority. It almost didn't matter that the Liberal majority on the committee offered a low-key knuckle-rapping report on the egg scandal while formally sparing CEMA the knife. It was apparent that B.C. producers were themselves inclined toward the task of doing the agency in. They were followed a month later by the Newfoundland Egg Marketing Board, who also announced their withdrawal effective February 1, 1976.

The CEMA rotten egg scandal was not simply an issue of egg marketing. It was a test of relations between producers and the market generally, with as much application to other poultry commodities, dairy, livestock, and grains. The conflict between producers and agribusiness over short-term objectives was represented by CEMA and the egg processing industry. But the egg processors or 'breakers' are not typical of agribusiness. They are small in relation to most agribusiness interests and they were at the time of the CEMA hearings not integrated into basic egg production. Their fortunes depended on their monopoly advantage as the sole market for an extremely perishable commodity, i.e. surplus 'table eggs' about to go rotten. The creation of CEMA as a pricing mechanism meant they would be expected to pay a minimum price. (This minimum price set by CEMA was itself well below the cost of production to farmers.) As single-level agribusiness, Export Packers could gain no benefit from farm marketing boards. Canada Packers or other major integrated firms could easily expand into farm factories to share the price stability of marketing boards, but Rubenstein and his smaller rivals had to count on defeating the marketing board concept through whatever tactics were at their disposal. The difference is simply that large agribusiness can tolerate marketing boards in the short-term and exploit them to advantage in the long-term. Smaller agribusiness will 'suffer' in relation to their previous open market advantage in both the short term and the long term.

The tactics of the egg processors effectively sabotaged the CEMA concept. They first used imported eggs from the United States to cause a build-up of surplus in Canada so that CEMA would be forced to lower their price of 'breaker' eggs. CEMA continued to store eggs rather than give in and drop the price. Eventually the federal government was persuaded in May to restrict the import of eggs from the U.S. but the move was about four months too late.

Secondly, the processors, still refusing to buy from CEMA at CEMA prices, actually closed their plants down, hoping to break the price floor. This added to the CEMA held surplus. The normal market for Canadian surplus eggs was taken away from CEMA by a boycott of Canadian processors. Finally, CEMA was forced to lower their prices because they discovered that eggs were spoiling in inadequate temporary storage. The processors once again were getting eggs for as low as 25¢ per dozen and CEMA was faced with defending itself in a major political scandal.

In Retrospect

The outside critics of CEMA, including Mrs. Plumptre, Maryon Brechin (former president of the Consumers Association), and Herb Gray, charged that CEMA was offering farmers too high a price for surplus eggs. This, they claimed, had the effect of over-stimulating production. But this alleged oversupply of eggs did not have the usual supply-demand effect of decreasing the wholesale and retail price of eggs. The price level of eggs should have been allowed to collapse in a market glut according to the logic of this position.

This argument assumes that supply and demand forces should be left unchallenged in agriculture when they are regulated in all other sectors. In this case the assumption is that an oversupply of eggs should be allowed to force the wholesale price down to whatever level necessary to dispose of surpluses. To expand egg consumption sufficiently, the price might drop by as much as 40 per cent. But who absorbs the losses? Free market proponents would say the producer.

Assuming that chicken farmers haven't been lying about their cost figures (something the Food Prices Review Board hasn't contended), a drop in price means a cut-back in farmers' family income. People who try to make their living looking after chickens are expected to accept that their efficiency as producers should be rewarded by an income cut and potential bankruptcy.

Secondly, it remained unclear even after the rotten egg scandal that there *was* an oversupply of Canadian production in 1974. When the sharp increase in imported U.S. eggs is taken into account, along with the refusal of the major egg processing firms to utilize available supply, the 'surplus' issue becomes clouded. If in fact the surplus of eggs was artificially created through imports and the processor boycott it would have been disastrous for CEMA to allow the price to Canadian producers to drop. As it was, they cut prices to a break-even level and many egg producers were claiming they would have to go out of production. In January 1975, the price of eggs in B.C. was cut to a 51¢ return to farmers and the B.C. Egg Board claimed they were losing 19¢ per dozen sold. The cost of initiating new poultry and egg operations when current producers are forced out of the market is staggering to contemplate, given rising land prices.

And finally, even if there was overproduction in 1974, it is not accurate to assume it came in response to the price offerings of CEMA. Hens just can't be cranked up or down in production levels every month to suit the whims and opportunities of the market. They require at least a year to be ordered, hatched, grown and put into a regular laying pattern. CEMA purchase offers in late 1973 had been sharply adjusted upward to cover higher feed costs (see graph) but this could have had no effect toward expanded production before spring 1975. Even then, production expansion would only be possible if provincial marketing boards were not enforcing their quotas on producers. There is evidence to suggest that some provinces *have* been ineffective in supply management. Ontario, for example, with apparent overproduction of some magnitude, was faced with a new situation in 1972-73. The anticipation of the CEMA purchasing program on a quota basis starting in 1973 gave Ontario producers one

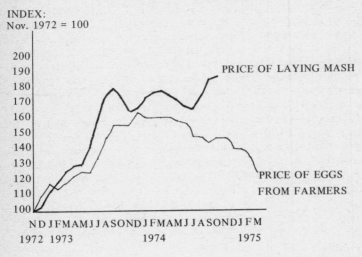

FIGURE 19

**COMPARATIVE PRICE TRENDS: FEED COSTS AND EGG PRICES,
NOVEMBER 1972 TO MARCH 1975**

INDEX:
Nov. 1972 = 100

PRICE OF LAYING MASH

PRICE OF EGGS
FROM FARMERS

N D J F M A M J J A S O N D J F M A M J J A S O N D J F M
1972 1973   1974   1975

---

last chance to expand their flocks before marketing quotas came into effect. This development in Ontario, if it *did* contribute to later overproduction, cannot really be blamed on CEMA.

Notwithstanding all these points, there is an aspect of CEMA policy and the whole egg marketing system which is a rip-off of consumers. The cost to CEMA of eggs bought up from producer marketing boards in each provice is paid for through a levy of 6¢ per dozen on every dozen eggs sold on the wholesale market. This levy is included in the price of wholesale eggs when it is set by each provincial marketing board. It is a cost, therefore, within that of every dozen eggs bought in the store although it has nothing directly to do with the production, handling, and distribution of the eggs being purchased.

The 6¢ levy doesn't go to the farmer, the distributor, or the supermarket. Nor does it go to maintaining the CEMA bureaucracy in Ottawa except in very small measure. It goes to buy eggs at regular or 'break-even' prices from farmers which are then sold to processing companies for 25-30¢ per dozen lower — or as little as one-half the costs of production. The big cost for consumers then has been not the

28 million eggs which were destroyed in 1974 but the 1.7 billion eggs processed annually into other products like shampoo and egg powder. The rip-off is that Export Packers and other companies can exploit every *consumer* since creation of CEMA where they once exploited farmers directly. CEMA has streamlined the process through a check-off on every dozen eggs. And farmers, rather than destroying hens or surplus eggs, have been prepared to market them at the CEMA price. The more eggs marketed, the more upward pressure on the check-off levy as CEMA goes into the red. Consumers pay in a substantial way for marketing inefficiencies.

A partial solution would be to tighten up the quota system on producers and allow a proportion of the Canadian egg supply to go to processing companies at regular market prices. Eggs which are surplus to the combined table and processing markets should be used for export markets for human consumption. Under no circumstances should they be sold at subsidized prices to large private profit ventures. Nor should these private processing companies have license to import egg supplies from other countries undercutting Canadian production as they have in the past.

In Conclusion

The issues surrounding the great egg scandal were broader than the destruction of one day's production of a single commodity. What was at stake was the short-term advance of the marketing board concept as part of a general federal strategy of supply management. The minor skirmishing and resistance of the egg processing companies reflected a self-interest not necessarily shared by the food industry as a whole, particularly in the long term. It is significant that Whelan successfully held his ground against his critics. Clearly the arguments in support of supply management had a certain logical appeal to the overall agribusiness community. However much agribusiness prefers the speculation and manipulations of the open market system in the short run, it also appreciates the risks. If agribusiness has serious intentions of further integrating into basic production, its security of investment demands some variant of the marketing board concept. If farmers are given temporary advantages and stability in the short term, agribusiness will accept the change and pass it on in inflation to consumers. In the long run it can buy out or squeeze out the farmer and replace him with an industrial wage-labour force.

Notes to Chapter 7

1. Vernon Fowke, *Canadian Agricultural Policy: The Historical Pattern* (Toronto: University of Toronto Press, 1947).

2. H. Buckley and E. Tihanyi, "Canadian Policies for Rural Adjustment: A Summary of Conclusions," in *Social and Cultural Change in Canada*, I (Toronto, Copp-Clark, 1970).

3. Members of the Task Force were as follows: Dr. David L. Macfarlane, Agricultural Economist, McGill University; Dr. J.C. Gilson, Agricultural Economist, University of Manitoba; Mr. Pierre Comtois, Chartered Accountant, Sherbrooke; Dr. D.R. Campbell, Political Economist, University of Toronto; and Dr. D.H. Thain, Professor of Business Policy, University of Western Ontario.

4. Federal Government Task Force, *Canadian Agriculture in the 1970s* (Ottawa, Queen's Printer).

5. In this regard William Sherman, president of Loblaws Groceterias, stunned observers at an October 1974 Retail Grocers meeting by demanding a Royal Commission to investigate "rip-offs" in the food industry. It turned out he didn't have retail supermarkets in mind. He said the country's 26,000 food store operators were being unfairly maligned as "profiteers and price gougers," while the real cause of inflation lay with marketing boards. This outburst from the president of the third largest retail food chain in Canada was skeptically received even by the 26,000 grocers allegedly maligned. Sherman, as head of one of the three grocery empires which control up to 80 per cent of the market in some Canadian cities and engage regularly in collective price leadership, is not credible as a critic of marketing boards. Marketing boards, for all their faults, were at least structured for some degree of public accountability.

6. Statistics Canada, *Production of Poultry and Eggs* No. 23-202 (annual) and No. 23-003 (monthly).

VIII

The Politics of Investigation: Royal Commissions, Inquiries and Review Boards

The federal government's image as protector of the public interest in a private 'free market economy' has been painfully and persistently portrayed over the years through the tactics of public inquiry. Government investigations of the food industry are at one and the same time both fraudulent and useful. They are fraudulent because they are presented as 'coming to grips with issues' when in reality they are intended to postpone and avoid them. They are useful from the public's point of view, however, because they necessarily involve information-gathering at a level beyond the scope of individuals or private interest groups. Despite their role in the politics of avoidance, they often serve to fan the flames of discontent they were meant to extinguish.

There are two important and overlapping sources of investigation which typify the relationship between government and agribusiness over the four decades since the 1930s. One is the special 'single-issue' inquiry which is set up by an Act of Parliament to conduct specific investigation as mandated and report back. The other is the permanent investigative machinery of the Anti-Combines administration, responsible to the Minister of Consumer and Corporate Affairs (formerly to the Minister of Justice), with a general and permanent mandate "... to assist in maintaining free and open competition ... in a system of free enterprise."

The Royal Commission

A favourite target of Royal Commissions or 'parliamentary inquiries' has been the thorny political issue of inflation. This subject has brought the investigative bodies repeatedly into discussions of agri-

business and the role of oligopoly power as evidenced by the
following sample conclusions:

> On closer study however, it became clear that many of the
> grievances complained of, and the problems disclosed, were mani-
> festations of one fundamental and far-reaching social change, the
> concentration of economic power.
> > —from the Royal Commission on Price Spreads 1934-35

> It would seem that in the long run, the greatest hope for reduction
> of margins and mark-ups lies in reducing the costs of distribution
> . . . there is a growing tendency towards monopolistic competition
> [sic] through brand names and special advertising, price leadership
> by a few large firms and resale price maintenance whereby a
> manufacturer sets the retail price for his product.
> > —from the Royal Commission on Prices 1948-49

> Abnormally high profits (. . . among retail food chains and break-
> fast cereal manufacturers of 17.1 per cent and 29.1 per cent
> respectively) . . . illustrate the consequences of industrial structure
> and practices which are certainly not confined to the preparation
> of breakfast foods or large scale retailing. . . .
> > —from the Royal Commission on Price Spreads of
> > Food Products 1958-59

> . . . grocery retailing today is seriously deficient on at least four
> counts: profits are excessive; excess capacity has added to costs;
> advertising has favored a concentrated structure, created monopoly
> power and increased costs; the promotion of the luxury store has
> inflated gross margins.
> > —from the Royal Commission on Consumer Problems
> > and Inflation 1967-68 (prairie provinces)

If the purpose of Royal Commissions, House Committees, and Prices
Review Boards was really to discover the mysterious forces behind
inflation and provide solutions, it would be hard to understand why
we haven't made more progress in the forty years since 1935. The
monotonous round of hearings and probes have uncovered repeatedly
the fact of monopoly control over markets, the existence of administered prices, vertical integration, and excessive profits. The strongest
and clearest indictment was probably that of the Bennett government
Commission on Price Spreads in 1934-35. If its message had been
noted at the time and its contents reviewed by successive Parliaments,
we could have dispensed with the numerous repetitions of the exercise
since that time.

Royal Commissions dealing with food have been a staged and
cynical exercise in Canadian politics aimed at assuring the Canadian
electorate that all is well with the free market system. They have
rarely escaped revealing more than they intended.

The past half-century has seen recurring cycles within capitalist economies. A prosperous expanding economy is overtaken by a rising rate of inflation causing a slow-down. This recession, with declining incomes for workers, a drop in consumption of goods and services and a rise in unemployment, is followed eventually again by an expanding economy. This inflation-recession cycle was repeated in the 1929-39 period, the late 40s, the late 50s, and now the 70s. Each time it led to a broadly-based political attack on the food policies of the government of the day, which responded with an agreement to investigate through a parliamentary committee, a Royal Commission, or both. The inquiries would conduct hearings for 12-18 months, getting the views and evidence of both the business class through industry lobbies, and the working class through trade unions and consumer organizations. When the reports were made, they tended to try to merge conflicting testimonies of management and workers, but they consistently recognized the absence of competition in the corporate food industry.

The dilemma of federal politicians, especially in the governing party, has been that they cannot come to grips with the class divisions which the issue of inflation necessarily creates. On the one hand, public protest demands very strongly that government intervene to control prices. But corporations generally oppose the application of controls as a nuisance factor (even though they have shown they can undermine them when they are applied). So instead of 'controls' the government prefers the tactic of investigation and exposure. It's a way of channeling public protest to one side while seeming to do something about the questions raised.

R.B. Bennett stumbled on the formula for inflation fighting almost by accident in 1934. In the depths of depression the Tory Bennett government was facing a political crisis in which the country was polarized along class lines, as was the Tory party itself. One of Bennett's cabinet ministers, H.H. Stevens, made a widely publicized speech in Toronto in which he attacked the practices of "big retailing corporations and the packing and milling industries." Stevens became a national hero almost overnight as his office (Trade and Commerce) "received hundreds of letters from all over Canada detailing what were claimed to be injustices both as to methods of buying and selling, and the rate of wages prevailing in many industries" (Toronto *Globe*, February 5, 1934).

Bennett, sensing a way out which could preserve the government's creditibility without directly interfering with or alienating business support, set up a Royal Commission with the rebel Stevens at the head. In announcing the Commission, Bennett stated: "The matter has been forcibly presented in recent months and it is desirable that it should be investigated" (Toronto *Globe*, February 1934).

The Commission was generously awarded broad powers ("... investigation of business capital structures with a view to uncovering financial pirating"), as well as making specific examinations of price spreads in industry.

The 1934 Commission hearings were well received by the public. Wide-ranging testimony was given on everything from minimum wage violations and factory speed-ups to monopoly power over retail prices. By the time the Commission reported, Harry Stevens, its original chairman, was so tied to reformist recommendations he had to be removed by Tory Committee members. Reported the Toronto *Globe:*

> ... The regular government supporters of the Committee are seeking to tone down the findings to avoid giving offence to big business contributors to party funds.

And a week later:

> Drastic proposals to remedy alleged evils in the Canadian economic system as disclosed to the Price Spreads Commission were submitted by H.H. Stevens today, and if they are not incorporated in the recommendations of that body, Mr. Stevens will include them in a minority report which he will submit himself.

Stevens was successful in winning compromises from the committee even though he was ousted as chairman, but he could not persuade the cabinet to act on his many reform proposals, which included an excess profit tax, direct taxation of incomes over $10,000, and control over refinancing schemes to prevent 'financial wizardry.' Eventually Stevens broke with the Conservatives and ran successfully as an independent and head of the Reconstruction party. His defection was a major contributing factor to the Tory election loss to Mackenzie King in 1935.

As with later examples, the use by Bennett of the Royal Commission contained political liabilities as well as assets. Although he successfully avoided the demands for reforms which emanated from in and outside of the Commons, it was at the cost of defeat at the polls. The analysis and conclusions of the Stevens Commission fanned discontent and split the Tory party. By 1935, Bennett's defeat was inescapable. But Mackenzie King was not about to implement the Stevens recommendations either.

Mackenzie King's ideology and political style muddied the contradiction between the growing evidence of monopoly and the traditional competitive enterprise myth. It was King who introduced the Anti-Combines Act to Parliament in 1923. He seemed to be inspired by the sense of cleanliness which competitions law implied and he was undoubtedly influenced by the example of U.S. anti-trust measures which predated the turn of the century.

In 1934, when the Bennett government proposed the parliamentary inquiry into Price Spreads, King, as leader of the opposition, made his usual 'on-the-one-hand-on-the-other-hand' attack. On the one hand, he wanted the Commission to have broad powers to investigate 'large industrial concerns' and 'loss through reckless financing that is being passed on to the consumers.' On the other hand, he contended that the previous Liberal government through its anti-combines legislation had created all the machinery which the government required to carry out an investigation into the matters under consideration. There was no need, he said, for either parliamentary committee or Royal Commission.

King was returned to power, the depression passed, eventually, and the country was plunged into a war economy, all without serious regard by government to the findings of the soon-forgotten Stevens Price Spreads Commission. But in 1947 and 1948, when post-war inflation got out of hand, it was the same Mackenzie King who produced the solution of *both a parliamentary inquiry and a Royal Commission*. The political situation was not altogether different from 1934. In three weeks in December-January of 1947-48 the price of essential food items like meat, cheese, milk and butter rose 20 per cent. Prices had increased 135 per cent since 1939. Consumer militancy led to demands for re-imposition of wartime price controls. Unions began to demand cost-of-living bonuses as the cost of essentials outstripped average weekly wages. In by-elections in urban Ontario in 1948, the CCF swept to power with a mandate to curb inflation through any means including government take-over.

King established a parliamentary committee, first to investigate specific problems like a 44 per cent increase in bread prices. Under pressure from backbenchers and the opposition, the Committee mandate was broadened. Eventually, when the Committee reported in June 1948, it proposed price controls, payment of subsidies, removal of 25 per cent luxury excise tax, and excess profits tax. CCF members were so pleased with the tenor of the report they decided not to submit a minority report. But two days later, in a six-hour debate in the House, it became clear that the government had no intention of acting on the recommendations. Instead they established a Royal Commission on Prices, gave it a $50,000 budget and asked it to report back in a year with its findings. By May 1949 the inflationary spiral had levelled for a time and the political crisis was passed. King was able to face an election, successfully turning the earlier feared CCF gains to a loss of over half their seats. The Liberals won the largest election majority since Confederation, with 190 seats.

King had roughly followed the Bennett formula for avoidance of anti-inflation measures which he had ridiculed in opposition. But King added an important innovation, which had it been included in 1934-35 might have saved the Tories from defeat. King moved the focus of investigation as quickly as possible outside the arena of Parliament and parliamentary committees into the 'judicial inquiry' format of a full-time independent Royal Commission. The King government avoided open class divisions and partisan political debate in the process of investigation. By so doing they avoided the rupturing which the Stevens Commission, made up of Members of Parliament, had caused for the Conservative Party. The King formula for inquiry was one which could work parallel to the Combines Investigation Branch, an agency he had once argued was "all the machinery necessary."

The Liberal Party in the 1950s under C.D. Howe and nominally headed by Louis St. Laurent never possessed the touch which Mackenzie King had for co-opting the protests of opposition parties and extra-parliamentary forces. Their relationship with capitalist interests in the United States and Canada was more openly and honestly expressed. The St. Laurent government was perceived as arrogant and overbearing, placing the rights of corporations over those of people. Their attitude in the pipeline debate in 1956, when they invoked closure on the opposition and forced through a bill to help finance a U.S. pipeline consortium, typified their political style. It led directly to their upset at the polls by the Progressive Conservatives in 1957.

Diefenbaker came to power in the midst of a period of continuing inflation leading into a mild recession. As a veteran of the 1940s parliamentary debates, he reverted to the King formula. Presenting a decisive 'let's get to the bottom of this' attitude, he established a Royal Commission on Price Spreads of Food Products. This was within three months of taking office and before going to the polls in 1958 to win the largest majority ever. (The Diefenbaker government majority surpassed even the high-water mark of Mackenzie King in 1949.)

Following hearings throughout 1958 at which, according to the Commission ". . . the food industries were well represented . . . ," a Report was presented to Parliament in September 1959. Among its major recommendations was one calling for action by the Combines Investigation Branch. Based on a finding that some sectors within the food industry had "abnormally high profits," the Commission proposed that the Director of Investigation and Research under the Combines Investigation Branch

. . . extend inquiries into the buying practices and the selling practices of large business organizations in the food industries and give the results the widest possible distribution and publicity.

Anti-Combines Administration

The Combines Investigation Branch of the federal government, established under the Anti-Combines Act of 1923, has two protective agencies. One is the Investigation and Research agency with a permanent Director and a small research budget. The other is the Restrictive Trade Practices Commission.

The Director of Investigation conducts inquiries informally at the request of the House of Commons or a group of citizens (at least six) who petition his services. He publishes the results of all his requests and inquiries in an annual report to the Minister of Consumer and Corporate Affairs. The RTPC is a more formal body which may be activated by Parliament on the basis of recommendations from the Director of Investigation, the Minister of Consumer Affairs, or the cabinet as a whole. It conducts hearings, subpoenas witnesses, and considers violations of the Act. If its findings are sufficient to lay charges under the Act it will submit its evidence to the courts on behalf of the Crown. The intent and effectiveness of the Director of Investigation and Research and the Restrictive Trade Practices Commission are made clear by their record on issues concerning the food industry over the past twenty years. Some of the best detailed critique of the Anti-Combines Administration in Canada has been provided in articles by Gideon Rosenbluth. Writing for the *Canadian Journal of Economics and Political Science* in the early 1960s, he showed that an unmistakeable pattern has emerged in the history of Combines Investigation since the 1920s. There is a direct correlation between the effectiveness of the (two) agencies of the Combines Investigation Branch and the size of firms involved. Investigation and prosecutions are aimed primarily at local markets and small firms. More specifically he showed that the size of firms investigated with successful prosecution was small, firms investigated but with no action taken somewhat larger, and firms of high concentration with national markets, (like the retail food chains) have generally avoided investigation altogether.

Two possible conclusions emerge. One is that small businessmen are more 'crooked' than the nation's corporate elite. The other, more obvious answer, consistent with the evidence of the Director of Combines Investigation below, is that the Anti-Combines Administration is neither able, nor willing, nor intended to influence the real forces which run the economy.

The point, after all, is not that the Combines Branch has failed in its job or that the Director of Investigation and Minister of Consumer Affairs should be replaced by someone else. The point is that the jobs themselves are unreal. The approach by which mergers and combines become a legal, police problem, rather than an economic fact characteristic of modern capitalist enterprise, is artificial to the point of being absurd. Rosenbluth makes this point effectively;

> This concept (of policing) is of course at variance with reality since monopolistic practices are the normal activities of businessmen seeking profit in an environment in which the number of competitors is limited and there are barriers to entry. It serves the purposes of compromise, however, since it leads to a policy of enforcement which provides *a few spectacular court cases to which the attention of voters can be directed, while leaving most business activity unmolested.* Moreover, the high standards of proof required in criminal proceedings lead to an emphasis on documentary evidence, which provides relative immunity to the verbal agreements among a few large firms. Thus, big business is protected. It opposes the Combines Investigation Act, but can live with it. [emphasis added]

The illustration of Rosenbluth's critique emerges best from a review of the record of the two agencies of the Combines Investigation Branch. Their attitude in response to both general monopoly trends in the food industry and specific allegations of anti-combines violation is a pathetic and revealing commentary on government-industry collusion.

In 1959, in apparent response to the Diefenbaker Commission on Food Price Spreads, the Director of Research and Investigation, T.D. MacDonald, initiated an investigation in the food industry. This investigation was delegated to one academic researcher on leave from university and never fully completed. The researcher returned to university and the study was 'officially discontinued' in 1963. Since the study was not fully completed it was not published. An analysis of partial results led David Henry, the Director from 1960 to 1972, to conclude in his annual report of 1963 that "a critical degree of concentration did not exist in any market. . . ." (for food retail chains).

This boldly-stated conclusion took four years and an incomplete one-man study to arrive at. It was part of a continuing pattern. First parliamentary committees or commissions were established under political pressure. They observed and commented urgently on the obvious and growing concentration or market power. They would call for deeper and more systematic probes by the agencies of the Combines Investigation Branch. Then the Director of Investigation without staff or resources to follow through would assume the role of

corporate defender. As apologist he would explicitly deny the existence of monopoly trends and practices in contradiction to the Royal
Commission.

Public concern about concentration continued through the 1960s.
In 1965 the massive financial holdings of the Weston family empire
became a matter of public knowledge for the first time. This caused
the special Joint Committee of the Senate and House on Consumer
Credit Prices) to express some alarm. In their 1966 interim report the
Committee observed:

> The five great corporate food chains and the voluntary chains
> control more than 75 per cent of the grocery business in urban
> areas and their percentage is increasing.

And in April 1967, noting the Director of Investigation had
discontinued the previous inquiry on concentration in the food
industry, they endeavoured to restoke the coals, recommending

> . . . that this study be resumed on a continuous basis and broad-
> ened to cover both food, retailing and manufacturing in Canada
> with a particular view to examining concentration, market power
> and trading practices in the relations between retailers and
> suppliers.

This might have been a valuable exercise to engage the Director of
Investigation. Obviously the politicians could not accept Mr. Henry's
1963 statement that a critical degree of concentration did not exist.
But in his 1967 annual report he again dismissed the recommendation
for a study saying it was "beyond the capacity of a staff of the size
and character now available to the director."

Director Henry abandoned a food inquiry in 1963 and in 1967 he
pleaded a staff shortage as an excuse for inaction. Yet without an
investigation he dismissed the concerns of the Joint Committee. He
defended the competitive nature of the industry, including the newly
publicized Weston holdings, about which he had prior knowledge.
This was the man assigned as the guardian of the public to 'police'
against breaches of free competition. Instead he used his Annual
Report to lecture the public representatives about their over-reaction
to the splendour of corporate agribusiness:

> The Joint Committee was influenced in its findings by the
> disclosures which it had elicited from the complex of companies
> under the financial ownership and control of George Weston
> Limited, which includes Loblaws and other companies at all levels
> of production and distribution. This group had kept private the
> facts about its holdings and when the Committee's initiative caused
> the group to make them public there was wide public concern. The
> Director is now at liberty to disclose that these facts had already

been ascertained by him, under the disclosure powers of the Combines Investigation Act in connection with his discontinued study of concentration in food retailing. After studying them he felt bound to hold them in confidence in view of the privacy provisions of the Act, and the fact that they had been obtained through use of statutory powers, especially since they did not disclose an offence under the Act.

In other words, the Director of Combines Investigation knew back around 1960 that Weston had a fully integrated milti-billion dollar operation which controlled a large segment of food processing and retailing. This was unknown to a public already alarmed about concentration and clamouring for action. Yet Mr. Henry failed to reveal the facts from his first discontinued study, on the basis of which he was prepared to conclude that "a critical degree of concentration did not exist."

The first real documented challenge to the corporate food retailers was left to the 1968 Royal Commission on *Consumer Problems and Inflation* which was established by the governments of the three prairie provinces. The fact that it operated outside of Ottawa without the combined influences of the national agribusiness lobbies or the federal consumer bureaucracy may have saved it from fudging on all the critical questions. It is a much clearer statement than anything produced since the days of Harry Stevens and his Price Spreads Commission.

The "Batten Report," (named after its chairman, Judge Mary Batten) found in contradiction to the Director of Investigation that there *was* a critical degree of concentration, up to 75 per cent in some prairie cities by three chain store owners, Dominion, Safeway's and the Weston stores. They were increasing their combined market share 1 per cent a year at the expense of independent grocers. The existence and exercise of oligopoly powers by the major chains led, according to the Batten findings, to excess profits, excess capacity in stores, and advertising practices which create and reinforce monopolies.

The authors of the Batten Report were directly critical of the role of the Combines Investigation Branch. They took note of the 1967 Director's Report which for lack of staff and lack of shared concern dismissed a Joint Committee request for a full investigation into the food industry. Economist Peter Dooley, author of a Batten support study entitled *Oligopoly in the Retail Grocery Trade*, observed that

. . . The deficiencies in the performance of the grocery trade either cannot or will not be remedied by existing combines legislation and methods of enforcement.

Although critical of the performance of the Combines Branch, the

Batten Report was not critical of the idea that somehow the market system might be reformed by an investigative agency of government without direct intervention or ownership by the state. The Batten Report's final recommendations included a renewed call for an immediate investigation of grocery retailing in Canada by the Combines Investigation Branch. They also called for broader powers under the Act:

> That in the event correction to the inadequacy of the grocery trade's operation fails to be secured under existing legislation and procedures, the governments of the three prairie provinces urge the initiation of an immediate study and action to provide the necessary legislation so that cases of inadequate industry performance on account of concentration can be examined and corrected.

The response of David Henry to the Batten Report was interesting. (His own track record, remember, consisted of one abortive study discontinued after four years, and a refusal to initiate a second requested study because of staff shortages.) First he ignored the demands for investigation with the simple conclusion that "the evidence did not justify the commencement of an inquiry under the act." Secondly, he ignored the proposal for broader powers under the Combines Act, presumably because that was a political matter and not an administrative one. But the main response of Mr. Henry was to attack the evidence and findings on grounds of methodology. He dismissed the entire research effort and summation of briefs presented to the Batten Report because he disagreed with some of the research assumptions of its authors.

This incident demonstrates that the role of the Combines Branch is to avoid and diffuse the issue of market concentration. The Branch refused to investigate it and attempted to discredit those who did. But they also make a pretense of not having any position when they write off documented reports and conclusions as providing 'no convincing evidence':

> The foregoing conclusion should not be taken as a judgement of the actual performance of the grocery trade on the prairies. . . . It might be possible for them to operate in a predatory fashion and to enjoy discriminatory buying advantages. However the Commission has not provided any evidence that the big chains have in fact done so in the prairie provinces.

As well as being inaccurate (there *was* evidence provided), this statement by the Director was unusual in that it acknowledged the possibilities "*it might be possible . . . to operate in a predatory fashion*" while refusing to acknowledge the primary obligation of the

Federal Combines Branch to find out if it was so acting.

The final irony was that by 1971 the Director of Investigation was reporting figures from Statistics Canada which confirmed some of the Batten Report findings on concentration levels. He reported these without acknowledging the coincidence with the Batten Report figures or taking action:

> It should be noted that the power of the large corporate chains increased substantially in the Western provinces from 1958-68. . . . In addition there remains a great deal to be learned about food distribution, especially at the wholesale level. It is the intention of the Director of Investigation to keep the situation under active review.

Eventually there was some limited action directed toward retail marketing practices, at least in the province of Alberta. But the Director of Investigation did not play a major role in the investigation or court proceedings.

The basic problem with the Director of Combines Investigation has been with the conception of the job itself as analyzed above by Rosenbluth. But the selection of personnel has contributed to the ineffectiveness of the role. Henry, who held the post until his appointment to the Ontario Supreme Court in 1972, reflected a pro-business bias in his judgements and approach to the job which watered down in practice an already impotent piece of legislation.

Henry defined his job as being both defender and prosecutor for corporations faced with potential violations of combines laws. He took great pains to cultivate his contacts in the Canadian Manufacturers Association and other corporate lobbies to ensure that he would be seen as 'a friend.' He didn't want the nuisance of combines laws which he was obliged to administer to interfere with the normal pattern of business activity. A short feature in the *Financial Post* of August 3, 1968, revealed much about Henry's role and assumptions. Under the headline *Combines Cop — both a confidant and advisor* the story said in part:

> . . . David Henry thinks he is succeeding in his eight year struggle to win the confidence of business and help it steer clear of him in his role as combines top cop. As evidence Henry points to the hundreds of businessmen and groups that have accepted his open door invitation, disclosed their plan for merger, pricing or marketing and sought his opinion on the legality of the move.

Henry explained to the reporter that where there might be a difference between the 'letter of the law' and the 'spirit of the law' he advised companies on the letter of the law. He reasoned that if the law provided loop-holes it should perhaps be changed. But it wasn't up to him to apply a broad interpretation and discourage company actions which could be successfully defended in courts. In short he provided a service, while on the public pay-roll, of advising companies how to beat the intent of the law.

> Henry cannot guarantee his advice will be upheld in the courts. But he can claim that never has he advised a firm which proceeded accordingly, and then found itself on the wrong end of a combines act court judgement.

In addition to his unofficial role as private advisor to companies engaged in 'suspect' marketing practices or anticipated mergers, David Henry tried generally to improve the image of the Combines Branch within the business community. For example he was distressed at the generally held view that anti-combines laws were biased against the trends toward centralization. He pointed out that even pure monopolies were not illegal provided they were not taking unfair advantage of their market power. In an article he wrote for *Financial Post* in 1968, he tried to debunk the interpretation held by businessmen that combines laws treated 'bigness as badness.' This was most assuredly not the case, he said:

> More than 2500 mergers have taken place in Canada in the post-war period and of these not more than a handful has been challenged by the director of investigation and research and *none has been struck down by the courts.* . . . Look at the 100 largest Canadian firms. A number of them have been convicted for conspiracy, but a restrictive agreement can scarcely be called bigness. None has been convicted of a merger, or monopoly offense or of predatory pricing. [emphasis added]

Such assurances coming from the Director of Combines Investigation hardly stand out as a deterrent to market concentration, which of course in not their intention. But the boast that mergers restricting competition have not been disallowed in courts is a misleading assessment, as Mr. Henry was in a position to know. The facts were that mergers *were investigated and found to be restricting competition* by the Restrictive Trade Practices Commission. But they *weren't even taken to court* because government lawyers felt the loopholes in the law meant a prosecution could not be won despite the evidence. Henry was aware of exactly this assessment of the case against Canada Packers in 1962-63 (discussed below). Had the law been effective so that prosecution could proceed, Henry would have been robbed of his boast that "no mergers have been interfered with." The Director of Investigation, who should have wanted tougher provisions under the law, developed an investment in maintaining the loopholes.

Mergers, Price-Fixing and Monopoly Practices: Some Case Studies

The record of the Combines Branch in running interference in general for big business was amplified around specific charges and allegations under the protections of the Anti-Combines Act. Four examples involving agribusiness and alleged violations of business law are not a complete record, but they provide a useful cross-section.

A case of 'mergers reducing competition' followed allegations in the House of Commons against Canada Packers Limited concerning the acquisition of Calgary Packers Limited of Calgary in 1957 and Wilsil Limited in Montreal in 1958. The Director of Investigation inquired into the matter and decided that a more formal inquiry was warranted. He referred the issue to the Restrictive Trade Practices Commission in September 1959. The RTPC conducted an investigation, calling witnesses and examining company records. In August 1961 they completed and filed a 450-page report and a recommendation of prosecution. The report was thorough on all aspects of the meat packing industry in Canada over a thirty-year period. It went beyond the question of mergers to illustrate how Canada Packers was involved in dumping of livestock from one region to another to depress farm market prices. It also provided evidence of price fixing:

> The evidence contains instances when Canada Packers attempted by prior consultation with other packers to ensure that a particular policy with respect to prices or other market action would be generally followed.

On the general question of the effect of mergers the Commission report stated:

> ... the acquisition of Calgary Packers Ltd. and Wilsil Ltd. by Canada Packers *significantly lessened the competition previously existing in the trade in livestock* on the markets where the purchases of Calgary Packers and Wiksil Ltd. were made, and because of the inter-relationship of markets could be expected to lessen the competitive effect resulting from such independent buying on Canadian livestock markets generally. It also appears to the Commission to be likely that *competition in the distribution of meat products was also lessened* as a result of such acquisitions. . . . [emphasis added]
>
> In view of the limitations on competition which become evident when competitors are few in number and anxious to avoid active competition with respect to price, *it does not appear to the Commission that the public interest will be best served if the disappearance of independent firms in an industry already highly concentrated proceeds unchecked.* The evidence in the present

inquiry with respect to the manufacture of shortening and fertilizers makes it clear that when producers become few in number
*there is a reluctance, as one witness put it, "to change prices relative
to competitors."* [emphasis added]

This report was a refreshing change emanating from the Combines
Branch, in contrast to the apologies offered each year in the Director
of Investigations Report. This study detailed the situation and seemed
determined, in an almost unprecedented show of aggressive intent, to
prosecute Canada Packers and disallow the mergers. However, in his
1962 report Director Henry stated that

> the matter has been referred to counsel with instructions to
> proceed with prosecution or other appropriate legal proceedings
> *unless he comes to the conclusion that the evidence is insufficient.*
> [emphasis added]

Obviously the Director was anticipating a course of action other
than that proposed by the Commission report. After an unexplained
lapse of two years, during which nothing further was heard on the
matter of prosecuting Canada Packers, the Director of Investigation
reported in 1964:

> After consultation between counsel and departmental officials, the
> opinion was ultimately received that having regard to the juris-
> prudence on the merger section of the Combines Investigation Act
> legal proceedings would be unlikely to succeed. *It was accordingly
> decided not to institute any court proceedings in the matter.*
> [emphasis added]

In other words, in anticipation of an unfavourable court decision
against the documented and conclusive evidence of a two-year
investigation, the Combines Investigation Branch of the Department
of Justice dropped the case without even a challenge in the courts.
The pretense was either that the Act is so loosely worded that it
provided loopholes you could drive a meat truck through, or else the
evidence was really not as damning and substantial as the Restrictive
Trade Practices Commission believed. In either case if the Combines
Branch was serious about its role the matter should have been tested
in the courts. The case would have clarified the meaning of the section
on mergers. But even more incredible than the case being dropped
uncontested was the fact that this informal backroom judgement *was
then used as a precedent* by the Director of Investigation to avoid
other inquiries on mergers.

In 1964, the controlling interest in Burns Foods (40 per cent of the
shares) was purchased by Alexander Hill of Toronto and Imperial
Trust Company of Montreal. Questions on the purchase in the House
of Commons led to demands for an inquiry under the Combines Act.

The Minister of Justice referred it to the Director of Investigation, who stated in his annual report:

> After seeking information concerning the identity of the group reported to have gained control of Burns and Company Ltd. the Director concluded, in the light of the jurisprudence and of counsel's opinion in the Canada Packers case, that the reported change in control did not warrant initiation of a formal inquiry under the Act.

The determining factor, then, in decisions about whether to restrict company mergers or even to inquire into them was not the accumulated evidence of a two-year study into the meat-packing industry. It was in this case an untested judgement that the existing legislation would be ineffective anyway. All the factors which entered into the decision not to prosecute were never known and could have been the subject of an investigation as well.

A second area in which Canadians are 'protected' by the Anti-Combines law is 'price-fixing.' It is illegal for companies to openly arrange to set their price levels so as to avoid competition. They are assumed by law to base their prices on their real costs, plus a modest return to profit. Under pressures of competition in the marketplace there is a presumption prices are not going to be identical among firms. But there is nothing illegal about identical pricing unless it can be proven there is more than a coincidence involved. Such proof is difficult to establish.

The role of the Combines Branch in the face of allegations of price-fixing is to directly defend the corporations involved and explain to the consumer involved why price competition cannot exist and identical pricing is justified. They refuse to launch an inquiry or invite proof of the allegations. A case in point was the alleged price fixing by fertilizer manufacturers in Ontario in 1970.

In May 1970, the NDP agriculture critic Alf Gleave asked in the House of Commons for a Combines Branch investigation into identical pricing by fertilizer manufacturers in Ontario. His request followed a call for an investigation by the local president of the Charlotteville Federation of Agriculture whose members had asked for tenders on a bulk purchase to fill their collective needs. They received 'substantially identical tenders.' When the request for an inquiry was referred to the Director of Investigation, he dismissed it. His logic was quite simple. No provisions of the Act had been violated just because there were identical bids, and the absence of price competition was quite rational. His explanation in the 1971 Annual Report is instructive on why oligopoly practice will be unchallenged by the state:

... It was explained that quotations of identical or similar prices by a number of sellers do not establish the existence of a price-fixing agreement in contravention of the Combines Investigation Act. In a market where there are relatively few firms supplying a homogenous product such as tobacco fertilizers, any difference in price which the firms regularly sell the product can only be temporary unless some unusual factor is present. *In such markets firms have a tendency to refrain from price reductions since these are likely to be followed by competitors with the result that the firm initiating the reduction may in the end simply retain its original share of the market at a lower profit margin.* In addition, if the market shares held by several competitors are altered in the process, a seller whose share has decreased may attempt to regain his original position by a further price cut thereby triggering further price cutting. *To avoid such instability, companies in such a market avoid making price concession that may be detected by competitors. Such independent but parallel action does not of course, constitute a violation of the Combines Investigation Act.* [emphasis added]

The Ontario farmers originally were less concerned about the fact that they got identical tenders than they were about the high price of fertilizer. They put down high prices to a lack of competition in the industry, and made the point about identical tenders simply to illustrate collusion among rival firms. But what the Director of Investigation told them with perfect candor was that of course there is an absence of price competition. Such a phenomenon as undercutting your competitor's price after all would eat into profits and spoil the business for everyone. The notion of 'free and open competition' is interpreted to mean that which is necessary to protect and enlarge profits. Since the price level must protect the most inefficient firm by covering his costs and allowing a profit, it tends to be very generous in the returns given to the more efficient manufacturer which is often larger and more centralized. Price cuts are subject to misinterpretation by rivals, and a price war might emerge. Under such a system the price can only move up and not down.

In slight contrast to the total inaction and avoidance which characterize the Combines Branch's response to the practices of the meat-packing and fertilizer oligopolies, there have been successful and happier episodes. The 1963 prosecution of the eastern Canadian sugar refineries and the 1973 restrictions on Canada Safeway operations in Alberta represent the high points in an otherwise dismal anti-combines record. The sugar industry case also demonstrates the limited impact which the laws provide even where 'guilt' is established.

The investigation of the three major sugar refineries in eastern Canada ran parallel to the investigation of the meat-packing industry discussed earlier. As with the Canada Packers 'mergers' inquiry, the investigation of Atlantic, Canada and Dominion, and St. Lawrence sugar companies took ten years from the original violations of combines laws to a conviction decision. By the time the issue had gone through all stages of judgement and appeal, the same refineries were engaged in actions which would again lead to court trials on monopoly practices.

The original events on which the investigation was based occurred between January 1, 1954, and January 20, 1955. The Restrictive Trade Practices Commission of the Combines Investigation Branch conducted an inquiry with hearings between March 1956 and February 1959. On February 3, 1960, they filed their report with the Minister of Justice, recommending charges under the Anti-Combines Act. On April 3, 1962, formal charges were laid against the three companies based on the Commission Report. The companies pleaded guilty one week later. On March 18, 1963, there was a judgement on the case and the companies were fined $25,000 apiece. They were issued an Order of Prohibition which prevented the companies and their officials from

> . . . conspiring, combining, agreeing, or arranging together with any
> other person,
>   a) to fix a uniform price
>   b) to fix uniform package and grade price differentials
>   c) to fix agreed transportation charges
>   d) to arrange their respective sales policies so that the propor-
>   tion of total sales should remain . . . substantially constant, etc.

Atlantic Sugar appealed the Order of Prohibition on April 6, 1963, and on December 13, 1965, they lost the appeal and were included in the Order of Prohibition.

The case of the sugar refineries amply illustrates the pathetic character of anti-combines administration. After ten years of procedural developments, the companies received what amounted to a wrist tap and a restraining order which they proceeded to ignore. The process had to be repeated, leading to the trials of the sugar refineries in 1974-75. But, as with the example of the inquiry into meat-packing, the valuable part of the exercise was the exposure which the investigation provided of the absolute market power of the sugar oligopoly.

The 1960 Report of the Restrictive Trade Practices Commission set out the wide-ranging powers of the refiners, including price fixing which denied consumers the advantage of changing cost and efficiencies. The Commission's conclusion underlined the raw power of the sugar oligopoly as it operated in the 1950s and continued to operate in the 1970s:

> ... It is the conclusion of this Commission that the practices engaged in by the three eastern refineries with respect to common basic prices, equalized freight rates, common package differentials, and the use of price concessions, have limited competition ... to the detriment of the public. The maintenance of non-competitive conditions have been assisted by private arrangements ... by the three eastern refineries with respect to purchase of raw sugar from Cuba. ... The eastern refineries received further protection from the practice of sugar producers in potential areas of supply refusing to make available types of semi-processed sugar which could be used by certain manufacturers. Such restriction was encouraged by C & D through its relationship with sugar brokers.

> ... The principal feature of competition is that it compels suppliers to seek the most efficient methods of production and marketing and, equally important, it compels suppliers to pass onto consumers in the form of lower prices gains which are made in efficiency. The maintenance of non-competitive conditions in the sugar industry suspended the latter process. There was no way in which an individual refiner could pass on gains in efficiency because of the way in which a common structure of prices was maintained. ... the practice of seeking only a traditional share of the market meant there could not be an active price competition. ... Each refiner could increase his own profits by reducing his own costs but there was no compelling reduction in selling prices where savings in cost could make this possible.

> [For example] ... When C & D found in 1953 that it achieved some savings in its raw sugar purchases by utilizing the services of Tate and Lyle, the management clearly indicated that there was no intention to allow this factor to influence the price level of refined sugar. When C & D and St. Lawrence secured reductions in cost by shipping refined sugar to Toronto and Hamilton by boat no consideration appears to have been given by either company to a change in price which would pass such savings on to the consumer.

Instructions in the practices of oligopoly by the Restrictive Trade Practice Commission were useful but the practices were still treated as exceptional. This remains so although the reputation of the international sugar cartel has reached the point where any notion of 'exceptional' behaviour by way of price-fixing becomes a naïve assessment. In 1971 a Canadian Tariff Board inquiry concluded that:

> The price of refined sugar in Canada does not appear to be related to domestic forces of supply and demand. . . . One company is the price leader and the others follow.

In 1972 a European Common Market anti-trust inquiry described the business methods of European sugar companies, lead by Tate and Lyle of London, as 'a text-book case of how a cartel and lobby operate." Meanwhile, in Canada, the three refineries were back before the courts for breach of anti-combines laws in trials in Montreal in 1975.

The three Canadian refineries, Redpath Industries (formerly Canada and Dominion), Atlantic, and St. Lawrence, are integrated agribusiness operations which have used their near-monopoly position to rapidly expand their capital base in Canada from earnings in the sugar market. For example, Redpath (C & D), a subsidiary of Tate and Lyle of London, went from being just a sugar refinery in 1964 to producing its own packaging, to engaging in agricultural consulting, plastic pipe, and housing development around the sugar beet fields in western Canada. Atlantic Sugar diversified after 1965 into the Atlantic fishing industry under the generous corporate welfare of the federal government and the profits of the sugar trade. The company received $12 million toward the $26 million cost of fishing vessels outright from DREE and another $7 million in income tax deductions because of capital cost allowances under the Income Tax Act. In addition, the Marystown plant of Atlantic Fish Processers is located in a designated area and "exempt from income tax on profits derived from the plant for a period of three years commencing June 1st 1967."

St. Lawrence Sugar, a family company owned by the McConnel family is a private company and not required to divulge details of holdings. It is known that the McConnel family acquired a 20 per cent interest in Crush International, a soft drink manufacturer and a major user of sugar. The Canadian refineries joined in squeezing advantage from the disruption of world sugar prices in 1974, as discussed in Chapter 9.

The final example of the Combines Branch in action was the 1973 case of Safeway in the province of Alberta. This was the first attempted action against a major retailer for monopoly marketing practices. It developed following a report of the Restrictive Trade Practices Commission which documented price discrimination between Safeway's stores in the same city according to neighbourhood market conditions. Charges were first laid against Safeway on October 1972 after the case had been remanded three times.

The prosecution's case was never tested as a settlement was agreed to in the course of a preliminary hearing. A restraining order was issued by the Alberta Supreme Court and agreed to by Safeway without an admission of guilt. In agreeing to the out-of-court settlement, Crown prosecutor P.J. McCaffery explained that, had the monopoly charges been pressed, it ". . . would involve the calling of some 800 witnesses and the introduction of some 9,000 to 10,000 documents."

The legal action would have taken three years. The court order agreed to by Safeway avoided financial penalties. The company agreed to practice uniform pricing in all its outlets within each city (Edmonton and Calgary) and restrict their expansion of outlets to one in each city until 1977, and one per year in each city after that date.

Safeway had grown from 22 to 42 stores in Calgary between 1965 and 1974 and from 25 to 36 in Edmonton. In both cities they had more stores and a greater proportion of the market than all of their combined rivals.

The out-of-court settlement was a slap on the wrist to Safeway but critics pointed out that the imposed restrictions on expansion of stores only applied to the municipal boundaries as existed for the cities in 1973. With suburban expansion, Safeway had power to accelerate growth even within the terms of the agreement. Safeway agreed not to buy out any competitor for five years (to 1978) but they had already eliminated most independent competitors. Safeway was also restricted in the total volume of advertising they could apply within the Alberta city markets.

The Alberta Safeway case was significant, not in terms of its impact on Safeway operations in Alberta, but in its precedent for controlling marketing excesses generally. It spoke to many of the issues outlined by the Batten report as causes of monopoly power and inflation. Such issues as unrestricted advertising, price discrimination, and over-capacity of supermarkets, were at least recognized by the Alberta decision. While the restrictions were laughable in their degree of impact and enforcement, they served to expand public jurisdiction by their precedent. To that extent they must be seen as positive. With only two convictions under the monopoly sections of the Combines Act since 1923, the 'controlled maximum' innovations represent progress, of sorts.

Current Government Strategies on Inflation and Competition

In January 1973, the Trudeau government grimly faced the country on the question of inflation. The government had scarcely survived the election of October 1972 and needed to appear strong and decisive in a precariously balanced minority parliament. It first established a committee of 25 M.P.s to conduct a parliamentary inquiry into food prices. The Committee on Trends in Food Prices would, according to Herb Gray, be ". . . useful in dealing with the serious issue of current trends in food prices, a matter of concern to the government of Canada."

"Dealing with the serious issue" meant avoiding it for six months while yet another series of briefs were read into the record on the matter of inflation. In its first quarterly report, the Committee on Trends in Food Prices made a single firm recommendation which was to create an on-going *Food Prices Review Board*. The Board would have a full-time chairman and research staff and a mandate to inquire into causes of increases and make recommendations to parliament — a sort of mobile Royal Commission. The pattern was similar to that of Bennett, King, and Diefenbaker except that the Food Prices Review Board was a more permanent creation than the investigative bodies set up traditionally.

Where the Committee on Price Trends was bland and insignificant, the Review Board under Beryl Plumptre was colourful and alive. It served no role towards substantial changes by way of economic reforms, but it provided useful information on agriculture and food in its special and quarterly reports. The Food Prices Review Board, and Mrs. Plumptre specifically, became a central participant in virtually every sub-crisis within a general crisis of rising food prices from 1973 onwards.

The FPRB in its first two years of existence from May 1973 to mid-1975 fulfilled the mandate expected of it by the Trudeau cabinet. It monitored price trends, provided plausible explanations to the public for what was happening, and generally drew attention and criticism away from the cabinet itself. The political role of the FPRB was not unlike that of past Royal Commissions or the continuing role of the Combines Branch of Consumer and Corporate Affairs. It provided information and interpretations which were useful in elaborating the problems of inflation but did not contribute directly to solutions. The predictions of the Board on price trends was generally, if not always, off the mark. For example, on June 29, 1974, the board confidently announced that "food price increases could ease this summer." The prediction, made ten days before the 1974 federal election, was contradicted by an average price rise of one-and-a-half per cent per month for the remainder of 1974.

The Board had no power to act directly but could make action recommendations to government. These recommendations, while often ignored in legislation, served to give some focus to the cut-and-thrust of parliamentary debate on the food price issue. Among the recommendations which *were* heeded were those in August 1973, calling for the government to cushion consumers against the impact of rising raw material prices for milk and cereal products. In the case of cereals, the government applied a two-price system on wheat to cushion the impact of rising world grain prices on domestic flour and bread. For fluid milk, the federal government applied a one-year-only 5¢ per quart subsidy. Both of these were recommendations advanced by the Prices Review Board. The seating of consumers on national farm products marketing boards, agreed to by Parliament in November 1974, was also a recommendation of the FPRB.

The FPRB and Mrs. Plumptre have been accused of playing a politically supportive role for the Liberal government in Ottawa. Their announcements during the 1974 federal election campaign, referring to an easing of consumer prices and to corporate profits as not being a factor in the pattern of higher food prices, were favourable to the Liberals. Conservative M.P. Jim McGrath (his party's consumer affairs critic), said Mrs. Plumptre was making an 'unwarranted intrusion' into the election. He was particularly distressed about her publicly-declared opposition to price and wage controls, a main plank of the P.C. platform.

The persistently apologetic role which the Board performed on behalf of food corporations cost it more in credibility than all other positions combined. The position taken repeatedly that "corporate profits were not a factor in inflation" was inconceivable to a public made aware of substantial profit increases in both 1973 and 1974 as reported in company annual reports. Although profits were not *the* central factor in inflation, the evidence of the FPRB's own special report on corporate profits in June 1974 suggested they were an important one.

According to the FPRB survey of fifty food corporations engaged in either processing or distribution, their returns "were not out of line with what was happening elsewhere in the economy." Mrs. Plumptre thereby entered a plea of 'not guilty.' This conclusion was despite the fact the Review Board survey showed a 29.7 per cent increase in the rate of return on investment in 1973 over 1972. A similar study by an Ontario government Commission showed a 46 per cent profit increase in the companies surveyed, and *they too* felt food corporations were unjustifiably fingered as a villain. The standard of measurement for government watchdogs seemed to be "what was happening elsewhere in the economy." In other words, if the monopoly sector was generally exploiting inflation as an opportunity to increase surplus at the expense of declining real incomes for workers there was no reason to point the finger specifically at the food industry. This logic makes little sense to low-income families and pensioners, however. It was their plight, in the first place, which was given by Herb Gray as part of the reason for setting up the Review Board.

There was another factor overlooked in the Review Board survey of Corporations. Some of the companies were subsidiaries of other companies in the same survey. Fifteen of the companies had direct ownership links with one or more of the other companies. In other words, although the Board chose to treat each company and its level of profits as a distinct and separate entity, in reality they were part and parcel of larger empires which accumulate surplus through non-productive holding companies. For example, B.C. Packers, West-fair Foods, and Kelly-Douglas were included as separate profit earners, when all of them are tied into George Weston Limited, the major holding company of the Weston family empire (Chapter 4). George Weston Limited increased its profits 86 per cent in 1973 and had a profit return on investment of 16.1 per cent. In general, the Review Board in this survey and in all its reports chose to ignore the reality of concentration and vertical integration as these related to prices and profits. The largest food chains and food processors had the highest profit returns, not necessarily because of efficiency but because of the advantage gained through ownership links and flexibility in marketing practices relative to smaller firms.

In the final analysis the role of the Prices Review Board was to avoid challenging the existing market structure. It was consistent with the politics of investigation since the days of Mackenzie King. The torpedoes are aimed at farm marketing boards, and the petty abuses of the retail system such as double ticketing, display advertising, and inadequate federal inspection standards. The major abuses of a monopoly market structure are spared, and the Review Board avoids recommendations which smack of direct state intervention. Mrs. Plumptre, like her boss André Ouellet, maintained an enthusiasm for the 'free market system.'

André Ouellet was appropriately the man in charge in 1974-75 not only of the Prices Review Board but all the agencies under Consumer and Corporate Affairs including the Combines Branch and its investigative arms. He was perfect for the job, the right man at the right time, like a missionary in a period of religious doubt. Unquestionably, the faith of the masses had been shaken by inflation and no one was more aware of it than the young Ouellet. In his maiden speech as Minister after displacing Herb Gray, Ouellet called for tougher measures against those who would engage in price-fixing or other violations of the competitive ethic. Ouellet stated bluntly, "If we don't act now, we will lose the free enterprise system . . . because the public will insist that the government intervene." Horrified at the thought of encroaching socialism (although he admits he was a delegate to the NDP founding convention in 1961), Ouellet called for a hard-line Combines Investigation Act, which, as in the U.S., would jail company executives for offences. He reintroduced amendments to the Act to promote truth in advertising and protect small businessmen from the depradations of large corporations. These, he promised, would "go a long way to restoring the public's faith in the free enterprise system."

Ouellet illustrates that neither the ideology nor the tactics of the federal government have advanced much since the days of Mackenzie King. As both a crusader and an opportunist, Ouellet embodies perfectly the qualities demanded of a corporation front-man within the federal state. On the one hand he took a strong 'principled' stand in support of the free market idelogy he adheres to by suggesting businessmen be jailed for Combines Act violations. In contrast he confessed to reporters that the anti-profiteering bill may be just window-dressing and may never be applied. His contradictions match nicely the contradiction built into a single government department charged with both consumer and corporate affairs.

Like Mackenzie King, Ouellet at thirty-six hoped to make his name in history by the introduction and enforcement of competitions law. In 1974 he inherited the stewardship of the long-awaited Competitions Act, a liberal reform measure with a pretense of toughening up the existing anti-combines law.

It was in 1967 that the Pearson government first began to prepare a new bill. In the eight years following the Competitions Act was prepared and presented to Parliament four times under four different cabinet ministers and never allowed to come to a vote. The lobby by industry had the government continuously reworking the legislation after it was first introduced by Ron Basford in 1971. Why the major corporations should give the Competitions Act heed when the government's Combines Branch has earned such a reputation for timidity is not altogether clear. It may have been that they took the reform rhetoric of Herb Gray and André Ouellet seriously and wanted to avoid future hassles. In any case they set out to dismantle the legislation in a process well described by Henry Aubin in the *Montreal Gazette*.

According to Aubin, 39 of the 40 witnesses who appeared before the Senate committee on Banking, Trade and Commerce (charged with reviewing the bill), were industry and business groups. The other was the Consumers Association of Canada. An eleven-corporation 'study group' included Canada Packers, the breweries, and major department stores among its members.

The new Competitions Act was to come in two parts, the first dealing with 'shady business practices' like double-ticketing, pyramid selling and misleading advertising. This part was to be passed in 1975 as a 'code of ethics' for Canadian business. The second part purported to control monopolies and aimed (in its original draft under Basford in 1971) to review mergers, monopoly practices, and interlocking directorships under a *Competitive Prices Tribunal*. The 'Tribunal' provision was withdrawn from the Bill after a howl of industry protest. As an alternative, the Restrictive Trade Practices Commission was to be given wider latitude. How much change in legal power would be given the Combines Branch awaited final redrafting under the careful scrutiny of industry observers. By spring 1975 it appeared as if the second stage of the bill might not surface before late 1976, almost ten years after the process was begun by Lester Pearson.

Whatever the outcome of the Competition Bill debates, the relationship between government and industry would not be substantially affected. The politics of avoidance and investigation would continue to be the basis of government's relationship to the massive power of corporations. The dilemma of the federal government remains as public investigative bodies have to investigate issues like inflation, price-fixing, and mergers and continue to acknowledge monopoly power. But the Combines Branch, charged with preserving 'free and open competition', will have to continue to present a fantasy world of an aggressive and competitive business environment.

Behind the formalized relations of government agencies and corporations, the politicians and businessmen are overwhelmingly of one class and one political persuasion. The interconnections of business and government in Canada have been detailed by social analysts such as John Porter in *The Vertical Mosaic*. Those links with public agencies are as impressive in agribusiness as in any other field. James Richardson is a direct pipeline from the Winnipeg private grain trade to the cabinet. Eugene Whelan, a bona-fide farmer himself, had a general manager of H.J. Heinz Limited spearheading his election campaigns. The McCain brothers of New Brunswick are prominent Liberals who run the potato empire of the Atlantic region and thrive off federal DREE grants, when they aren't running as Liberal candidates. Rod Bryden of the Bryden Consulting company learned his tricks as a deputy minister of DREE and a co-ordinator of the federal government's Grains Group. Then he quit and went into private consulting. One of his first major projects was a feasibility study for the Weyburn Inland Terminal Association, financed in part by a $35,000 grant from former colleagues in DREE.

The connections between government and private industry need not be intimant, although to a considerable degree they are. It is sufficient that they accept as the basis of a common working relationship the assumption of 'non-intervention' by the state in the market determinations of a private economy. From that basis of understanding, the gamesmanship of protecting the public interest can be tolerated by business whatever its nuisance implications. Business-men know that without the credibility of 'public watch-dog' earned for government by the rhetoric of the Herb Grays, Beryl Plumptres and André Ouellet's things could be much worse. The issue of inflation might be drawn more clearly along class lines, with consequences frightening for the average business executive to contemplate.

Notes to Chapter 8

The major references in this chapter are included in the Bibliography. They can be listed in summary here. They include a sizeable number of public documents plus an article by Rosenbluth and Thordburn in the *Canadian Journal of Economics and Political Science* entitled "Canadian Anti-Combines Administration," published in November 1961.

Government documents include the Royal Commissions of 1934-35, 1948-49, 1958-59 and 1967-68, all on increases in prices for food and other commodities. They also include Reports of the Restrictive Trade Practices Commission into the meat packing, sugar refining and retail grocery industries. And they include the Annual Reports of the Director of Investigation and Research for the Combines Investigation Branch from 1958 to 1973. And, finally, they include the quarterly and special reports of the Food Prices Review Board in the period from 1973 to 1975 as well as the minutes of the Committee on Trends in Food Prices in 1973.

IX

Canada and the World Food Crisis

The world food crisis encompasses the twin problems of inflation and starvation. In 1974-75 the food issue shared the focus of formal international politics with the energy crisis and disturbed the comfort of developed capitalist economies as well as crippling the Third World. But the nature and definition of the problem were sharply different in the United States and Canada from the character it took in the colonized areas of Asia, Africa, and Latin America. In Canada the issues were inflation and shortages in the domestic market and a humanitarian concern for the plight of massive starvation among people in the Third World.

The causes of both the domestic and international features of the world food crisis have been described as 'international' by Canadian political leaders. In other words, Canadians are the victims and not the cause, and our national government and its agencies are incapable of single-handedly protecting Canada from food supply and price problems. On the domestic front, Beryl Plumptre and the Food Prices Review Board have repeatedly emphasized that the basic causes of food price inflation were international. In its representations to the World Food Conference held in late 1974 the Canadian delegation consistently avoided debate over basic trade and tariff policies and emphasized the need for more food aid to cope with the short-term crisis of starvation. The Americans did not even go that far.

As one Canadian non-governmental delegate summarized the position upon return from Rome: "Canada was the moral leader among developed countries, but that was in a contest in which no one else was bidding."[1] Two months before the Rome conference, the U.S. had been urging the priority of a global strategy on the twin issues of energy and food. This was the thrust of Gerald Ford's September address to the U.N. general assembly. But two months later, in spite of pressure and urging from U.N. officials and conference delegates, the U.S. refused to make commitments. Agriculture Secretary Earl Butz even denied that any crisis existed.

The Canadian role at the Conference was less crude and less cynical than that of the United States. Eugene Whelan, co-chairman of the Canadian government contingent to Rome, announced on his return that "politics won and food lost." Whelan's intended meaning was not altogether clear from this remark, but the comment was appropriate. International politics *was* a factor in the world food crisis before, during, and after the Rome conference. But it wasn't the 'international squabbling" variety implied in Whelan's comment. It had more to do with the extension of the national economic objectives of some countries into the affairs and destinies of others.

Nationalism and Imperialism

National and international problems in the production and distribution of food are interrelated. Canada, for example, has a major export and import role in food products which ties us specifically to the economies of other countries. The nature of our economic ties with other countries shapes our contribution to the world food crisis. Despite our diplomatic offensive in Rome with its pretense of becoming central to the solution, we remain part of the problem through our relationship to the United States.

The *national* economic policies of all countries would seemingly be the most critical arena in solving problems of more equitable food production and distribution. This is obvious in light of the fact that the vast majority of world food resources are produced and consumed *within national boundaries*. Less than 10 per cent of cereal grains, for example, are involved in import or export over national boundaries. Furthermore there are very few areas of the world which do not have the natural resources necessary to be fully self-sufficient in the provision of basic food-stuffs.

Do we then conclude that distribution problems exist because the social and political systems in some countries are inadequate to the task of feeding their own people? To some extent this may be a fair conclusion. For example, the comparison is often made between the nations of India and China. Both have large populations and large agricultural land masses to feed them. But India faces continuous shortages which are intensified by inequitable distribution of available food supplies along lines of caste, class, and region. Since the Chinese revolution of 1949, however, the built-in social inequities in food production and distribution within China have largely been eliminated.

But the inequality of nationally-determined policies on food production and distribution is not restricted to countries such as India, which has open starvation in some provinces. Both Canada and the United States have growing incidence of malnutrition among certain sectors of the population and a generally widening disparity of diet standards between rich and poor as a result of inflation. These circumstances are primarily but not exclusively the product of national governments and national priorities.

In world agricultural production and trade, countries do not trade on the basis of simply exchanging what they can best produce for what other countries can best produce in some spirit of mutual advantage. There is in no sense a 'pooling' of production from diverse climates and resource capabilities into some kind of international co-operative bread basket.

With a double role as both food colony and food colonizer, Canada has a complicated place in world food trade. In general Canada is dependent on the United States for markets for food exports, and as a supplier of food imports. Also, Canadian production and trade policies are heavily influenced by the United States. But Canada also plays a role of colonizer in relationship to some resource exporting countries of the Third World.

Colonial relationships in food trade are directly connected to world hunger. The developed capitalist countries of North America, Europe and Japan are consuming a disproportionate amount of food per capita relative to world standards. It is estimated that 210 million Americans consume as much food in grain equivalent as the 1.5 billion people who live in the most populated nations, India and China. (Grain equivalent is a measure of food consumption which starts with actual food consumption in a country and then calculates the amount of grain required to produce the beef, chicken, milk, bread, and other food consumed.) In total, the 20 per cent of the population living in the most industrialized countries consume as much food as the other 80 per cent of the world's population.

To support the consumption habits of the industrialized countries, the world's agricultural resources have been gradually converted toward the production of 'luxury' high-protein food commodites. Through colonized plantation agriculture in commodities such as sugar, tea, coffee, and fruits, the resources of third world countries are drained to feed the already-overfed populations of developed countries. Their own populations may be starving. In 1974, for instance, H. J. Heinz was encouraging production of beans for export in hunger-ravaged Ethiopia.

In more general terms, the Canadian Council for International Co-operation (CCIC) claimed in 1974 that

Rich countries export 3 million tons of average protein high profit grains to poor countries each year while 4 million tons of high protein foods flow from pour countries to rich countries each year. The rich have the power to command food from the market which is denied to the poor.[2]

The international market for food has the same character as the Canadian domestic market in terms of disparities along class lines. Nations can be ranked as consumers in the same way that consumers within a capitalist market economy can be measured and distinguished by class. Industrial nations are the 'middle class' consumers in global terms, while underdeveloped nations achieve the status of 'welfare dependents.' As in a national capitalist economy, the rich stay rich by virtue of their control over the production and consumption patterns of the poor.

Interpretations from the Rome Conference

The burst of publicity surrounding the World Food Conference in 1974 had all the moral fervour of an international 'war on poverty'. From the perspective of the advanced capitalist countries it was a time to voice humanitarian concern for the plight of the starving masses. There was no sense of blame or self-criticism on the part of western political leaders who saw food shortages as a consequence of natural disasters, lack of population control, and poor management of economic resources in the countries affected.

For their part, political leaders of the third world set out both moral and political dimensions to the food crisis. On the moral question they pointed to the decadence of industrial nations which were wasting, hoarding and destroying food resources while sharply cutting back on food aid. Politically, third world and socialist countries challenged the trade and development policies of the U.S. and other western powers. The channelling of food resources from the third world through international agribusiness to the developed capitalist markets of Europe and North America was clearly seen as a major factor in the present situation.

Press coverage of the Rome Conference emphasized the moral questions and largely ignored the political questions. News reports concentrated on the contradictions of a world of affluence and starvation and appealed to sentiments of liberal guilt. This reinforced the 'welfare' response to the crisis and was a boost to the continuing efforts of international relief agencies like Red Cross, Oxfam, and the straight religious charities. It also lent credibility to the Canadian government's position of expanded food aid. But the coverage failed to present the political and economic analysis of the problem despite the efforts of some non-government delegates to raise that perspective.

The response of liberal charity faces a seemingly bottomless pit of direct and extreme human suffering. U.N. agencies were estimating in October 1974 that 450 million people were weakened from severe malnutrition and as many as 10 million would die before spring without massive aid.

In contrast to the staggering dimensions of the food shortage, liberal journalists commented extensively and repeatedly, around the time of the food conference, on the decadence and waste of North America. For example 1½ million tons of fertilizer poured annually onto the lawns, cemeteries and golf courses of North America would produce enough additional grain in third world countries to feed an additional 80 million people per year. Millions of tons of protein-rich food are marketed to pet owners and unavailable for human consumption. Meanwhile the human eating habit of North Americans enabled us to consume an average of 2,000 pounds of grain equivalent annually by 1973.

The liberal guilt position reinforced by the media was both positive and negative as an interpretation of the world food crisis. It was unquestionably healthy in terms of creating awareness and building public pressure on government to at least take its 'welfare' role seriously. The extent of Canadian government aid would prevent some loss of life in the short term. But liberal guilt also served to confuse the issue by placing the blame on the mass of undifferentiated individuals who happen to be born into an industrialized capitalist economy. As individuals they could solve nothing by contributing to the Red Cross or becoming vegetarians except perhaps the nagging of their conscience. By dwelling on the moral issues instead of national trade and foreign development policies of the U.S. and Canada, the media reduced the possibility of any collective solution of a political nature coming from the mass of Canadian people. All the major political institutions from political parties to churches and trade unions accepted the media interpretation of the issue as a moral one. It appeared as if most Canadians were satisfied that their government's commitment in 1975 of 1 million tons of food-aid in wheat per year was not only adequate but generous.

Canada as Bread Basket

The Canadian reputation as a major supplier of world food reserves is somewhat distorted. It is true that Canada, along with the United

States, produces a healthy proportion of the world grain reserves. But Canada also serves increasingly with the U.S. as a key market for specialized food commodities from third world countries. And, finally, we serve as a branch-plant partner of the United States to provide a home base for the international food corporations which shape production patterns, prices, and eventually markets of food commodities.

In the role of supplier, the Canadian contribution to world food markets is substantial. We are second in volume as a food exporter to the United States. But the nature of our contribution contradicts to some degree the pattern of world needs. We produce less than our capacity, we produce for markets which are least in need of our resource and we trade in terms which disadvantage this country's industrial development potential in secondary food processing. Our position as an agricultural exporter is not different from our general trading role as a supplier of resources and raw materials to developed industrial countries.

Canada's $3 billion in food exports in 1973 was about 12 per cent of total exports. Half of the food total was in wheat. In world terms we were in 1973 small as a producer, our wheat crop making up less than 5 per cent of world production. But because we have such a tremendous land mass and such a sparse population we contribute disproportionately to food exports. Our wheat exports account on the average for about 20 per cent of all wheat exports.

The recent shift in agricultural exports by Canada from grain to other commodities has come as a result of demands from our primary trading partners. Contrary to the myths about feeding the hungry masses of the world, 80 per cent of our agricultural exports go to European, Japanese, and American markets. Their demand is shifting from cereal crops to protein crops, animal feed grains, and beef and pork products directly. Canadian production planning has responded accordingly.

Wheat, which accounted for 60 per cent of total export value in the 1960s, had by the early 1970s been reduced to 40 per cent.[3] Britain and Western European countries which were traditionally the biggest buyers of Canadian food exports had by the 1970s been displaced first by the United States and then Japan. The U.S. and Japan, which between them in 1973 absorbed 35 per cent of our total exports, registered most of their increased volume in the purchase of livestock and oilseed crops.

This overall shift in food exports reflects a combination of federal supply management policies, the influence of U.S. trade policy on Canadian exports, and the shift in consumption patterns for food among industrial nations throughout the world.

From Wheat to Meat: 1966-73

Agriculture resource planning in North America in the late sixties concentrated on policies to systematically reduce wheat surpluses. By 1966 both Canada and the United States had come to view their unsold wheat stocks as a major domestic problem. This was despite 1967 FAO predictions which projected shortages of 41 million tons by 1975. Since Canada and the U.S. combined represented 65 per cent of all world wheat reserves, the consequences for the global community of reducing production and eliminating surpluses were potentially great. It meant the loss of insurance against potential world shortages for both the developed importing countries, like Britain and Japan, *and* the underdeveloped Third World countries who had received a substantial proportion of U.S. export grain by way of food-aid prior to 1966.

Two ways for the grain-exporting countries to reduce their inventories were to sell wheat at below market value to enlarge sales or to encourage production shifts by farmers into other commodities.

The two countries applied variations of policy as suited their circumstances. In the United States wheat exports had been less central to the overall economy than was the case in Canada. The American economy, with a much broader proportion of its production anchored in an industrial base, had no great dependence on agricultural exports. The U.S. government was inclined to use wheat as a flexible instrument of foreign policy. Food-aid programs to developing countries became an instrument of establishing and maintaining dependency on U.S. trade and investment as early as Roosevelt.

Throughout the 1950s and up to 1966, U.S. trade policy was primarily to direct its wheat exports through 'concessional sales' to Third World countries. This was a system of partial food-aid in which countries were able to get access to U.S. cereal grains at prices and conditions much more liberal than those available from other major exporting countries like Canada, Australia and Argentina. The result was that U.S. export volumes were substantial but without greatly interfering with the sales of Canada to traditional overseas markets not eligible for 'concessional sales' such as Britain and Western Europe. By 1965-66 U.S. aid shipments in wheat had reached a peak of 583 million bushels, more than half their total exports. But despite the food-aid strategy and a policy of discouraging wheat acreage through farm payments, grain stocks were building up in storage.

In 1966, U.S. policy changed dramatically. They abandoned their liberal policy of concessional sales, shed their passive attitudes to traditional markets and moved aggressively into commercial sales. They increased wheat acreage allotment in 1966 by 30 per cent. Suddenly the U.S. needed to improve its balance of trade with other industrialized countries. Concessional sales dropped in a single year from 583 million to 414 million bushels while commercial sales increased from 277 to 333 million bushels. The U.S. increased its wheat exports by 15 per cent in 1967-68, while the other wheat exporters, Canada, Australia, and Argentina, whose markets were being invaded, dropped 40 per cent in total combined exports. The Americans gained market sales in Britain, western Europe, and the Soviet Union, all major Canadian markets of the early sixties.

The impact of the shift in American policy in the mid-sixties was of major importance to the food crisis of the mid-1970s as it had something of a domino affect. The first impact was to enlarge the role of private international grain brokers in manipulating world markets and prices. Responsibility for stock-piling grain and negotiating trade deals shifted from government bureaucrats to the private grain trade. By 1972 the Nixon Administration had reduced government food-aid commitments to 150 million bushels and 80 per cent of the grain supply was authorized for sale by the private grain brokers through the mechanism of the 'open market.' This was to lead inevitably, and catastrophically, to higher world grain prices.

Secondly, the policy of withdrawing food-aid to Third World nations was coupled with initiation of 'the green revolution.' This was a process which purported to reduce dependence of Third World countries on imported food by encouraging the mechanization of their domestic agriculture with American technology. It had the effect generally of increasing agricultural production in these countries, but food became more expensive for the indigenous population than it had when they depended more totally on imports. Ironically some of these countries have increased their agricultural exports to industrial countries while their own peasant classes face starvation.

The third direct result of U.S. policy was the loss of markets for Canada and other wheat exporting countries, and the subsequent rapid build-up of their wheat reserves. The U.S. price for wheat was dropped below the established International Wheat Agreement Price of $1.96 ½ in 1966-67. With U.S. treasury export subsidies, the price to buyers for American wheat was only $1.70. Canadian market sales quickly evaporated as the Canadian Wheat Board attempted to maintain the basic international price. The Canadian share of total exports fell from 27 per cent in 1964-65 to 17.2 per cent in 1967-68. The Wheat Board eventually dropped its own export price to $1.70.

It was at this point that the Trudeau government, besieged by farmer protest over depressed prices and falling sales, produced its

Task Force Report on Agriculture. The main points and assumptions of the Task Force have already been discussed (in Chapter 7), but can be underlined here in terms of their impact on the international market.

The Task Force proposed a range of measures to reduce wheat stocks. These included conversion of wheatland to grassland for cattle, conversion to other crops, and taking land out of production altogether. All of these measures were enacted by the federal government with varying degrees of success. In general they contributed to a five-year pattern from 1969 to 1974 in which wheat acreage was reduced 30 per cent and cattle population was increased by 40 per cent. Similar patterns were apparent in Australia and Argentina. Even the U.S. increased its cattle population by 20 per cent in this time-period. Wheat available for export *had* to be reduced as a result.

(There is room for argument about how much the production shift in Canada was the result of 'free market forces' and how much was due to direct government incentive. Clearly both factors influenced producer choices in the late 1960s. But there is no doubt that had the federal government encouraged continued wheat production it would have been successful. If they had made payments on farm-stored grain, or bought wheat and held it off the farm in storage terminals, farmers would have continued to grow wheat. It is by far the easiest crop to produce from the standpoint of risk, and it involves a much less labour-intensive farming operation than the 'mixed' farming with cattle and hogs which farmers were encouraged into.)

By mid-1972, world wheat stocks were substantially reduced through the concerted actions of the governments of the United States and Canada. The U.S. had met their objectives through aggressive selling and the generosity of the federal treasury. Canada had gone the route of sabotaging production through operation LIFT, plus various incentive programs to produce commodities other than wheat. The conditions were set for panic and inflation in the summer and fall of 1972. The series of developments which began with a crop failure in the Soviet Union and ended with a tripling of grain prices and major inflation in all food commodities was unexpected, but might have been predicted with the knowledge of world conditions available to agricultural planners.

The point of which everyone was aware by 1971 was that world grain reserves as a proportion of total wheat production were critically low. They were proportionately low not simply because the exporting countries were *reducing their carry-over* stocks but also because total world *production and consumption had increased* so dramatically through the 1960s. The dramatic trend which saw wheat production increase 40 per cent from 1966 to 1971 and wheat consumption

TABLE 8

WORLD WHEAT PRODUCTION (IN MILLION TONS)

	1961-65 (Average)	1971	1972	
TOTAL PRODUCTION:	254.2	353.8	342.4	(TOTAL
DEVELOPED COUNTRIES	103.7	126.2	122.1	(SUB-TOTAL)
EEC block	31.8	40.1	41.4	
Other Western Europe	12.7	16.6	14.9	
Japan	1.3	.4	.3	
United States	33.1	44	42	
Canada	15.4	14.4	14.5	
Australia	8.2	8.5	6.5	
Others	1.2	2.2	2.5	
UNDERDEVELOPED COUNTRIES	48.9	71.2	78.9	(SUB-TOTAL)
Near East	17.6	23	26.2	
Far East	15.8	31	33.9	
Africa	3.9	5.3	6.4	
Latin America	11.6	11.9	12.4	
CENTRALLY PLANNED SOCIALIST COUNTRIES	101.6	156.4	141.4	(SUB-TOTAL)
U.S.S.R.	64.2	98.8	80	
Eastern Europe	14.8	24.7	26.6	
China	22.2	32.5	34.5	
Others	——	.4	.3	

SOURCE: UNITED NATIONS FAO–1973

increase at the same rate, was well underway when the Task Force made its recommendations to the federal government in Canada to divert to cattle from wheat. By 1971 the world was producing and consuming 350 million tons of wheat. But most of the increase came because both the underdeveloped countries and the socialist nations were becoming more self-sufficient. One of the myths had been that underdeveloped countries could not match population growth with production growth. But in the period 1952-62 population in these countries increased 2.4 per cent per year while food production increased 3.1 per cent. From 1962-72, population growth annually was 2.4 per cent while food production expanded 2.7 per cent. The problem for underdeveloped economies has been the inability to retain the benefit of improved production for home markets, and more recently the inability to obtain fertilizer and technology from developed countries to sustain production expansion.

In terms of Canada we can see that total wheat production was down about 7 per cent over a ten-year period while total world production was up 35-40 per cent and production in the developing countries was up over 70 per cent. Canada's status as a world wheat producer went down as production declined from 8 per cent of the world total to about 5 per cent.

China, the U.S.S.R., and Eastern European countries combined increased their production from 101.6 million to 156.4 million from the early 1960s to 1971. Developing countries similarly increased production from 48.9 to 78.9 million tons. But since all gains in production were totally offset by increases in consumption both directly as cereal and indirectly through animals, the world reserves of grain were not improved. By 1972, total world trade in grain amounted to only 14 per cent of total consumption. The stocks on hand in the exporting countries amounted to only a six-week world supply, where in 1961 they were a four-month reserve. By fall 1974 these stocks represented only a 27-day supply.

The point which was evident by the mid-1960s was that along with increased production of cereals in the world there was a growing level of consumption related to population growth and introduction of red meat diets. This in turn meant a much *greater* need for a world grain reserve given the potential of natural crop failure in any of a dozen major producing countries. But the warnings were ignored and the traditional exporting countries proceeded to reduce their stocks. Disaster finally struck in summer 1972.

Detente and the 'Great Grain Robbery': 72-73

The Soviet Union is the world's largest wheat producer. In 1971 they produced a record 98 million tons of wheat. But in 1972 the crop showed signs of disaster (it later turned out to be 80 million tons), so Soviet buyers began to look abroad for purchases. In the months of June, July, and August 1972 they moved quietly into the U.S. to negotiate with potential suppliers. In a matter of days they managed to contract to purchase a total of 12 million tons of wheat and 7 million of other grains. The volume of these purchases was without precedent, but they were made separately and independently with the major international grain brokers: Continental, Carghill, Dreyfus, Bunge, Cook, and Gamae. It was only later when these companies started to firm up their delivery contracts that the United States Government began to appreciate the extent of the total deal.

As the major grain companies attempted to meet their obligations they had to bid competitively for the available U.S. supply. This affected the price levels on the Chicago commodity exchange, driving wheat 'futures' up sharply. The world price went up from less than $2.00 per bushel to over $6.00 in a matter of twelve months. But the Soviet Union remained protected in their massive purchases, guaranteed the subsidized U.S. export price of $1.63 per bushel.

The sequence of events between Soviet buyers and U.S. sellers became known to Americans as the 'Great Grain Rip-off' and it was the subject of a senate inquiry a year later. It was disastrous for consumers all over the world, but for the executives of the grain companies involved it merely reflected the necessary risks of 'supply and demand' selling. Walter Folliott, Manager and Secretary for Louis Dreyfus' Canadian operations, discussed the deal in a 1974 Winnipeg interview:

> We had our pants taken down. It cost Carghill money, and Continental too. They do it to five of them. The next day we show up in the market all wanting to buy one million tons. That was the most astute piece of business the Russians ever pulled.[4]

Rather than viewing the U.S. pricing system as somehow being at fault for contributing so directly and drastically to international inflation, Folliott defended the system unquestioningly and attacked the Canadian Wheat Board for not being part of it.

> You must remember trading internationally, it's every man for himself. The Russians are as aware of that as we were. There was nothing dishonest about it. If Canada had been on the free market we would have got a piece of that action too. The Canadian farmer doesn't realize it was the best thing that ever happened to him. U.S. stocks had been keeping the price down. The Canadian Wheat Board had nothing to do with the appreciation of wheat prices since 1972.

There is little doubt that the price movements in the United States were the main cause of world price adjustments including those by the federally appointed Canadian Wheat Board. The background to the price rise and its impact are an important illustration of the dangers attached to an open market system of bidding on scarce resources.

The Soviet Union had several good reasons for choosing the U.S. as a source of supply rather than Canada, Australia, or Argentina. One was the pricing arrangements offered in U.S. trade policy. Subsidies on grain reduced the per bushel price 50¢ below the 1972 world price and would amount to a saving of $300 million on the volume of grain purchased in 1972. This amount was paid out from the federal treasury to American farmers to bring their returns up to the world price of $2.10. A second reason for choosing the U.S. was the general strategy of 'detente' being pursued by the major powers. Trade was a key aspect. The trade deal in grain was announced with much fanfare in Washington by Henry Kissinger and Earl Butz. It was portrayed as a concrete result of the Nixon-Brezhnev talks in Moscow in May 1972. The 'deal' as announced by the White House was a purchase-credit understanding whereby the Soviets would buy "at least" $750 million worth of U.S. grain over three years. No maximum was set and all purchases would be negotiated through the private grain trade.

This negotiation of trade contracts with private companies was the third reason for the Soviets choosing the U.S. market. It is ironic, given the socialist practice of central planning by the state, that the Soviets avoided dealing with Australia or Canada, which would have meant government-to-government negotiations. They knew this approach would raise questions as to the amount and price of the total purchase and its effects on other committed markets, including domestic needs. In the U.S. no such troublesome questions needed to arise. U.S. government involvement was restricted to a 'go ahead' on trade and credit arrangements. They were only concerned with 'minimums' of volume as a condition of trading. The Soviet buyers were free to deal independently and one by one with private international firms so that the scope and terms of the overall purchase were unknown to anyone but the buyers until it was too late.

The consequence of the deal was that the three-year purchase agreement of $750 million minimum was surpassed by August of the first year. This was at a time when world prices were low anyway, at roughly $2.10 a bushel. Then the price was further reduced by the U.S. treasury subsidy of $300 million. This deal affected not only world prices, which tripled, but also contributed to further massive food-aid cuts, higher domestic prices on bread flour, cereal products, and dairy, poultry, and meat products.[5]

The 'Great Grain Rip-off' was more than a failure of the commodity exchange system of buying and selling. It was a consequence of deliberate political objectives pursued through trading policies of the U.S. government and the U.S. based international grain trade. In four years they had managed to reduce food-aid in grain by a full two-thirds while still reducing and almost eliminating wheat reserves.

The political motives of Nixon and Earl Butz were bare-faced and obvious. They openly gloated in July 1972 when announcing "the largest grain deal as far as we know in the history of the world." The political scenario was to cut surpluses, raise farm prices, and harvest the votes in the fall 1972 presidential elections.

The motives of the Chicago-based grain brokers were not essentially different from the politicians, although they couldn't help but be better informed. They knew that the movement of more than $1 billion of U.S. grain to a previously limited market was bound to disrupt existing trade commitments and U.S. domestic reserves. But from the point of view of the grain trade this was essential. Grain buyers and speculators regarded the surpluses of the 1960s and the government-regulated food aid exports as a curse. In contrast, shortages would bring on a lively round of profit-taking on futures contracts.

As the paper price went up on the commodity exchanges, the real selling and purchase price rose throughout the world from around $2.00 in fall 1972 to $6.00 a year later. The Canadian Wheat Board adjusted its price, along with the Chicago price. Canadian market prospects improved sharply as the Soviet Union took its delivery of U.S. supply which was then unavailable to other buyers. Canada and the other exporters, Australia and Argentina, increased their sales primarily to the 'developed' countries. Canadian exports of wheat and wheat flour increased from a low of 310 million bushels in 1968-69 to 580 million in 1972-73. Gross income to prairie farmers doubled with the combination of higher sales volume and higher prices. By 1973-74 the world wheat reserves in exporting countries reached their lowest point in 25 years.

Obviously not all of the adjustment in world wheat prices can be blamed on the role of commodity exchanges. They exaggerate the impact of real or potential shortages. But other major influences in 1972-73 included the international realignment of currencies which forced the United States, and automatically Canada, to adjust their export values on commodities as much as 30 per cent in U.S. dollars. Prices for commodities exported rose to offset devaluation of the U.S. dollar in foreign currencies. This upward pressure was independent of direct increases in cost of production, world shortages in grain, or pending crop failures. But the combined influence of all the measurable inflationary pressures should not have totalled more than a 60 per cent increase in the international price of cereals. Instead, by virtue of the 'open market' pricing mechanism, there was a 200 per cent increase. Such inflation in a single year reinforced disparities in world cereal consumption but it also created a crisis in grain-fed agricultural commodities, such as the beef and dairy industries discussed earlier.

Canada as Luxury Market: The Sugar Trade

Sugar is in world terms a luxury market which caters to the diet of developed countries. It is one of Canada's major food imports.

Our import-export pattern in sugar is an interesting contrast to our role in the grain trade. In grain we are an exporter, and most of our exports go in raw unprocessed form rather than as flour or other cereal by-products. We are in essence a staple trading colony for the food processing industries of Europe or Japan. In sugar the opposite is true. Not only do our sugar refineries import 98 per cent of our sugar in raw form from producing countries, they actually process this raw sugar and re-export some of it for other markets. We exported 135 million pounds of refined sugar in 1973. Canadian sugar refineries, as part of the international sugar cartel, profited directly from the sweat labour of apartheid policies in South Africa, Canada's major supplier.

In Canada we consumed 100 pounds of sugar per capita in 1974. At that rate of consumption the world's 80 million tons of sugar produced annually would feed roughly one-third of the total world population. Obviously some people were eating less. If they weren't eating less in August 1973 when the price was $16 per hundred, they were by December 1974 when the price was $72 per hundred.

World production of sugar is largely consumed by the nations which produce it. About 70 per cent disappears domestically, with most of the industrial countries and many developing countries having some cane or beet sugar to draw from. Of the remaining 30 per cent, half is traded on the basis of government-to-government negotiated sales, and half is sold on the 'open world market.' But as with grain it is this 'open market' price which determines the refinery price and ultimately the retail price. As with grain the price is subject to distortions on the basis of speculation in the commodity exchanges.

Canada produces 12 per cent of its total market needs from sugar beets in western Canada. The rest of its requirements are filled by imports of cane sugar primarily from Australia, South Africa, and Fiji. The Canadian market consists of 40 per cent domestic 'bag' sugar for home consumption, and 60 per cent industrial sugar in canned fruits, ice creams, soft drinks, confectionaries, and baked goods. Obviously when sugar prices go out of control as they did in 1974, a great many consumer food items beyond sugar are affected. There is a multiplier effect in the processing stage because sugar is a widely-used additive.

The 'crisis' in the sugar commodity was strictly one of price from 1973-75. Prices increased five-fold in 1974 and increased ten-fold from 1967-74. But the issue of price did not become a problem just in 1974. Prior to that time the problem existed in a slightly different form. The world price of raw sugar was depressed for the producing countries. An International Sugar Agreement, which existed until it expired at the end of 1973, kept prices stable but low relative to costs of production. This encouraged and reinforced exploitive labour conditions in the producing countries. In South Africa, Canada's major supplier, the low sugar price reinforced plantation and state policies of hiring cheap black labour made available through apartheid policies. Mechanization in the production of sugar was slowed by the low world price. In Canada, where the sugar beet industry depended on migrant native farm workers each year, costs were too high to be covered by the pre-1974 world price for raw sugar. The federal government had to subsidize Canadian producers beyond the world price in order to allow them to sell their product to refiners at the world price and still meet costs.

Prior to 1974, then, the market for raw sugar was characterized by short booms and long depressions to the detriment of the producing countries, their producer owners and the exploited migrant cane cutters and beet pickers. But this did not mean that the North American price of *retail sugar* was necessarily a bargain. The problem for consumers over the long-term has been that the international cartel of sugar refineries has had the power to pass on inflationary price increases in the refined product *despite* their overly cheap supplies. In Canada the big three Eastern refineries of Atlantic Sugar, Redpath Industries (formerly Canada and Dominion Sugar Company), and St. Lawrence Sugar Refineries, have twice been dragged into federal courts for alleged price fixing at artificially high levels (see Chapter 8).

The price rises in 1974 resulted from open market speculative trading which involved both the refineries themselves and petty speculators. The trade fed on rumour and panic throughout the fall of 1974. There was no real shortage as production matched consumption of 83 million tons, but fears of purchasing and hoarding by Arab nations, holding of supplies by refineries, and threatened cutbacks in production by some sugar producing countries all pushed prices up.

One syndicated story from the *New York Times* News Service in November 1974 illustrated the character of the uncontrolled market at the peak of inflation. It read in part:

> Feverish speculation in the inflated sugar market has given rise to price-kiting through agreements to buy and sell millions of tons of sugar crops around the world that may not exist. . . .

> . . . The practice has involved sugar buyers for such major business users as candy, pastry, soft-drink and syrup producers. It involves offers of growers contracts for central and South American cane that has never been planted.

The practice is described by industrial sugar buyers as a world-wide activity in which prices for non-existent sugar are consecutively bid up. This activity inevitably influences the real price of the commodity.

The sellers play on an industrial buyer's need in a tight supply situation. They place cryptic telephone calls, ascertain a buyer's real interest and provide only vague information. Last week a sugar buyer for a large candy company received his 25th such call in a month. . . .

"Anybody who has a telex machine seems to be involved," another potential buyer said. These salesmen obtain a commitment from a sugar user, contact either a broker or wholesaler in a London Bank and report they have an order for 100,000 tons. The bank is asked to provide its guarantee and some in London have.

The successive selling of the contracts is said to produce heavy returns for the operators. Only an occasional delivery of an accidentally available quantity is forthcoming. . . ."

The article pointed out that the speculators involved here were not legitimate brokers. But the practice they were involved in of buying and selling future delivery contracts for non-existent sugar supplies, though less regulated, was no different in kind or effect from the role of legal trading in the New York exchange.

There is evidence to suggest that the sugar refineries exploited the price rise to extra advantage by moving the bulk of their refined sugar supplies onto the market at the peak price when there was a panic over impending shortages. November 1974 was the peak for prices in the U.S. market as raw sugar topped at $64.00 per cwt. on November 20. Consumption remained high because the industry was circulating rumours of impending shortages. But despite the reports of short-supply at the time it was later reported that U.S. refineries had shipped a near record 217,877 tons the week ending November 25, compared to 173,067 in the same week a year earlier. The refineries read the market perfectly. They took the refined sugar they had processed and stored when raw sugar prices were lower, and unloaded it onto the market when the speculated price was at its peak and consumers were panicked into increasing their consumption in spite of the price.

Two months later, the price had dropped to $40 per cwt. for raw sugar and the consumer market had fallen off, having stocked up at the high price. Retail prices in the U.S. dropped from a 5-pound price of $3.74 on November 25 to $2.48 on February 1, 1975. The 30 per cent decline at retail levels compared to a 40 per cent wholesale decline, so increasing the price spread from producer to retail.

The price to producers could be predicted to return toward minimum costs of production within a few months. The problem for consumers was that the refineries had no obligation to completely return to earlier price levels for refined sugar. When they decided to increase their margin, they had the power collectively to decide what the price of refined sugar should be.

Beyond the refineries, which were at least subjected to challenge for price fixing, there were the industrial users of sugar. The soft-drink and confectionary manufacturers, bakeries, canneries, ice cream plants and so on had all justified price increases throughout 1974 in line with the wildly inflationary sugar price. It would be unusual if any of the grocery products with sugar additives were decreased in price in recognition of a return to 'normal' sugar prices. The problem is not the dishonesty of manufacturers, it is their unwillingness as partners in oligopoly markets to engage in price cuts which could lead to retaliation by rivals. What could be hoped, at least, was that the deflation of sugar prices would slow the rate of increase in all the refined food products in which it plays a cost role.

The Open Market System

If the international food system has any single feature which is most cancerous and destructive to the whole of production and distribution it is the role of the speculator. The speculators, people who extract profits from the buying and selling of paper contracts, prey on the world food system. They produce nothing, and they gamble on the lives and miseries of others. For the speculator, bad news is good news. Crop failures, floods, an early frost — any of these catastrophes can be the source of immensely profitable trading. This is the main advantage which the promoters of commodity speculation hold up in contrast to stock exchanges. The Secretary of the Winnipeg Commodity Exchange has summed it up best:

> By and large, if you get some good healthy international disaster, they break the stock market downwards, while they break the commodities market upwards. People don't have to have IBM stocks; they do have to have bread.[6]

Toronto brokerage firms were wild with enthusiasm during the panic run on soybean futures in the fall of 1972. They claimed a 500 per cent increase in trade activity over levels in 1969. One broker explained a year later that if the housewife had put $200 into soybean futures in fall 1972 instead of filling her freezer with beef, she could have made $4,000-$5,000 by now and could afford the higher prices for steak.

The professional speculator keeps track of world conditions as diverse as the winter snowfall in the Ukraine to the grasshopper hatch in western Canada. He knows what the probabilities of human suffering are and he is more than a little prepared to transfer his knowledge into hard cash. By investing in contracts which can be expected to rise sharply in price over a three-or-four-month period he can sell them for a simple net gain or he can re-invest in a rising market to pyramid his earnings. The tricks of petty speculation on a large scale and small are laid out by Morton Shulman in his popular book *Anyone Can Make a Million.*

The arguments against the commodity exchange markets as the method of pricing are growing. The examples of grain prices in 1973 and sugar prices in 1974, each of which in their respective years was the greatest single contributor to overall food prices, stand out as an indictment against an irrational carry-over from nineteenth-century capitalism. These prices bore no relationship to changes in cost of production nor to real patterns of supply and demand. In the case of sugar, industry spokesmen themselves continuously emphasized there was no world shortage.

The commodity exchange system has been around since the mid-nineteenth century. Based in the United States with branches through the world, these centres, like stock exchanges, do not themselves buy, sell, or produce anything. They are simply trading facilities used by agencies wishing to buy or sell 'futures contracts' in grain, minerals, sugar, beef, eggs, or whatever.

In Canada, the Winnipeg Commodity Exchange functions as a branch-plant operation to the Chicago exchange and is primarily engaged in the grain trade. As outlined in Chapter 4, the control over grain marketing and pricing has been a major source of conflict between prairie farmers and the private grain-trade.

The United States price is the strongest influence on world grain prices. This is because it is such a major exporter and it houses the major trading exchanges. The Canadian Wheat Board can maintain an independent price from the fluctuating Chicago futures price, but only within close limits and at its own peril. If the Americans are underselling the Canadian price, as they have generally since 1966, then the Wheat Board in Canada is forced to come into line to generate sales. On the other hand, if the Chicago exchange is a source of exaggerated high prices, as it was in 1973, the Wheat Board is under pressure from producers in Canada to rise to that price level.

The issue between government-to-government selling agencies and open-market commodity exchanges is one of control, rather than of basic function. As defenders of the Commodity Exchange will argue, the Canadian Wheat Board is itself engaged in speculation. When it sets price levels for wheat and commits contracts to export markets in advance of deliveries, it is taking certain calculated risks on behalf of farmers and the Canadian taxpayer, both of whom could lose if the Board miscalculated. For example, if a 100 million bushel sale is negotiated for delivery over a two-year period, the Wheat Board must guarantee a price which may well increase the next year, causing farmers a loss relative to what they could have sold wheat for in the second year of the delivery. On the other hand the Board could lose money for the federal treasury if it paid farmers a higher price for the grain they delivered to the elevator system than the Board eventually sold the wheat for to export customers. This possibility is protected against by the system of initial and final payments. The Wheat Board pays farmers for their grain deliveries initially at a price which it feels is the minimum possible export price. In 1974 this was $2.35 per bushel, compared to export prices of $4.50. Then it makes a final payment after the end of the crop year which makes up the difference between the initial payment price and the price at which the Wheat Board eventually sold the grain.

For the producer, the main point about the Wheat Board system is that he gets a price based on the average price over the full crop year rather than the price on the day he sold it. Also he gets a full return from the sale of export grain minus specified deductions on freight rates and handling charges by the elevator. He may or may not be happy with the total export price of wheat but at least he knows his fair portion of the returns is guaranteed.

Under the open-market system, the price tends to be lowest when harvest is completed by farmers and supplies are heavy. He sells to a depressed market and watches the price rise later in the season. This is what tends to happen in the United States. Finally, in the 1974-75 crop year, U.S. grain farmers decided to withhold their product until better prices were offered by the grain buyers. This exacerbated an already apparent supply shortage but also had the effect of keeping the price on the Chicago market down. The U.S. price for wheat was lower than the Canadian price throughout 1974, waiting for producers to deliver. Without guarantees to producers that their returns will be a fair proportion of the final market value they cannot themselves co-operate in good faith. But if *producers* have suffered by the open-market system of world food pricing in the long-term, *consumers* have been the major victims of the period 1973-75. Since there are more food consumers than producers, the political pressure to reform the system has got more response after 1973, at least in terms of investigation, and particularly in the United States. Senator Henry Jackson headed a senate sub-committee to probe the issue, which failed to propose scrapping the open-market system, but did propose more controls on price movements. Jackson estimated that the 1973 cereal price rise and the round of speculation on soybeans (in which the price went from $3.50 to $12.90 per bushel) may have added 15 per cent to the food bill of every American.

For consumers of food, the problem was not so much the commodity exchange system of boom-and-bust pricing directly. It was the one-two punch which commodity price hikes delivered in conjunction with the general pricing structure of food oligopolies. So far as commodity prices themselves go, they have if anything tended over the longer term to be depressed on the side of producers. The markets, especially for Third World commodities like sugar, coffee and cocoa, tended to be characterized by short booms and long depressions. It is not difficult to understand why these commodities (whose prices are determined on the U.S. commodity exchanges although they are produced elsewhere) should be generally depressed. The buyers of delivery contracts are the major food processing companies.

But the one-two punch for final consumers can be understood quite simply in the examples of sugar and wheat. Bursts of inflation due to real or imagined shortages of commodities affect the basic commodity in raw form as a result of heavy speculative trading. This sets in motion more controlled and permanent price rises in all of the manufactured or processed foods which use these basic commodities in any form. In the North American diet sugar and grain are included in virtually every major article of consumption with the exception of fresh fruit and vegetables. The oligopolies affected by the rising cost of the raw material include basic processing firms like sugar refineries and flour mills, but also meat packers, canneries, wineries, breweries and distillers, bakeries, confectionery manufacturers, soft drink firms and so on. Where the basic commodity price on the open market will necessarily return to a depressed market price, the secondary price of processed or refined foods will not deflate in the same way. All the by-products of sugar and wheat increased in part in 1973-75 because of the rising cost of the raw material. But when wheat prices declined $1.00 per bushel from the peak price or when the Canadian price for wheat flour was subsidized there was no decline in the price of by-products. Similarly the surge in price increase for confectioneries, baked goods, and canned foods using sugar were not deflated when sugar prices were again reduced on the open market.

The advantage gained by widening the price spread between producers and consumers may not appear as direct profit gains to agribusiness middlemen. Surplus is fed as well into capital expansion in new plants and facilities, research, new technology and so on. The point is that the open market commodity exchange system gives agribusiness a tremendous ability to manipulate producers into surrendering their commodities at low prices. It also enhances the processor's ability to manipulate consumer prices by holding them at inflated prices in a period of declining raw material costs. The critics of the open market system have not included sugar refineries and grain companies, even when the price of the raw product to them goes temporarily out of control as it did with sugar in 1974. They know they can avoid losses directly as a hedge and by exploiting the price of refined products in the consumer marketplace. (It is also obvious, however, that if marketing boards expand their role as discussed in Chapter 7 or if Third World producer-states apply Organization-of-Petroleum-Exporting-Countries-type strategies to food marketing; the processors are capable of adjusting to maintain their advantage. The sugar cartel is no more likely to suffer from the bargaining strength of sugar producing states than the petroleum industry suffered from the OPEC price hikes for crude oil in 1973-74.)

In Conclusion

The world food crisis is not a creature of recent discovery. Some features of the disparity in food distribution became more pronounced since 1972, but its essential characteristics have been with us throughout the current century. What changed substantially was the disappearance of world grain stocks to the point where threat of shortage came to affect the developed countries' markets as well as the food-hungry nations of the Third World. The short-fall in grain reserves led to the inflationary spiral in grain prices, forcing some traditional buyers out of the international consumer market.

The solution to the crisis may lie in part in the establishment of a world food bank in which grain would be purchased and stored during times of market surplus for use in case of natural production failures. But such a solution assumes a great deal about the willingness of the grain exporting countries, particularly the United States which is the largest, to surrender their control over grain marketing for profits to an international authority. The concept of food distribution according to need is so foreign to the basis of international trade that it is extremely unlikely as a political solution.

A more lasting long-term solution lies in the strengthening of the economies in those nations which lack the financial resources and political power to fully exploit their own natural agricultural wealth. By initially gaining more control over the pricing systems for their commodities, as the OPEC have done, they could sell for higher returns to the developed markets and use their improved trade wealth to re-organize their production for local and national needs. Land could be shifted at least in part from the luxuries of sugar, tea and spices to intensive production of cereals, vegetables, and orchard fruits.

For developed agricultural economies such as Canada, higher prices for imported foods from the Third World would be inflationary to some extent, the same way as higher oil prices from Venezuela pushed up consumer costs in Eastern Canada. But this development would encourage greater self-sufficiency in agricultural commodities in the Canadian market, a necessary and healthy development in itself, for vegetables, red meats, and even sugar.

Greater independence in the Third World or underdeveloped economies may require national revolutions against foreign control. The possibility of more Vietnams fought on the basis of control over basic agricultural wealth hung as a backdrop to the Rome Conference in 1974. The most sensitive to this possibility are the Americans, who are the most integrated into these countries through their strategy of the 'green revolution.' A *Time* Magazine special on the eve of the Conference reflected on the disturbing possibilities from an American bias:

> ... This deteriorating situation poses a dilemma for the wealthy, food-surfeited citizen of the developed world. ... Morals aside, out of sheer self interest he must ponder whether the hungry half-billion will allow him to live peacefully enjoying his wealth. He must realize that there is a chance that the impoverished might resort to war to take his wealth and food.

The reality of course is not that colonized peoples are going to demand and seize American domestic resources. It is that they may increasingly challenge U.S. claims to the food and other resources of the Third World through corporations and government programs operating in those countries.

For Canadians the issue of our contribution to world markets is tied to the class nature of our own society, and to our dependence on U.S. markets. Our resources are under-utilized. Our consumption patterns are in general wasteful and inefficient. Our internal distribution of food is so distorted by class and income disparities that we have different people in our midst dying of both overconsumption and malnutrition.

Obviously Canadian policy initiatives will not greatly reverse the world disparities in food distribution. They might at least serve to re-organize and re-direct our own production and consumption priorities. Specifically we need to arrest the trend of supply management which has been shifting production from cereal commodities to red meats. But food resource planning cannot be done within the framework of the profit-oriented 'free market' system of retail markets. Nor can it be done without a greater measure of independence from U.S. market demands. Some of the stages required to

establish a more rational system of food resource planning are
suggested in the next chapter.

Notes to Chapter 9

International Trade statistics are taken from the 1972-73 report of
the Department of Agriculture on *Trade In Agricultural Commodities.*

1. Pat Mooney, delegate from non-governmental organization to the
Rome World Food Conference, quoted in Regina in November 1974.

2. Canadian Press story, October 1974.

3. The value of grain exports recovered its position somewhat in
1973-74 because of the unusually high price for wheat on the world
market, even though the volume of exports was down from the peak
years of the mid-1960s.

4. Comments from interviews conducted in May 1974 among private
grain trade officials in Winnipeg.

5. These consequences were specifically ruled out by Secretary of
Agriculture Butz at the White House press conference announcing a
Soviet trade deal on July 8, 1972. He contributed three misleading
impressions to the American people. First, he said he was "sure" the
Russians would not exceed the $750 million agreed purchase in the
first year of a three-year agreement (which they had by September
1972); secondly, he underestimated the impact on North American
food prices, saying they "won't have any impact on the price of
bread" and "an imperceptible result if any result at all" on the price
of livestock; and thirdly, he underestimated the cost of sales to the
U.S. treasury by stating it "does not involve subsidy to the Russians."

6. Interview with Percy Huffman, Secretary, Winnipeg Commodity
Exchange, May 1974.

X

The Future of Food Policy: Two Alternatives

Changes in the organization of agriculture and food are occurring rapidly. The acclerating rate of change in agriculture since World War II continues, guided increasingly by federal government policies. The question for Canadians to ask is not whether changes will occur but what the impact of the changes already occurring will be and what the alternatives are. The days of the half-section homestead, the general store, and the water-powered grist mill are already long-gone. Some aspects of earlier stages of agriculture, food processing, and distribution may well be forgotten; others are sorely missed in the plunge to total centralization. In food distribution the era of the 'hyper-marche' has come to replace the luxury supermarket. In processing, the withdrawal of processing facilities from agricultural regions continues. Flour mills, packing-plants, and canneries continue to be centralized to the metropolitan markets.

Some elements of agriculture are more or less constant regardless of the particular social and political organizations which are built up. For example Canada will continue to enjoy the advantage of a tremendous diversified agricultural land mass. This provides the potential for food abundance throughout the present century even at the levels of waste and conversion of agricultural land apparent in the 1970s. Secondly, despite the underdevelopment of agriculture we in Canada will continue to have an available core of skilled farmers and farm workers to provide the labour power for food production. Finally, we have the technological capacity to ease the labour demand in agriculture allowing either for more leisure among producers or fewer producers.

These combined elements of land, labour and technology can be organized to fit more than one set of assumptions or objectives. The federal government's Task Force on Agriculture provided one future model on the basis of trends already in existence or viewed as necessary for capitalist organization of production in a period of growing centralization:

1. There will be a substantial reduction in the number of commercial farms. Some will be family farms but all will be rationally managed, profit oriented businesses. Farm mergers and consolidation will result in much larger units, not primarily for increased production efficiency but to structure units that are large enough to afford better management.
2. Farm organizations, marketing boards, co-operatives and similar organizations will be much larger, more professionally managed and users of much more sophisticated management, data processing, research and planning techniques.
3. Because of a drastic reduction in farm population, (probably to about 3 per cent to 4 per cent of population), the balance of power among farmers, consumers, and taxpayers, will change substantially. The government will become less involved in agriculture. Farm subsidies will be cut and the entire private sector of the agricultural system will be required to accept a much greater degree of independence.
4. Management, survival and cost-price realities will force a more effective rationalization of the relationships of production and sales; sales, costs and profits; and return on investment in agriculture from the smallest farm to the largest corporation.
5. As governments encourage agriculture to rationalize its management processes and organizational structure, a clear-cut separation of welfare and commercial farm policy programs will emerge. Some form of guaranteed annual income will be taken for granted.
6. As the necessity for planning increases, the drive for security will be manifest in increasing formal and informal integration.
7. As the size of units increases, financial requirements multiply and operating problems increase in complexity, ease of entry into commercial farming will be drastically cut allowing much greater rationalization of supply-demand relationships.
8. As a high and rising proportion of farm workers become employees working for salaries and wages, farm employee unions may emerge and become a factor in the bargaining process.

The Task Force model of corporate centralized agriculture is of course attached to assumptions that the capitalist system of profit-earning markets will continue to be the rationale of any political programs introduced. They explicitly reject any hints of socialist planning:

In sketching out this kind of model for agriculture circa 1990, *we are of course rejecting the "public utility" or socialized concept of agriculture.* Members of the Task Force sincerely hope that option is avoided. [emphasis added]

The rejection of socialized concepts for agriculture applies to the Task Force thinking toward the trends in agribusiness as well. Although the Task Force did not analyze these trends in detail, its view was that profit-motivated vertical integration is desirable, as is centralization of processing and distribution facilities.

An alternative set of projections must begin where the Task Force leaves off, i.e. consideration of food as a 'public utility.' From that point a number of possibilities suggest themselves as ingredients in a 1990 alternative model.

1) *Food as a renewable resource could be owned and controlled through an integrated public food corporation.* As an essential source of human energy, food can be removed from the uncontrolled marketing and pricing practices aimed at private profit and placed under public planning and marketing. Like medical care, the food services related to proper diet could be moved in stages to the position of a universal shared-cost public service borne by the public treasury. Disparities in food consumption and the incidence of malnutrition could be eliminated by basic food standards.

2) *National self-sufficiency in basic food commodities.* This objective could be met for meat products, vegetables, animal feed grains, and even sugar as a means of ensuring guaranteed markets for Canadian producers and guaranteed supplies for Canadian consumers during a period of increasing uncertainty of international supplies and higher transportation costs. Self-sufficiency in the major commodities would not eliminate Canada from import and export trade in agricultural commodities. It would reduce our overall dependency and shift the trade emphasis to limited and specific commodities not easily produced here. (Future imports would not include milk products, beef products, and vegetable products, all of which were net imports in 1974.) Self-sufficiency would necessitate a national transportation policy involving east-west railway movement and development of the railways as a public service. Import tariffs would be strengthened to prevent dumping of food commodities by food-exporting countries, particularly the United States.

3) *Farm Product Marketing Boards could be established in all domestic and export commodities, and the 'open market' commodity exchanges would be eliminated by law.* Prices for agricultural commodities could be stabilized and administered in response to cost of production factors (including farmers' income) and to conditions of supply and demand. Marketing boards would include producer repre-

sentation but would not be the primary bargaining agency for farm income.

4) *Farmers' incomes could be separated from farm product prices by the development of industrial-type bargaining agencies.* These 'farmers' unions' would bargain for income levels reflecting family needs, cost of living adjustments and productivity. They would bargain with Farm Products Marketing Boards for guaranteed negotiated contracts which would not be affected by the boom-and-bust cycles in the market price of farm products. The state would absorb losses in depressed market circumstances and accept windfall gains during inflated market prices. Both of these conditions could be reduced by production planning.

5) *Centralized production planning could result from researched information about potential market conditions and domestic and international needs.* Quotas would be negotiated with farmers as part of the contract bargaining between marketing boards and farmers' unions. Resources could be channeled to meet national policy objectives of improved domestic consumption or international food-aid and trade, rather than the traditional free market dependence on 'effective demand.'

6) *Positive discrimination in land ownership and tenure policies could prohibit direct corporate, absentee or foreign ownership of farm land.* Land tenure for agricultural purposes would be restricted to working farmers, farming either individually or collectively. Maximum limits of farm size would be legislated on a regional and commodity basis and would establish upper limits on gross income and acreage.

7) *Crown land-assembly through the government purchase of farm land (voluntarily offered on the market) for leasing back to farmers could provide an alternate system of land tenure.* Land-banking of agricultural land at a national level could provide the combined advantages of protecting and conserving the land resource for agricultural purposes, reducing the land cost as an inflated and accelerating cost in food production, and planning of future rural communities through the organization of co-operative production units.

8) *Co-operatively run integrated farm production units could provide the potential for a new agrarian social base.* As an alternative to the large isolated commuter farms and the decimated communities around them, multi-family co-operatives could provide an integrated social and economic base. They provide for both diversified production in various commodities such as grain, livestock and poultry as well as integrating production with service industries, and small-scale processing (depending on the commodities produced). Services integrated into the farm with its base of ten to fifty families would include mechanics, retail trade, education and health care. Processing might

include such areas as a community abattoir, cheese plant, or tannery depending on the size, resources and local marketing possibilities surrounding the co-operative. Co-operative production units would be established on public land with a collective lease. All farm workers and their families could share equally in decision-making power.

9) *Food processing could be integrated (through public ownership) with the production and marketing priorities of basic agriculture.* Although some small-scale processing would be decentralized into agricultural communities for local markets, the bulk of processing could remain regionally centralized. High volume processing plants would service the major urban markets through publicly owned packing-plants, canneries, flour mills and so on.

10) *Worker control could be applied as a management concept throughout the state-owned food industry.* Just as farmers' unions would bargain production planning along with income, industrial workers in food processing could enlarge their power to management of plant operations, production levels and prices in conjunction with government authorities. 'Consumer issues' of food quality, use of additives, and packaging standards would all be publicly accountable and a matter of negotiation within the limits of federal standards.

11) *Reorganization of food distribution at two levels.* First there could be the expansion of 'farmer's market' facilities in agricultural regions to allow direct farmer-to-consumer transactions for unprocessed farm products. These could be supervised by producer marketing agencies to determine minimum and maximum price levels, quotas, space rentals and so on. Such markets might have some impact on major urban markets for some commodities such as fresh vegetables.

The second level of retail distribution could be through *neighbourhood food outlets.* These would be low-cost direct-purchase facilities as part of an integrated public food corporation. They would replace luxury supermarkets and would sell basic food essentials at cost, eliminating advertising and reducing packaging costs, product differentiation costs and capital costs on buildings and equipment. These outlets could be organized and maintained in much the same way some provinces have organized public liquor outlets. If free food vouchers were distributed as a means of guaranteeing a minimum diet standard for all Canadians they could be honoured through these neighbourhood grocery outlets. Related services such as centralized locker plants for bulk meat storage could also be located in such neighbourhood centres.

12) *Government organization could be deepened to provide for a more comprehensive Department of Agriculture and Food to oversee and co-ordinate public policies.* Farm products marketing boards and

an integrated public food corporation would be semi-autonomous agencies under such a department.

These twelve elements of an alternative approach to food production and distribution only propose the broadest outline of a direction of change. They are no detailed blueprint for the future. But even accepting that such changes are within the range of possibility over the fifteen years from 1975, the preconditions which would bring them into affect are less than apparent. A plan or strategy which can cope with the short-term limitations of a market system of oligopolies while laying ground-work for more substantial long-range reforms does not now exist in Canada. Rising food prices, depressed and erratic farm income, and lay-offs in the food processing sector are all issues of short-term priority for political parties and interest groups alike. But their response has failed to give root to alternatives to be established in the longer term.

This political expression of the need for an alternative approach would have to come about at two levels. The first is through the interest groups within the agriculture and food system — the trade unions and farmers' organizations. In the case of farmers, as noted in Chapter 2, the National Farmers Union represented in the 1970s the best potential for advancing self-interest solutions for the rural communities. The pro-capitalist assumptions of the major commodity groups like the Canadian Cattlemen's Association and Palliser Wheat Growers draw them into a compromising partnership with agribusiness.

The second level of needed political expression is a political party or parties which will integrate the demands of farmers and workers in the food industry into a single national program for the food resource. This clearly did not exist in 1975. By 1975 it was clear that inflation in food and other commodities was giving way to recession. Workers in the food industry, as elsewhere, had to temper their concerns about declining real income with the threat of lay-offs and unemployment. The tensions generated against the free market system of oligopolies by both inflation and recession were not being expressed by the existing political parties. In short there is in Canada no class-based party to respond to working class interests, not even the New Democratic Party — in spite of its official links with the Canadian Labour Congress.

Until an open working-class party emerges on a broad base and at a national level in English Canada, reform politics can emerge mainly from specific interest groups. For food industry workers, the demand for public take-over of processing facilities could be accelerated during the time when corporate mismanagement is leading to industry dislocations. Lay-offs in meat-packing and other industries in spring

1975 reflected the assumption that any costs of a down-turn in markets due to recession should be borne fully by the workers. The public take-over demand in such cases needs to be attached to the argument that provincial governments should be willing to absorb short-term operational losses to obtain long-term benefits.

Agricultural reforms such as income bargaining, land policies, and organization of co-operative production units, were not within the program of existing farmers' organizations in 1975. Such reforms were, however, in the discussion and debate stages, and could be given wider support if the necessary organizing and persuasion were carried out. Limitations of program and ideology in the National Farmers union in this respect are minor in relation to the pro-capitalist assumptions of the commodity groups.

In the final analysis, the biggest obstacle to change may be the ideological stumbling block which blinded the economists on the federal Task Force. Canadians will have to be persuaded that the food resource is too socially vital to be left to private profit-marketing. An integrated public food corporation is only a solution if it is contained in a program of complete socialization of the food resource. Profit-seeking crown corporations, such as Air Canada or the Canadian National Railway, can be as burdensome and inefficient as the 'private' multinationals. But approaches to improving the nation's diet standards by creative and efficient public food distribution could be a boon to agriculture. It would also be a great advance toward establishing preventive health care and social equality.

The suggestions for change in the twelve points outlined need debate and elaboration. This part of the discussion must go on in a less abstract forum than a book such as this represents. A political program needs to be the basis of community organizing and education around the concerns now felt about the food industry. Many people across Canada have much to contribute to this process. Meanwhile, however, the Task Force's scenario of corporate centralized agriculture is steadily being implemented by the combined power of government — particularly the federal government — and agribusiness. Unless the rest of us act, they will have made all the decisions for us. Their record, detailed in this book, should leave no one in any doubt about who will gain — and who will lose — if they have their way.

APPENDIX

THE WESTON FOOD OCTUPUS

OCTUPUS NUMBER	REPORTING CORPORATION	OCTUPUS NUMBER	HOLDING CORPORATION	PER CENT OWNED BY
2	Willington Investments	1	Weston W. E. Charitable Foundation	81.8
4	Weston George Ltd.	2	Wittington Investments	51.7
3	Wittington Realty & Construction	2	Wittington Investments	100.0
5	Dicoe Ltd.	4	Weston George Ltd.	100.0
6	Diversified Research & Sales Ltd.	4	Weston George Ltd.	100.0
7	Eddy Paper Co. Ltd.	4	Weston George Ltd.	100.0
8	Marven's Ltd.	4	Weston George Ltd.	100.0
9	McCormick's Ltd.	4	Weston George Ltd.	100.0
10	Megargy Investments	4	Weston George Ltd.	100.0
11	Neilson William Ltd.	4	Weston George Ltd.	100.0
12	Paulin Chambers Co. Ltd.	4	Weston George Ltd.	100.0
13	Perrin Investments Ltd.	4	Weston George Ltd.	100.0
14	Sayvette Ltd.	4	Weston George Ltd.	100.0
15	Weston Bakeries Ltd.	4	Weston George Ltd.	100.0
16	Willards Chocolate Co. Ltd.	4	Weston George Ltd.	100.0
17	Eddy, E. B. Co.	7	Eddy Paper Co. Ltd.	99.4
18	Hamilton G. J. & Sons Ltd.	8	Marven's Ltd.	100.0
19	B.C. Packers Ltd.	10	Megargy Investments Ltd.	69.0
20	Duart Investments Ltd.	10	Megargy Investments Ltd.	100.0

21	Universal Cooler Co. (1964) Ltd.	10	Megargy Investments Ltd.	100.0
22	Eplett Dairies Ltd.	11	Neilson William Ltd.	100.0
23	Eplett Ice Cream Ltd.	11	Neilson William Ltd.	100.0
24	Loblaw Companies Ltd.	13	Perrin Investments Ltd.	51.2
25	Somerville Industries Ltd.	13	Perrin Investments Ltd.	100.0
26	Westfair Foods Ltd.	13	Perrin Investments Ltd.	100.0
27	Sayvette (Ontario) Ltd.	14	Sayvette Ltd.	100.0
28	Lane's Bakeries Ltd.	15	Weston Bakeries Ltd.	100.0
29	Boyle J. E. Ltd.	17	Eddy E.B. Co.	100.0
30	Upper Ottawa Improvement Co. Ltd.	17	Eddy E.B. Co.	42.8
31	B.C. Packers (Nfld.) Ltd.	19	B.C. Packers Ltd.	100.0
32	Nelpack Fisheries Ltd.	19	B.C. Packers Ltd.	50.0
33	Packers Steamship Co. Ltd.	19	B.C. Packers Ltd.	100.0
34	Todd J. H. & Sons Ltd.	19	B.C. Packers Ltd.	50.0
35	Western (Canada) Whaling Co. Ltd.	19	B.C. Packers Ltd.	50.0
36	Connors Bros. Ltd.	20	Duart Investments Ltd.	53.1
37	Alservice Ltd.	21	Universal Cooler Co. (1964) Ltd.	100.0
38	Sno-Boy Coolers Ltd.	21	Universal Cooler Co. (1964) Ltd.	100.0
39	Universal Cooler Acceptance Corp. Ltd.	21	Universal Cooler Co. (1964) Ltd.	100.0
40	Universal Refrigeration Ltd.	21	Universal Cooler Co. (1964) Ltd.	100.0
41	Loblaw Groceterias Co. Ltd.	24	Loblaw Companies Ltd.	99.3
42	Canadian Folding Cartons Ltd.	25	Somerville Industries Ltd.	99.8
43	Somerville Automotive Trim Ltd.	25	Somerville Industries Ltd.	100.0
44	Dominion Fruit Ltd.	26	Westfair Foods Ltd.	100.0
45	Ensign Stores Ltd.	26	Westfair Foods Ltd.	51.0

46	Foodwide (Canada) Ltd.	26	Westfair Foods Ltd.	45.3
47	Gateway Foods Factors Ltd.	26	Westfair Foods Ltd.	100.0
48	High-Low-Foods Ltd.	26	Westfair Foods Ltd.	33.3
49	Jenkins Groceteria Ltd.	26	Westfair Foods Ltd.	100.0
50	Malkin W. H. Ltd.	26	Westfair Foods Ltd.	100.0
51	McLean G. Co. Ltd.	26	Westfair Foods Ltd.	99.9
52	Mini Marts Ltd.	26	Westfair Foods Ltd.	100.0
53	Pacific Coast Packers Ltd.	26	Westfair Foods Ltd.	100.0
54	Western Grocers Ltd.	26	Westfair Foods Ltd.	100.0
55	Beaver Harbour Canning Co. Ltd.	36	Connors Bros. Ltd.	100.0
56	Black's Harbour Mfg. Co. Ltd.	36	Connors Bros. Ltd.	100.0
57	Connors Lewis & Sons Ltd.	36	Connors Bros. Ltd.	100.0
58	Fundy Cold Storage Co. Ltd.	36	Connors Bros. Ltd.	100.0
59	Fundy Marine Insurance Co.	36	Connors Bros. Ltd.	100.0
60	Robichaud & Co. Ltd.	36	Connors Bros. Ltd.	49.9
61	Seal Cove Canning Co. Ltd.	36	Connors Bros. Ltd.	60.0
62	Shippegan Cold Storage Co. Ltd.	36	Connors Bros. Ltd.	40.7
63	Creland Equipment Lessors Ltd.	41	Loblaw Groceterias Co. Ltd.	100.0
64	Dunedin Investments Ltd.	41	Loblaw Groceterias Co. Ltd.	100.0
65	Food Markets Holdings Ltd.	41	Loblaw Groceterias Co. Ltd.	100.0
66	Display Fixtures (Manitoba) Ltd.	44	Dominion Fruit Ltd.	100.0
67	Northern Potato Ltd.	44	Dominion Fruit Ltd.	100.0
68	Shop-Easy Stores Ltd.	44	Dominion Fruit Ltd.	100.0
69	Brim Products Ltd.	46	Foodwide (Canada) Ltd.	98.8
70	Chess Brothers Ltd.	50	Malkin W. H. Ltd.	100.0

71	Shop-Easy Stores (B.C.) Ltd.	50	Malkin W. H. Ltd.	100.0
72	Fundy Cold Storage Co. Ltd.	57	Connors Lewis & Sons Ltd.	80.0
73	Welch H. W. Ltd.	59	Fundy Marine Insurance Co.	31.2
74	Donlands Dairy Ltd.	64	Dunedin Investments Ltd.	99.8
75	Douglas E. Investment Co. Ltd.	64	Dunedin Investments Ltd.	100.0
76	Federal Distributors Ltd.	64	Dunedin Investments Ltd.	100.0
77	Kemac Investments Ltd.	64	Dunedin Investments Ltd.	100.0
78	Tamblyn G. Ltd.	64	Dunedin Investments Ltd.	51.0
79	Zehr's Markets Ltd.	64	Dunedin Investments Ltd.	85.0
80	Harbour Investments Ltd.	65	Food Markets Holdings Ltd.	100.0
81	Kambly (Switzerland) Canada Ltd.	65	Food Markets Holdings Ltd.	100.0
82	National Grocers Co. Ltd.	65	Food Markets Holdings Ltd.	73.7
83	Pickering Farms Ltd.	65	Food Markets Holdings Ltd.	100.0
84	Power Super Markets Ltd.	65	Food Markets Holdings Ltd.	100.0
85	Sobeys Stores Ltd.	65	Food Markets Holdings Ltd.	40.0
86	Yeates Charles & Co. Ltd.	74	Donlands Dairy Ltd.	100.0
87	Kelly-Douglas & Co. Ltd.	75	Douglas E. Investments Ltd.	33.3
88	Federal Farms Ltd.	76	Federal Distributors Ltd.	78.7
89	Kelly-Douglas & Co. Ltd.	77	Kelmac Investments Ltd.	33.1
90	Tamblyn (Alberta) Ltd.	78	Tamblyn G. Ltd.	99.0
91	Tamblyn (Western) Ltd.	78	Tamblyn G. Ltd.	100.0
92	Atlantic Wholesalers Ltd.	80	Harbour Investments Ltd.	99.8
93	Foodwide (Canada) Ltd.	82	National Grocers Co. Ltd.	45.3
94	Gordons Super Markets Ltd.	82	National Grocers Co. Ltd.	50.0
95	Busy B. Discount Foods Ltd.	84	Power Super Markets Ltd.	100.0

96	Food City Ltd.	85	Sobys Stores Ltd.	99.9
97	T.R.A. Ltd.	85	Sobys Stores Ltd.	49.1
98	B.C. Food Service Associates Ltd.	87	Kelly, Douglas & Co. Ltd.	20.0
99	Cal-Van Camps Ltd.	87	Kelly, Douglas & Co. Ltd.	100.0
100	Cal-Van Caterers Ltd.	87	Kelly, Douglas & Co. Ltd.	100.0
101	Canus Camp Services Ltd.	87	Kelly, Douglas & Co. Ltd.	100.0
102	Cloverdale Paint & Chemicals Ltd.	87	Kelly, Douglas & Co. Ltd.	54.5
103	Dickson Importing Co. Ltd.	87	Kelly, Douglas & Co. Ltd.	100.0
104	Nabob Foods Ltd.	87	Kelly, Douglas & Co. Ltd.	100.0
105	Nabob Holdings Ltd.	87	Kelly, Douglas & Co. Ltd.	100.0
106	Pacific Cartage Ltd.	87	Kelly, Douglas & Co. Ltd.	33.3
107	Premier Packaging Ltd.	87	Kelly, Douglas & Co. Ltd.	50.0
108	Super Value Stores (B.C.) Ltd.	87	Kelly, Douglas & Co. Ltd.	100.0
109	Western Commodities Ltd.	87	Kelly, Douglas & Co. Ltd.	100.0
110	Fillmores Ltd.	92	Atlantic Wholesalers Ltd.	99.3
111	Harrison's Markets Ltd.	92	Atlantic Wholesalers Ltd.	99.9
112	Kitchen Bros. Ltd.	92	Atlantic Wholesalers Ltd.	98.8
113	McGregor R. & Sons Ltd.	92	Atlantic Wholesalers Ltd.	100.0
114	O'Reilly's Supermarket Ltd.	92	Atlantic Wholesalers Ltd.	100.0
115	Shamrock Stores Ltd.	92	Atlantic Wholesalers Ltd.	100.0
116	St. George Foods Ltd.	92	Atlantic Wholesalers Ltd.	98.8
117	Cal-Van Foods Ltd.	100	Cal-Van Caterers Ltd.	100.0
118	Tuxedo Foods Ltd.	103	Dickson Importing Co. Ltd.	100.0

Bibliography

Books

Chodos, Robert. *The CPR: A Century of Corporate Welfare*. Toronto: James Lewis and Samuel, 1973.

Fowke, Vernon Clifford. *The National Policy and the Wheat Economy*. Toronto: University of Toronto Press, 1957

____.*Canadian Agricultural Policy: The Historical Pattern*. Toronto: University of Toronto Press, 1947.

Lipset, Seymour Martin (ed.). *Agrarian Socialism: The Co-operative Commonwealth Federation in Saskatchewan*. 2nd ed. (revised). Garden City, New York: Doubleday, 1968.

Porter, John. *The Vertical Mosaic: An Analysis of Social Class and Power in Canada*. Toronto: University of Toronto Press, 1965.

____.*Canadian Social Structure: A Statistical Profile*. Toronto: McClelland and Stewart, 1967.

Yates, Samuel W. *History of the Saskatchewan Wheat Pool: Its Origin, Organization and Progress, 1924-1935*. Saskatoon: United Farmers of Canada, 1947.

Periodicals

Canadian Consumer, January 1972 to present.

Canadian Farm Economics (published by Agriculture Canada), 1972-1975.

Financial Post, January 1973 to present.

Regina *Leader-Post*, January 1973 to present.

Toronto *Globe and Mail,* 1934-35 and 1947-48. (Historical references.)

Union Farmer, (published by National Farmers Union, Saskatoon), January 1973 to present.

Western Producer (published by Saskatchewan Wheat Pool), January 1973 to present.

Articles

Aubin, Henry, Montreal *Gazette*, September 1974.

Buckley, H. and Tihanyi, E. "Canadian Policies for Rural Adjustment: A Summary of Conclusions," *Social and Cultural Change in Canada*, Vol. I, ed. W.E. Mann (Toronto: Copp Clark, 1970).

Fowke, Vernon C. and Fowke, Donald. "Political Economy and the Canadian Wheat Grower," *Politics in Saskatchewan*, ed. Norman Ward and Duff Spafford (Toronto: Longman, 1968).

McCrorie, James N. "Change and Paradox in Agrarian Social Movements: The Case of Saskatchewan," *Canadian Society: Pluralism,*

Change and Conflict, ed. Richard J. Ossenberg (Toronto: Prentice-Hall, 1971).

Rosenbluth, Gideon and Thorburn, H. "Canadian Anti-Combines Administration," Canadian Journal of Economics and Political Science, XXVII (November 1961) 498-508.

Silverstein, Sanford. "Occupational Class and Voting Behaviour: Electoral Support of a Left-Wing Protest Movement in a Period of Prosperity," Agrarian Socialism, ed. Seymour Martin Lipset (Garden City: Doubleday, 1968).

Warnock, John. "The Farm Crisis," Essays on the Left, ed. Laurier Lapierre, Jack McLeod, Charles Taylor and Walter Young (Toronto: McClelland and Stewart, 1971).

Public Documents

Canada. Census of Canada. Ottawa: Queen's Printer, 1971.

Canada. Agriculture Canada. Livestock and Meat Trade Reports January 1973 to present. (Weekly publication.)

Canada. Department of Consumer and Corporate Affairs. Annual Report: Director of Combines Investigation Branch. Ottawa: Information Canada, 1968-71 (selected years).

Canada. Department of Consumer and Corporate Affairs. Ron Basford, Minister. Concentration in the Manufacturing Industries of Canada. Ottawa: Information Canada, 1971.

Canada. Department of Justice. Annual Report: Director of Combines Investigation Branch. Ottawa: Queen's Printer, 1962-8 (selected years).

_____.Restrictive Trade Practices Commission. Report Concerning the Meat Packing Industry. Ottawa: Queen's Printer, 1961.

_____.Restrictive Trade Practices Commission. Report on Eastern Sugar Refineries. Ottawa: Queen's Printer, 1962.

_____.Restrictive Trade Practices Commission. Report Concerning the Sugar Industry in Eastern Canada. Ottawa: Queen's Printer, 1960.

Canada. Dominion Bureau of Statistics. Growth Patterns in Manufacturing Industries 1961-1967. Ottawa: Queen's Printer, 1969.

_____.Intercorporate Ownership 1969. Ottawa: Queen's Printer, 1971.

Canada. Food Prices Review Board. First Quarterly Report. September 1973.

_____.Report on Bread Prices. February 1974.

_____.Canadian Dairy Industry: Short-term Perspectives. March 1974.

_____.Feed Grains Policy Statement. April 1974.

_____.Report on Ground Beef. June 1974.

_____.Feed Grain Prices. June 1974.

_____.Beef Pricing. June 1974.

_____.Report on Egg Prices II. August 1974.

_____.Beef Pricing II. November 1974.

_____.Retail Beef Prices and Price Spreads. November 1974.

_____.A Review of the Canadian Beef Market. November 1974.

Canada. House of Commons. Special Parliamentary Committee on
Trends in Food Prices. *Minutes.* Ottawa: Queen's Printer, 1973.

Canada. *Report of the Royal Commission on Farm Machinery.*
Clarence Barber, Commissioner. Ottawa: Information Canada,
1971.

Canada. Royal Commission on Farm Machinery. *Special Report on
Prices of Tractors and Combines in Canada and Other Countries.*
Ottawa: Queen's Printer, 1969.

Canada. *Report of the Royal Commission on Price Spreads of Food
Products.* Ottawa: Queen's Printer, 1959.

Canada. Statistics Canada. *Dairy Products Industry* (annual publication). 1961 to present.

_____.*Employment, Earnings and Hours* (monthly report).

_____.*Grain Trade of Canada* (annual report). 1972, 1973.

_____.*Infomat* (formerly *Statistics Canada Weekly*). January 1973 to
present.

_____.*Inter-corporate Ownership,* 1969.

_____.*Prices and Price Indexes* (monthly report). 1961 to present.

_____.*Statistics Canada Daily* (formerly *DBS Daily*). January 1973 to
present.

_____.*The Dairy Review* (monthly report). January 1970 to present.

_____.*The Wheat Review* (monthly report). 1972 to present.

Dooley, Peter. "Retail Oligopoly in the Grocery Trade," Supporting
Study No. 3 of the Royal Commission on Consumer Problems
and Inflation. Regina: Provinces of Manitoba, Saskatchewan and
Alberta, 1968.

Garland, S.W. and Hudson, S.C. *Government Involvement in Agriculture: A Report Prepared for the Federal Task Force on
Agriculture.* Ottawa: Queen's Printer, 1971.

Manitoba. Department of Agriculture. *Fertilizer Marketing in
Manitoba: Report of the Commission of Inquiry into Manufac-
turing, Distribution and Pricing of Chemical Fertilizers in
Manitoba.* Topegon Group Limited, Consultants, May 31, 1973.

*Report of the Royal Commission on Consumer Problems and
Inflation.* Mary J. Batten, Chairman. Regina: Provinces of Manitoba, Saskatchewan and Alberta, 1968.

Saskatchewan. Department of Agriculture. *Annual Report 1970-73*
Regina: Queen's Printer, 1970.

_____."Summary of *Canadian Agriculture in the Seventies:* Report on
the Federal Task Force on Agriculture." Regina, 1969.

Saskatchewan. Executive Council Planning and Research.
Saskatchewan Economic Review 1972-74 Regina: Queen's
Printer,1972-73-74.

United Nations Food and Agriculture Organization. *Agricultural
Commodities Projections for 1975 and 1985,* Vol. I. Rome,
1967.

_____.*Commodity Review and Outlook* (annual publication), 1972-3,
1973-4. Rome, 1973, 1974.

Interviews

Stan Barber, Chairman, Saskatchewan Milk Control Board. July 1974.

Walter Folliott, official of Louis Dreyfus, Canada. May 1974.

Percy Huffman, Secretary, Winnipeg Commodity Exchange. May 1974.

Fred Longstaff, Producers' Egg Marketing Association, Saskatchewan. December 1974.

Clarence Lyons, Canadian Food and Allied Workers' Union. July 1974.

Other Sources

Bronson, Harold. "The Developing Structure of the Saskatchewan Meat Packing Industry: A Study of Economic Welfare." Unpublished Ph.D. dissertation, University of Saskatchewan, 1965.

Geshler, Ernest. "Study of the Structure and Politics of the Palliser Wheat Growers."Undergraduate paper.

Langer, Jeff. "Oligopoly in the Sugar Industry." Undergraduate paper.

Mitchell, Donald. "Oligopoly and the Cost-Price Squeeze: Assessing the Causes and Effects of Rural Decline." Unpublished M.A. thesis, University of Saskatchewan, Regina, 1973.

Financial Post Corporation Service. (Card index.)

Financial Post. Directory of Directors, 1970-71. Toronto, 1971.